REFLI

C000231224

DAILY PRAYER

ADVENT **2020** TO
EVE OF ADVENT **2021**

KATE BRUCE
RICHARD CARTER
ANDREW DAVISON
GULI FRANCIS-DEHQANI
PETER GRAYSTONE
LIZ HOARE
MICHAEL IPGRAVE
GRAHAM JAMES
DONNA LAZENBY
ANNA MATTHEWS
BARBARA MOSSE
MARK OAKLEY
SUE PICKERING
BEN QUASH
SARAH ROWLAND JONES
DAVID RUNCORN
MEG WARNER
MARGARET WHIPP
JEREMY WORTHEN

Church House Publishing
Church House
Great Smith Street
London SW1P 3AZ

ISBN 978 1 78140 179 8

Published 2020 by Church House Publishing
Copyright © The Archbishops' Council 2020

The opinions expressed in this book are those of the
authors and do not necessarily reflect the official policy of
the General Synod or The Archbishops' Council of the
Church of England.

Liturgical editor: Peter Moger
Series editor: Hugh Hillyard-Parker
Designed and typeset by Hugh Hillyard-Parker
Copy edited by Ros Connelly
Printed and bound by CPI Group (UK) Ltd, Croydon, CR0 4YY

What do you think of *Reflections for Daily Prayer*?

We'd love to hear from you – simply email us at

publishing@churchofengland.org

or write to us at

Church House Publishing, Church House,
Great Smith Street, London SW1P 3AZ.

Visit **www.dailyprayer.org.uk** for more
information on the *Reflections* series, ordering
and subscriptions.

Contents

Table of contributors

About the authors

Kate Bruce was Deputy Warden and Tutor in Preaching at Cranmer Hall, St John's College, until late 2017, and remains associated with Cranmer as Honorary Visiting Fellow. She now serves as an RAF Chaplain. She regularly offers day conferences in preaching around the country, and also preaches regularly. She enjoys running, and writes and performs stand-up comedy in her spare time; she performed at the Edinburgh Fringe in 2019.

Richard Carter is Associate Vicar for Mission at St Martin-in-the-Fields in London, where he works closely with homeless people and refugees, and organizes the lecture and formation programmes. He is the author of *The City is my Monastery: A Contemporary Rule of Life* and is a frequent contributor to BBC Radio 4 Daily Service. Previously, Richard was Chaplain to the Melanesian Brotherhood in the Solomon Islands, Vanuatu and Papua New Guinea; his experiences there through a violent conflict are described in his book *In Search of the Lost*.

Andrew Davison is the Starbridge Lecturer in Theology and Natural Sciences in the University of Cambridge, and Fellow in Theology and Dean of Chapel at Corpus Christi College. His publications include *Why Sacraments?*, *Participation in God*, and *The Love of Wisdom: An Introduction to Philosophy for Theologians*.

Guli Francis-Dehqani was born in Iran but moved to England following the events of the 1979 Islamic Revolution. Having studied music as an undergraduate, she worked at the BBC for a few years before training for ordination and completing a PhD. She was ordained in 1998 and has served as Bishop of Loughborough since 2017.

Peter Graystone works for Southwark Diocese, helping South London churchgoers become more confident in what they believe, how they talk about it, and the way they live it out. He is the author of many books and reviews theatre for the *Church Times*.

Liz Hoare is tutor for spiritual formation at Wycliffe Hall, Oxford. Prior to this she was in parish ministry in Yorkshire. She is especially committed to giving and receiving spiritual direction and has written *Using the Bible in spiritual direction* (SPCK, 2014). She has a doctorate in Church history and is currently working on women's writing in spirituality.

Michael Ipgrave is Bishop of Lichfield, and has previously ministered in Rutland, Japan, Leicester and South London. He has a particular interest in ecumenical, Christian–Jewish and interfaith issues.

Graham James was Bishop of Norwich for almost 20 years until his retirement in 2019. Since then he has chaired the Paterson Inquiry, an independent inquiry for the Government on patient safety in the NHS and private healthcare. Earlier in his ministry he was Bishop of St Germans in his native Cornwall and Chaplain to two Archbishops of Canterbury. His most recent book is *A Place for God* about the relationship between location and faith.

Donna Lazenby is the Director of St Mellitus College, South West, and Tutor and Lecturer in Christian Spirituality and Apologetics. Her doctoral thesis won a John Templeton Award for Theological Promise in 2011. She is the author of *A Mystical Philosophy: Transcendence and Immanence in the Works of Virginia Woolf and Iris Murdoch* and *Divine Sparks: Everyday Encounters with God's Incoming Kingdom*.

Anna Matthews has been vicar of St Bene't's, Cambridge since 2012, prior to which she spent six years as a Minor Canon at St Albans Cathedral. From 2012–19, she was also Director of Ordinands for the Diocese of Ely, and she retains an interest and involvement in vocations work and spirituality

Barbara Mosse is a writer and retired Anglican priest. Prior to retirement she was a lecturer on the MA in Christian Spirituality at Sarum College, Salisbury. Earlier ministerial posts included some parish work, alongside chaplaincy experience in prison, university, community mental health and hospital. She is the author of *The Treasures of Darkness*, *Encircling the Christian Year* and *Welcoming the Way of the Cross.*

Mark Oakley is Dean and Fellow of St John's College, Cambridge, and Honorary Canon Theologian of Wakefield Cathedral in the Diocese of Leeds. He is the author of *The Collage of God* (2001), *The Splash of Words: Believing in Poetry* (2016), and *My Sour Sweet Days: George Herbert and the Journey of the Soul* (2019) as well as articles and reviews, usually in the areas of faith, poetry, human rights and literature. He is Visiting Lecturer in the department of Theology and Religious Studies at King's College London.

Sue Pickering is a New Zealand Anglican priest, writer and spiritual director. Her publications through Canterbury Press include books on spiritual direction practice, retreat resources and ministry with older people. Sue is energised by beauty, creation, contemplative prayer and spending quality time with family and friends.

Ben Quash has been Professor of Christianity and the Arts at King's College London since 2007, and is Director of the Centre for Arts and the Sacred at King's (ASK). Prior to that he was Dean and Fellow of Peterhouse, Cambridge. He runs a collaborative MA in Christianity and the Arts with the National Gallery in London, and is also Canon Theologian of both Coventry and Bradford Cathedrals.

Sarah Rowland Jones was a mathematician, then a British diplomat with postings in Jordan and Hungary, before ordination in the Church in Wales. After 11 years as researcher to successive Archbishops of Cape Town, she returned to Wales, and is now the Dean of St Davids. She serves on international Anglican think-tanks, broadcasts regularly, and writes on spirituality, public theology and ecumenism.

David Runcorn is a writer, speaker, spiritual director and theological teacher. He lives in Devon.

Rachel Treweek is the Bishop of Gloucester and the first female diocesan bishop in England. She served in two parishes in London and was Archdeacon of Northolt and later Hackney. Prior to ordination she was a speech and language therapist and is a trained practitioner in conflict transformation.

Meg Warner is Tutor in Old Testament at Northern College, Manchester. She is a Reader in the Church of England, a regular guest speaker at synods, festivals and other church gatherings around the UK and internationally, and author and editor of several books, most recently *Tragedies and Christian Congregations: The Practical Theology of Trauma* and (writing as Meg Warner) *Joseph: A story of resilience*.

Margaret Whipp is an Anglican priest and spiritual director based in Oxford. Her first career was in medicine. Since ordination in 1990, she has ministered in parish and chaplaincies and served in theological education. Her books include the *SCM Studyguide in Pastoral Theology* and *The Grace of Waiting*.

Jeremy Worthen is a priest in the Church of England and is currently the Secretary for Ecumenical Relations and Theology at the Council for Christian Unity. He previously worked in theological education and has written on a range of subjects, including Jewish–Christian relations. His publications include *Responding to God's Call* (2012).

About *Reflections for Daily Prayer*

Based on the *Common Worship Lectionary* readings for Morning Prayer, these daily reflections are designed to refresh and inspire times of personal prayer. The aim is to provide rich, contemporary and engaging insights into Scripture.

Each page lists the Lectionary readings for the day, with the main psalms for that day highlighted in **bold**. The collect of the day – either the *Common Worship* collect or the shorter additional collect – is also included.

For those using this book in conjunction with a service of Morning Prayer, the following conventions apply: a psalm printed in parentheses is omitted if it has been used as the opening canticle at that office; a psalm marked with an asterisk may be shortened if desired.

A short reflection is provided on either the Old or New Testament reading. Popular writers, experienced ministers, biblical scholars and theologians all contribute to this series, bringing with them their own emphases, enthusiasms and approaches to biblical interpretation.

Regular users of Morning Prayer and *Time to Pray* (from *Common Worship: Daily Prayer*) and anyone who follows the Lectionary for their regular Bible reading will benefit from the rich variety of traditions represented in these stimulating and accessible pieces.

This volume also includes both a simple form of *Common Worship* Morning Prayer (see inside front and back covers) and a short form of Night Prayer – also known as Compline – (see pp. 326–7), particularly for the benefit of those readers who are new to the habit of the Daily Office or for any reader while travelling.

Building daily prayer into daily life

In our morning routines, there are many tasks we do without giving much thought to them, and others that we do with careful attention. Daily prayer and Bible reading is a strange mixture of these. These are disciplines (and gifts) that we as Christians should have in our daily pattern, but they are not tasks to be ticked off. Rather they are a key component of our developing relationship with God. In them is *life* – for the fruits of this time are to be lived out by us – and to be most fruitful, the task requires both purpose and letting go.

In saying a daily office of prayer, we make the deliberate decision to say 'yes' to spending time with God – the God who is always with us. In prayer and attentive reading of the Scriptures, there is both a conscious entering into God's presence and a 'letting go' of all we strive to control: both are our acknowledgement that it is God who is God.

> *... come into his presence with singing.*
>
> *Know that the Lord is God.*
> *It is he that has made us, and we are his;*
> *we are his people, and the sheep of his pasture.*
>
> *Enter his gates with thanksgiving...*
>
> *(Psalm 100, a traditional Canticle at Morning Prayer)*

If we want a relationship with someone to deepen and grow, we need to spend time with that person. It can be no surprise that the same is true between us and God.

In our daily routines, I suspect that most of us intentionally look in the mirror; occasionally we might see beyond the surface of our external reflection and catch a glimpse of who we truly are. For me, a regular pattern of daily prayer and Bible reading is like a hard look in a clean mirror: it gives a clear reflection of myself, my life and the world in which I live. But it is more than that, for in it I can also see the reflection of God who is most clearly revealed in Jesus Christ and present with us now in the Holy Spirit.

This commitment to daily prayer is about our relationship with the God who is love. St Paul, in his great passage about love, speaks of now seeing 'in a mirror, dimly' but one day seeing face to face: 'Now I know only in part; then I will know fully, even as I have been fully known' (1 Corinthians 13.12). Our daily prayer is part of that seeing in a mirror dimly, and it is also part of our deep yearning for an ever-clearer vision of our God. As we read Scripture, the past and the future converge in the present moment. We hear words from long ago – some of which can appear strange and confusing – and yet, the Holy Spirit is living and active in the present. In this place of relationship and revelation, we open ourselves to the possibility of being changed, of being reshaped in a way that is good for us and all creation.

It is important that the words of prayer and Scripture should penetrate deep within rather than be a mere veneer. A quiet location is therefore a helpful starting point. For some, domestic circumstances or daily schedule make that difficult, but it is never impossible to become more fully present to God. The depths of our being can still be accessed no matter the world's clamour and activity. An awareness of this is all part of our journey from a false sense of control to a place of letting go, to a place where there is an opportunity for transformation.

Sometimes in our attention to Scripture, there will be connection with places of joy or pain; we might be encouraged or provoked or both. As we look and see and encounter God more deeply, there will be thanksgiving and repentance; the cries of our heart will surface as we acknowledge our needs and desires for ourselves and the world. The liturgy of Morning Prayer gives this voice and space.

I find it helpful to begin Morning Prayer by lighting a candle. This marks my sense of purpose and my acknowledgement of Christ's presence with me. It is also a silent prayer for illumination as I prepare to be attentive to what I see in the mirror, both of myself and of God. Amid the revelation of Scripture and the cries of my heart, the constancy of the tiny flame bears witness to the hope and light of Christ in all that is and will be.

When the candle is extinguished, I try to be still as I watch the smoke disappear. For me, it is symbolic of my prayers merging with the day. I know that my prayer and the reading of Scripture are not the smoke and mirrors of delusion. Rather, they are about encounter and discovery as I seek to venture into the day to love and serve the Lord as a disciple of Jesus Christ.

+ Rachel Treweek

9

Monday 30 November
Andrew the Apostle

Psalms 47, 147.1-12
Ezekiel 47.1-12
or Ecclesiasticus 14.20-end
John 12.20-32

John 12.20-32

'Sir, we wish to see Jesus' (v.21)

Advent has begun. In very different circumstances from a year ago, we embark on the season of looking back and looking forward: reflecting on Christ's first coming in great humility and his second coming in glorious majesty. Yet our perspective lies between the two, here and now 'in the time of this mortal life' as the Advent Collect says.

Our Advent desire is therefore not so different to the request made through Philip and Andrew by the devout Greeks, 'we wish to see Jesus'. In the midst of all the familiarity of Advent and Christmas, what better longing than to have our eyes opened to see afresh both the child in the manger, and the ruler and judge of all, and hear them speak into our own time.

To do this, Jesus' words are perhaps the guide we need now. We need to be prepared to let go of life, to receive new life; to let a seed die to bear new fruit. What if we are called to lay aside old comfortable understandings of Jesus, that have become too small or old or dry, so that we can receive Jesus in new ways, more deeply, more fully, in a fresh Advent coming? Let's be open to letting go, and letting him reveal himself to us in renewed personal encounter, in whatever ways he desires. May our prayer this Advent be a radical requesting, 'We want to see you, Jesus'.

COLLECT

Almighty God,
who gave such grace to your apostle Saint Andrew
that he readily obeyed the call of your Son Jesus Christ
    and brought his brother with him:
call us by your holy word,
and give us grace to follow you without delay
    and to tell the good news of your kingdom;
through Jesus Christ your Son our Lord,
who is alive and reigns with you,
in the unity of the Holy Spirit,
one God, now and for ever.

   Reflection by **Sarah Rowland Jones**

Psalms **80**, 82 *or* **5**, 6 (8)   **Tuesday 1 December**
Isaiah 43.1-13
Revelation 20

Revelation 20
'Then I saw ...' (vv.1,4,11)

We want to see Jesus – and now we must let the testimony of one who has seen, paint an amazing picture for us. From the very first chapter of the book of the Revelation, where we read 'I saw one like the Son of Man ...' we are given a vivid depiction of Jesus, the Christ, the promised Messiah, and of his cosmic and eternal victory over evil, sin and death – including pandemics and all their consequences.

It might be said that apocalyptic Scripture is closer to parable than prophecy. Just as Jesus taught that the kingdom of God is like a mustard seed, or wise and foolish bridesmaids, or a farmer sowing seed, and more besides, so John tells us that the salvation of Christ is like earthquakes and tempests, angels and trumpets, mythical creatures and great battles, and most of all, of the ultimate triumph of redemptive, all-sacrificing love.

Here we see Jesus, not as the sort of therapeutic problem solver that so much of contemporary culture seeks. He's not encouraging us to get our act together and find self-fulfilment, if only we follow him more closely. Rather, we're invited to dwell on the enormity of the catastrophe that is evil, invading and infiltrating every aspect of creation, ourselves included – and then to discover the even greater majesty and glory of what God Almighty has done for us in Jesus Christ. It's quite an eye-opener!

Almighty God,
give us grace to cast away the works of darkness
and to put on the armour of light,
now in the time of this mortal life,
in which your Son Jesus Christ came to us in great humility;
that on the last day,
when he shall come again in his glorious majesty
to judge the living and the dead,
we may rise to the life immortal;
through him who is alive and reigns with you,
in the unity of the Holy Spirit,
one God, now and for ever.

COLLECT

Reflection by **Sarah Rowland Jones**   11

Wednesday 2 December

Revelation 21.1-8

'... a new heaven and a new earth' (v.1)

In life we experience both continuity and change in time's inexorable unfolding, and we expect something of this in our spiritual lives too. To pray as Jesus taught us, 'your will be done, on earth as in heaven' seems to imply a sense of commonality between the two. But now John sees our old familiar earth, and the heaven we think we know, passing away completely (together with the sea, so often a symbol of the dangerously chaotic and alien in Old Testament writing and culture).

There will be a new heaven and a new earth – both utterly transformed through the revolutionary change of this all-encompassing victory over Death and Hades, and all that comes with them. This year, it's been particularly hard to know where to begin in finding concepts through which to conceive this redeemed, restored, and entirely recreated existence, so different from our experience. Yet whatever it looks like, at the heart of it we will find that we are God's and God is with us, and we shall know the sheer love, comfort and security of God's embrace.

Our physical and spiritual eyes alike are so often clouded by the tears of life's struggles. In Advent, we turn to the coming Lord, asking him to wipe them away, so that we can begin to see this promise he sets before us: 'See, I am making all things new.'

COLLECT

Almighty God,
give us grace to cast away the works of darkness
and to put on the armour of light,
now in the time of this mortal life,
in which your Son Jesus Christ came to us in great humility;
that on the last day,
when he shall come again in his glorious majesty
    to judge the living and the dead,
we may rise to the life immortal;
through him who is alive and reigns with you,
in the unity of the Holy Spirit,
one God, now and for ever.

Reflection by **Sarah Rowland Jones**

Psalms **42**, 43 *or* 14, **15**, 16
Isaiah 44.1-8
Revelation 21.9-21

Thursday 3 December

Revelation 21.9-21
'... the glory of God and a radiance' (v.11)

After leaving university I went to work in London, and over the following 15 years there and in other capitals of the world, I had more than my fill of commuting, traffic pollution and other downsides of the metropolis. Living now in all the rural beauty of Pembrokeshire in west Wales, close to the coastal path and its spectacular scenery, I must admit that a picture of heaven as a return to city life is definitely unappealing.

But this new heavenly Jerusalem is no urban jungle. The key is in the phrase that it has 'the glory of God and a radiance like a very rare jewel'. And then the description goes on to picture what seem to be ideals of theological and aesthetic completeness, symmetry, riches and beauty – an utter perfection.

Perhaps it's easy for us to come up with pictures of a very personal ideal of perfection – birdsong and rainbows, perhaps. I might be tempted by a long, deep, hot bath with a good book and a glass of full-bodied red wine, accompanied by jazz-blues. But I recognize that for some that would be purgatory!

Yet this I know, or at least dare to believe, that whatever in me grasps at this imagined picture of something heavenly will be more than satisfied, beyond my wildest dreams, by what truly lies ahead. And it is in seeking to see Christ more fully, that my eyes will be opened to find it.

Almighty God,
as your kingdom dawns,
turn us from the darkness of sin to the
light of holiness,
that we may be ready to meet you
in our Lord and Saviour, Jesus Christ.

COLLECT

Friday 4 December

Psalms **25**, 26 *or* 17, **19**
Isaiah 44.9-23
Revelation 21.22 – 22.5

Revelation 21.22 – 22.5

' .. the leaves of the tree are for the healing of the nations' (22.2)

One weakness of the English language is that, because the singular and plural 'you' are the same, we too often individualistically read the promises of Scripture and of salvation as if they were for each of us alone, rather than for us corporately.

Here, we are reminded that God's redemptive love in Jesus Christ touches peoples and nations. There will be no more night, no darkness of the shadow of evil and death, not merely 'for me' but 'for us'. Yet grasping the breadth of that 'for us' is hard.

In her poem 'What they did yesterday afternoon', British-Somali poet Warsan Shire writes of holding an atlas in her lap, running her fingers across the whole world, and whispering, 'where does it hurt? it answered, everywhere, everywhere, everywhere.' This year we've been seeing illness, suffering and death touch us individually, nationally and globally in ways that we could not have imagined. However deeply we've been affected, we know there's far more pain and sorrow than we can ever comprehend.

But our Jesus is the one who does not shy away from any suffering, anywhere in creation. He looks it in the eye, shoulders it on the cross, and bears it into the new Jerusalem, so it will find healing salve. This Advent, how can we learn to see, to recognize, this Jesus and his redeeming love at work in the wider pains we see about us?

COLLECT

Almighty God,
give us grace to cast away the works of darkness
and to put on the armour of light,
now in the time of this mortal life,
in which your Son Jesus Christ came to us in great humility;
that on the last day,
when he shall come again in his glorious majesty
    to judge the living and the dead,
we may rise to the life immortal;
through him who is alive and reigns with you,
in the unity of the Holy Spirit,
one God, now and for ever.

Reflection by **Sarah Rowland Jones**

Psalms **9** (10) *or* 20, 21, **23**   **Saturday 5 December**
Isaiah 44.24 – 45.13
Revelation 22.6-end

Revelation 22.6-end
'Amen. Come, Lord Jesus!' (v.20)

There are times when the cynic within me is tempted to read words in Scripture such as the repeated phrase 'I am coming soon' with considerable scepticism. Almost two millennia after this was written in Revelation, we might claim that the predicted coming is showing no signs of being imminent. And so we read these words, perhaps for the umpteenth time, and might feel our eyes glazing over just a bit.

Therefore, it's all too easy to let myself off the hook of anticipating Jesus' coming and to pour rather more of my focus and energies into my own ambitions and aspirations for this life. In the narrow perspective of the here and now, there are all sorts of things I'd really quite like to see and do, achieve and experience, without being interrupted and thwarted by the second coming of Jesus Christ.

Yet at the same time, I recognize myself as most certainly among those who thirst for something more eternally satisfying; among those who, when the chips are down, want nothing more than to take the water of life as a gift. And so I know I must join in the Advent prayer of 'Come. Come, Lord Jesus!'

I still can't say with any certainty what that coming might mean, or how I might recognize it – but when it happens, I'm confident I'll know for sure. So I'll dare to keep on asking.

Almighty God,
as your kingdom dawns,
turn us from the darkness of sin to the
light of holiness,
that we may be ready to meet you
in our Lord and Saviour, Jesus Christ.

COLLECT

Monday 7 December

Psalm **44** *or* 27, **30**
Isaiah 45.14-end
1 Thessalonians 1

1 Thessalonians 1

'We always give thanks ... and mention you in our prayers' (v.2)

This is probably the earliest of Paul's known letters, sent from Corinth around AD 51, to the young church at Thessalonica. Paul and Silas (also known as Silvanus) had been forced to flee after only a short time in this major port city (Acts 17.1-10), so now he writes to encourage the congregation left behind. He shares his pastoral concern, offers prayerful support for their steadfastness and develops the teaching he was unable to complete while with them.

Though Paul spent only a limited time with these new Christians, they forged a lasting place in his heart, such that he now remembers them frequently, praying for their wellbeing and giving thanks for all they are to him. The example of their lives – rooting themselves deeply in Jesus Christ and keeping on growing in faith despite being so briefly under Paul's wing – is also influencing others they have never met, and never will, this side of heaven.

It's a welcome reminder that even our most fleeting of contact with others can have lasting spiritual impact – on them, and on us – which can re-echo more widely. It's an encouragement both to give thanks for those who have influenced us in our journey of faith, and to pray that we might have a similar influence on those we meet, whether or not we ever learn what impact we have had.

COLLECT

O Lord, raise up, we pray, your power
and come among us,
and with great might succour us;
that whereas, through our sins and wickedness
we are grievously hindered
in running the race that is set before us,
your bountiful grace and mercy
may speedily help and deliver us;
through Jesus Christ your Son our Lord,
to whom with you and the Holy Spirit,
be honour and glory, now and for ever.

Reflection by **Sarah Rowland Jones**

Psalms **56**, 57 *or* 32, **36**
Isaiah 46
1 Thessalonians 2.1-12

Tuesday 8 December

1 Thessalonians 2.1-12

'... to please God who tests our hearts' (v.4)

It took me a long time to recover from being brought up to 'be a good girl'. This seemed to equate to developing habits of pleasing others that lasted long past the need to follow the wise counsel of parents and teachers. Into adulthood I found myself jumping through real and imagined hoops held out by others, who might have little or no claim on my life, or what they supposed were my best interests at heart.

Somewhere along the line, the penny resoundingly dropped that pleasing God fell into an entirely different category from 'pleasing mortals'. For God truly does understand us better than we understand ourselves, and knows and desires what is best for us. And therefore, to please him is not constraining, but, I discovered, offers a far greater liberty and encouragement to 'be myself' than I'd ever guessed could be possible. The complement to this was learning to desire that others also should find themselves drawn to please God, and discover this freedom of the gospel, even if this meant doing other than what I might hope of them.

Instead of being daunted by the thought that God tests my heart, I've come to find it a reassurance. Through the lens of Advent, I'm praying to know more fully Christ's tender gaze upon me. Come, Lord Jesus!

> Almighty God,
> purify our hearts and minds,
> that when your Son Jesus Christ comes again as
> judge and saviour
> we may be ready to receive him,
> who is our Lord and our God.

COLLECT

Reflection by **Sarah Rowland Jones**   17

Wednesday 9 December

1 Thessalonians 2.13-end

'... God's word, which is also at work in you believers' (v.13)

Being grateful doesn't always come easily. Studies suggest that negativity impacts on us about five times as much as the positive. Bad emotions, experiences, comments and the like sink into us and stay with us. This over-alertness to adversity may be a legacy of our distant human past, when mistaking a stick for a snake, for example, might not be dangerous, but making the opposite error could prove fatal.

Paul's emphasis on constantly giving thanks echoes a similar call in many psalms, as well as by the Greek philosophers, and gratitude has long been seen as a mainstay of spiritual and societal wellbeing. Today, keeping a gratitude diary is thought to aid mental and emotional health, provided it reflects what genuinely deserves our thankfulness (and not, for example, feeling under obligation to accept what isn't authentically good for us).

As Christians, such habits of gratitude help us reappraise life, by attuning ourselves to be more alert to God's word in our lives, and to recognizing it 'at work among us who believe' in ways we might not otherwise have noticed. The presence of Jesus Christ, the Word of God made flesh and come among us, is limitless in the way he meets us in transformative, redemptive love. It's the Advent promise of Christ's coming, presented to us once again, in fresh perspective.

COLLECT

O Lord, raise up, we pray, your power
and come among us,
and with great might succour us;
that whereas, through our sins and wickedness
we are grievously hindered
in running the race that is set before us,
your bountiful grace and mercy
may speedily help and deliver us;
through Jesus Christ your Son our Lord,
to whom with you and the Holy Spirit,
be honour and glory, now and for ever.

Psalms 53, **54**, 60 *or* 37*
Isaiah 48.1-11
1 Thessalonians 3

Thursday 10 December

1 Thessalonians 3

' ... when I could bear it no longer' (v.5)

Paul honestly admits he could hang on no longer. Twice he says that waiting for news became unbearable. When Timothy returned with a good report, he recognizes that he had given in to unnecessary worry, whereas he should have had confidence that the Thessalonians would hold on in faith. Or perhaps this is another way of saying that he should have trusted that God's word at work among them would be sufficient.

There's a lovely prayer in the Anglican Church of Southern Africa's Prayer Book, which invites us to entrust all who are dear to the never-failing care and love of the God of everlasting mercy, 'both for this life and for the life to come, knowing that you are doing for them things beyond all that we can ask or think'. At first, I found this very challenging, because I realized that far too often, I neither trusted others to walk wisely in the paths of faith, nor trusted God enough to believe that they were safe in his hands, no matter what. It made me realize my reflections about faith at work were very self-centred.

Paul, having admitted his wobbling trust in their faith, is now set free to be encouraged and encouraging in turn. Now his prayers are driven by hope and trust, not fear. I can feel his joyful relief, as he prays all may abound in love.

Almighty God,
purify our hearts and minds,
that when your Son Jesus Christ comes again as
judge and saviour
we may be ready to receive him,
who is our Lord and our God.

COLLECT

Friday 11 December

1 Thessalonians 4.1-12

'God did not call us to impurity but in holiness' (v.7)

Paul's theological and spiritual reflections and teachings are seamlessly woven through with practical consequences. God calls us in holiness, and this mark of the new life he puts within us inevitably shapes how we live. Our sanctification doesn't come as a consequence of our actions. Rather, these flow from God's holy will, urging us into the paths of righteousness.

Even so, we are partners in this process, choosing to follow the call or not. Some aspects of holy living are clear wherever life takes us – always being honest, faithful in relationships, kind, just, and so on. But it can also be challenging to work out what shape holiness takes in response to our own contexts and circumstances. The Thessalonians are called to keep their heads down within this busy sea-port where it had been so easy to stir up a mob and start a riot (Acts 17.5). Theirs is to be a testimony of quiet and reproachless living.

But holiness doesn't mean prim, prudish withdrawal. Sometimes holiness can prompt us to stick our heads above the parapet, and to be God's salt and light in the world in more obviously evident ways of counter-cultural living. How do we know what to do when? American writer and theologian Eugene Peterson speaks of discipleship as 'a long obedience in the same direction' – it comes from cultivating lifelong habits of listening to the call of the Holy One, and, even if we sometimes stumble, keeping close.

COLLECT

O Lord, raise up, we pray, your power
and come among us,
and with great might succour us;
that whereas, through our sins and wickedness
we are grievously hindered
in running the race that is set before us,
your bountiful grace and mercy
may speedily help and deliver us;
through Jesus Christ your Son our Lord,
to whom with you and the Holy Spirit,
be honour and glory, now and for ever.

20 | *Reflection by* **Sarah Rowland Jones**

Psalm **145** *or* 41, **42**, 43
Isaiah 49.1-13
1 Thessalonians 4.13-end

Saturday 12 December

1 Thessalonians 4.13-end

'Therefore encourage one another with these words' (v.18)

The first three chapters of this letter all conclude with a reference to the Thessalonians living in anticipation of Christ's coming. Now Paul shifts his emphasis from practical instructions about how to pursue godly, holy living under such expectations, to what lies beyond. Questions of death and Christ's return take centre stage.

So what are the words, what is the reassurance, with which Paul wants us to comfort one another? He offers us an image of the living and the dead being caught up together in the clouds as we meet the descending Christ. This has echoes of Daniel's account of 'one like a son of man' (7.13, NIV), or 'a human being' (NRSV), and of Luke's description of the Ascension, where Jesus is lifted up and a cloud takes him from the sight of the disciples who are then told that he 'will come in the same way as you saw him go into heaven' (Acts 1.9-11).

Paul finds words from the narratives and concepts of his own culture, and of those to whom he is writing. Such analogies have limited traction in our own age of astronomy and cosmological science. But the nub of Paul's message remains the same: whether Jesus Christ's coming is in or beyond our lifetime, we will be caught up in his embrace and will be with him for ever. Encouragement indeed. Come, Lord Jesus!

Almighty God,
purify our hearts and minds,
that when your Son Jesus Christ comes again as
judge and saviour
we may be ready to receive him,
who is our Lord and our God.

COLLECT

Monday 14 December

1 Thessalonians 5.1-11

'.. whether we are awake or asleep, we may live with him' (v.10)

Our reading for today works through a long, extended metaphor. Or, to be more accurate, it works through a pair of contrasting metaphors, set out skilfully. One set is positive, and the other is negative. On one side, we have night, darkness, sleep, drunkenness, ignorance and nefarious doings; on the other side, Paul gathers together day, light, wakefulness, sobriety, knowledge and upright dealings.

As a piece of writing, this is quite a triumph but, at the end of our reading, Paul does something unexpected, something that makes the whole thing as much of a triumph of theology as it has been a triumph of writing. Paul takes what he has lined up against each other, and drives a coach and horses through his neat set of contrasts. Daytime and being awake suggest life; night and sleep suggest death. Jesus, however, disrupts all of that, redeeming sleep, redeeming night, giving hope in face of death, since his promise of 'life with him' applies also to those who have died: 'whether we are awake or asleep we may live with him'. Death, which we so rightly oppose, the 'last enemy' (1 Corinthians 15.26), becomes also a 'sleep.

In Christ, Paul writes, whether we are awake or asleep, alive or dead, we are safe, and live with him.

C O L L E C T	O Lord Jesus Christ, who at your first coming sent your messenger to prepare your way before you: grant that the ministers and stewards of your mysteries may likewise so prepare and make ready your way by turning the hearts of the disobedient to the wisdom of the just, that at your second coming to judge the world we may be found an acceptable people in your sight; for you are alive and reign with the Father in the unity of the Holy Spirit, one God, now and for ever.

22 | *Reflection by* **Andrew Davison**

Psalms **70**, 74 *or* **48**, 52
Isaiah 50
1 Thessalonians 5.12-end

1 Thessalonians 5.12-end

'... hold fast to what is good' (v.21)

Walking around Rome, you see that almost every church is associated with some cardinal or other, since every cardinal, anywhere in the world, has a church in Rome. The link is shown by the cardinal's coat of arms, displayed above the door, and each of them bears a motto, offering some declaration of faith, or principle to live by.

The second half of 1 Thessalonians 5 is a treasure trove of possible mottos, rich territory for phrases to write below a coat of arms: 'rejoice always', 'always seek to do good', 'to one another and to all', 'hold fast to what is good' – the list goes on.

One phrase, towards the end of our reading – 'The one who calls you is faithful' – appealed to someone in the history of the theological college where I trained for ordination and later returned to teach: Westcott House in Cambridge. In an inspired gesture, these words were cast, in Greek, into the bell that calls the community to prayer each morning and evening: 'The one who calls you is faithful'.

Growing up, my mother often repeated words from Romans 12 to me and my sister: 'So far as it depends on you, live peaceably with all.' These words have set the course of her life. We may not have coats of arms, or bells to cast, but adopting a scriptural motto for life is not a bad idea for any of us.

God for whom we watch and wait,
you sent John the Baptist to prepare the way of your Son:
give us courage to speak the truth,
to hunger for justice,
and to suffer for the cause of right,
with Jesus Christ our Lord.

COLLECT

Reflection by **Andrew Davison**   23

Wednesday 16 December

2 Thessalonians 1

'... according to the grace of our God and the Lord Jesus Christ'
(v.12)

Persecution can strengthen bonds between those who suffer under it together. We see that in our reading today. Within this persecuted Church, 'the love of every one of you for one another is increasing'. Persecution can also lead to bitterness towards persecutors, however, and a sense of distance from anyone who does not closely belong to our own group. That is also on view here, with the language of vengeance and separation.

That language can make our passage today difficult to read. Talk of vengeance and separation might seem a long way from the message of peace and forgiveness that we associate with the gospel, a long way, perhaps, from what might have drawn us to Christianity in the first place. If so, if the reading is otherwise difficult to connect with, one feature of it may offer us a toehold. Notice how central Jesus is: he is mentioned many times, six of them by name. Paul (or his follower, if Paul did not write 2 Thessalonians) tells us that judgement belongs to God and is in the hands of Jesus. We can take that to heart. Paul, or his follower, was equally sure that Christ's judgement will be one of widespread vengeance and destruction. We can leave that with Jesus, knowing that he came to save sinners. On the last day, mercy may triumph, more than was obvious to the writer of 2 Thessalonians.

COLLECT

O Lord Jesus Christ,
who at your first coming sent your messenger
to prepare your way before you:
grant that the ministers and stewards of your mysteries
may likewise so prepare and make ready your way
by turning the hearts of the disobedient to the wisdom of the just,
that at your second coming to judge the world
we may be found an acceptable people in your sight;
for you are alive and reign with the Father
in the unity of the Holy Spirit,
one God, now and for ever.

Reflection by **Andrew Davison**

Thursday 17 December

2 Thessalonians 2

'... the lawless one will be revealed, whom the Lord Jesus will destroy with the breath of his mouth' (v.8)

Our reading might sound similar in tone to the Book of Revelation, usually thought to be the final book of the New Testament to have been written. Both paint a picture of the world in its final phase, before the return of Christ and full of rebellion. In 2 Thessalonians, we have 'the lawless one'; in Revelation, the antichrist and the false prophet. In both, a sword comes from the mouth of Jesus. The shared imagery is striking.

These are raw visions. Until recently, they likely seemed a long way off. It was easy to distain apocalyptic writing, with its language of 'the day of the Lord', 'the lawless one', and 'lying wonders'. Richard Dawkins, for instance, reserves some of his sharpest dismissal of biblical texts for books with passages such as these.

The situation looks quite different since the arrival of COVID-19, and it has always looked different for the poor and downtrodden. Those who live at ease might find apocalyptic writing too extreme; not so those who live in poverty, or know daily extremity and loss. When we are comfortable, the idea of upheaval and overturning will sound unpalatable; for those with nothing, or seeing the world turned upside down, an apocalyptic reversal begins to sound more appealing.

That is reason enough not to dismiss apocalyptic passages. Here, as in Revelation, we find someone looking the horror of suffering, deceit and injustice in the face, and radiating a calm reassurance in the victory of God, the victory of justice and truth.

COLLECT

God for whom we watch and wait,
you sent John the Baptist to prepare the way of your Son:
give us courage to speak the truth,
to hunger for justice,
and to suffer for the cause of right,
with Jesus Christ our Lord.

Friday 18 December

Psalms 77, **98** *or* **51**, 54
Isaiah 51.17-end
2 Thessalonians 3

2 Thessalonians 3

'Anyone unwilling to work should not eat' (v.10)

These words may seem a bit out of place in the New Testament, which is otherwise such a communitarian document. Yes, we cannot deny that Paul is particularly worried about idleness, and has some sharp words for those who live that way. Why would that be?

One angle comes in the association of idleness with gossip, tittle-tattle and mischief. We find that, for instance, in 1 Timothy 5.13, a passage that censures those who 'learn to be idle, gadding about from house to house', adding that 'they are not merely idle, but also gossips and busybodies, saying what they should not say'. Idle people may be in danger of spending their time pulling members of the community down, not building them up. Paul's worry about idleness would turn out to be communitarian, after all.

We should also remember that life could be precarious in the ancient world, for all but the rich, and whole regions could be only one bad harvest away from starvation. That rings newly true for us too. Wellbeing and security for all called for the active participation of everyone.

Contribution to the common good, however, is not simply a means to an end. We grow as a community by working with one another and for one another – something again made clear in recent months – including those who have lost their jobs. In that way, again, Paul's great communal image of the Church as a body remains as important now as then.

COLLECT
O Lord Jesus Christ,
who at your first coming sent your messenger
to prepare your way before you:
grant that the ministers and stewards of your mysteries
may likewise so prepare and make ready your way
by turning the hearts of the disobedient to the wisdom of the just,
that at your second coming to judge the world
we may be found an acceptable people in your sight;
for you are alive and reign with the Father
in the unity of the Holy Spirit,
one God, now and for ever.

| *Reflection by* **Andrew Davison**

Psalms 144, **146**
Isaiah 52.1-12
Jude

Saturday 19 December

Jude
'... save others by snatching them out of the fire' (v.23)

The Letter of Jude stands out among the books of the New Testament. It is steeped in the Jewish literature we call the Pseudepigripha: books, often apocalyptic, that didn't make it into the Old Testament. Jude's letter itself is apocalyptic in tone, with scenes that would not look out of place in a Marvel Studios blockbuster. Jude also offers a magnificent line in denunciation: 'waterless clouds ... autumn trees ... wild waves ... wandering stars ...'

All that bleakness, however, all those warnings, feature in the end rather like Paul writing in the opening chapters of Romans, where he paints a darker and darker picture so that the message of grace may shine all the brighter. In that way, Jude goes on to urge his readers to have mercy and to seek salvation for those whose fate might otherwise have looked rather grim from the first half of the letter. In urging that, however, he is sober, adding a note of caution: reaching out to those who are on dangerous paths can be quite dangerous itself.

That endeavour is to rest upon the foundation of faith, or rather 'the faith', described here as 'your most holy faith' and as 'the faith that was once for all entrusted to the saints'. That is the foundation. The message of that faith, for all the fierce language early on, comes round to a message of mercy and of saving those we can (with that caveat about it not being a light matter).

COLLECT

God for whom we watch and wait,
you sent John the Baptist to prepare the way of your Son:
give us courage to speak the truth,
to hunger for justice,
and to suffer for the cause of right,
with Jesus Christ our Lord.

Reflection by **Andrew Davison** | 27

Monday 21 December

2 Peter 1.1-15

'... become participants in the divine nature' (v.4)

The first chapter of 2 Peter sets out the goal of God's purpose for us in extraordinary terms, in terms that we might take to be an exaggeration, simply going too far, were they not there in holy writ. The goal of salvation, we read here, is that we 'may become participants in the divine nature'.

This is an ideal passage to be reading in the run up to Christmas, when God shared our life, so that we might come to share his. 'He was made sharer in our mortality,' wrote Augustine, 'that we might also be made partakers in His divinity'.

The message of this season, we read in the Creed of St Athanasius, is that humanity and divinity are united in Jesus, not as if God were changed into flesh, but by taking our humanity into God. This phrase from the Creed can help us think through what this 'participation in the divine nature' might mean. It is not that we are to be turned into God and stop being human, any more than God turned into a human being and stopped being God. To be a participant in the divine nature is something that happens not by conversion of our humanity into divinity, but by taking of our humanity into God.

COLLECT

God our redeemer,
who prepared the Blessed Virgin Mary
to be the mother of your Son:
grant that, as she looked for his coming as our saviour,
so we may be ready to greet him
when he comes again as our judge;
who is alive and reigns with you,
in the unity of the Holy Spirit,
one God, now and for ever.

Reflection by **Andrew Davison**

Psalms **124**, 125, 126, 127
Isaiah 54
2 Peter 1.16 – 2.3

Tuesday 22 December

2 Peter 1.16 – 2.3

'... until the day dawns and the morning star rises in your hearts'
(1.19)

There is a fair bit of daystar imagery in the New Testament. 'I am the root and descendant of David, the bright morning star', Christ says of himself in the Book of Revelation (22.16). He is, Zechariah sang, the 'dawn from on high'. The date of Christmas, when the nights are longest, helps us, at least in the Northern Hemisphere, to appreciate Christ as the morning star, who dawned in the middle of our darkness, at the midnight of the year. Indeed, he was born at midnight itself, at least according to a tradition grounded in words from the Wisdom of Solomon (18.14-15, KJV): 'For while all things were in quiet silence, and that night was in the midst of her swift course, Thine Almighty word leaped down from heaven out of thy royal throne.'

Those who witnessed Christ's transfiguration were 'eyewitnesses of his majesty', we read today. That might seem the very opposite of the nativity, which took place not in glory, but in adversity; not in the day, among friends, but in the night, among animals; not on a mountaintop, but in a cave among the cattle. Yet, despite these differences, Christmas is a manifestation, a transfiguration. Mary and Joseph were also 'eyewitnesses of his majesty' in Bethlehem, as were the shepherds. The majesty of God is seen as clearly and profoundly in the humility of the baby as it was seen, by the chosen few, revealed in glory upon the mountain of transfiguration.

Eternal God,
as Mary waited for the birth of your Son,
so we wait for his coming in glory;
bring us through the birth pangs of this present age
to see, with her, our great salvation
in Jesus Christ our Lord.

COLLECT

Reflection by **Andrew Davison** | 29

Wednesday 23 December

2 Peter 2.4-end

'... people are slaves to whatever masters them' (v.19)

These words have a contemporary sound to them. They ring true as we look upon a world that has been mastered by possessions, fame, power, drugs, alcohol, pornography, adulation, and so much else; as we see human beings, created in the image of God, sometimes ourselves among them, behaving like 'irrational animals, mere creatures of instinct'. The nativity we are about to celebrate shows something very different: God coming into the world as a naked baby. Being helpless, he mastered nothing, but being humble, he was not mastered by anything either.

Infants are entirely dependent upon others, usually their parents most of all. The image of the Lord God as an infant lying in the arms of Mary or Joseph is arresting: the idea of God, the meaning of all things, lying without words. It teaches us an important message about slavery and mastery. Freedom from what might enslave us comes from simplicity, from knowing what matters most, which comes down to placing God first of all.

That freedom from slavery, however, does not mean the sort of self-mastery that the Stoics practised, with an attitude of indifference and detachment. In the infant Christ, whose birth we are about to celebrate, we see simplicity, but also a reminder that our lives are bound together, that we depend on one another, and that we need not, nor should not, try to shake that off. If that was ever in doubt, we have come to see it clearly over recent months.

COLLECT

God our redeemer,
who prepared the Blessed Virgin Mary
to be the mother of your Son:
grant that, as she looked for his coming as our saviour,
so we may be ready to greet him
when he comes again as our judge;
who is alive and reigns with you,
in the unity of the Holy Spirit,
one God, now and for ever.

30 | *Reflection by* **Andrew Davison**

Psalms **45**, 113
Isaiah 56.1-8
2 Peter 3

Thursday 24 December
Christmas Eve

2 Peter 3
'... all things continue as they were from the beginning' (v.4)

Do things continue 'as they were from the beginning'? What difference does Christmas make?

God is the goal of all things. With the nativity, the end of all things has come to us in the middle, while time still runs its course. Had God's attitude towards the world been one of wrath and fury, that coming would have unmade everything. At Christmas, however, we see that God came to seek and to save the lost. That God should come, and yet 'all things continue as they were from the beginning' is a sign of God's mercy. It also means that however cataclysmic the transition will be at the end of the world – a transition we read about in our reading today – it takes place within the embrace of Christmas. When Christ returns, it will be to a world that he has already made his own. 'All things continue as they were from the beginning': God took up the order of things, being born in our midst, rather than rubbing it all out and starting again.

In another sense, however, God has not left everything to continue as before. At Christmas, God did the supremely new thing, something so full of newness that only the resurrection and the creation of the world can compare with it for novelty. That supreme new thing was the birth of God as one of us: the end, appearing in our midst, so that the renewal of all things could begin.

Almighty God,
you make us glad with the yearly remembrance
of the birth of your Son Jesus Christ:
grant that, as we joyfully receive him as our redeemer,
so we may with sure confidence behold him
when he shall come to be our judge;
who is alive and reigns with you,
in the unity of the Holy Spirit,
one God, now and for ever.

COLLECT

Friday 25 December

Christmas Day

Psalms 110, 117
Isaiah 62.1-5
Matthew 1.18-end

Matthew 1.18-end

'... you are to name him Jesus, for he will save his people from their sins' (v.21)

In one sense, his name, Jesus, is just a name: common as Yeshua in Hebrew, or as Iesous in Greek. Having an ordinary name turns out to be part of what it means for God to be incarnate among ordinary people, in the matter, culture and humanity we share.

'Jesus' has not remained just one more name, however. Paul says that God: 'gave him the name that is above every name, so that at the name of Jesus every knee should bend, in heaven and on earth and under the earth, and every tongue should confess that Jesus Christ is Lord, to the glory of God the Father' (Philippians 2.9-11).

In the middle ages, and still today for some Christians, that meant never saying the name of Jesus (perhaps not even ever hearing it) without making some small act of reverence, such as bowing the head. The law of the Church of England recommended this well into the Reformation: 'when in time of Divine Service the Lord Jesus shall be mentioned, due and lowly reverence shall be done by all persons present, as it hath been accustomed; testifying by these outward ceremonies and gestures their inward humility, Christian resolution, and due acknowledgment that the Lord Jesus Christ, the eternal Son of God, is the only Saviour of the world.'

That may not be your custom, but one good way to meet the Christmas story with gratitude might be a resolution to greet the holy name with particular reverence in the year ahead.

COLLECT

Almighty God,
you have given us your only-begotten Son
to take our nature upon him
and as at this time to be born of a pure virgin:
grant that we, who have been born again
and made your children by adoption and grace,
may daily be renewed by your Holy Spirit;
through Jesus Christ your Son our Lord,
who is alive and reigns with you,
in the unity of the Holy Spirit,
one God, now and for ever.

32 | *Reflection by* **Andrew Davison**

Psalms 13, 31.1-8, 150
Jeremiah 26.12-15
Acts 6

Saturday 26 December
Stephen, deacon, first martyr

Acts 6
'Stephen, a man full of faith and the Holy Spirit' (v.5)

From the early days of the Church, we see that a degree of specialization grew up among its leaders, between practical service of the needy, and prayer and teaching. The distinction underlines how integral both are to the life of the Church, so central that each needed to be pursued with expertise, wholehearted diligence and attention. Both elements – service of the word of God and of the poor – stem from Christ: the Word Incarnate and the True Bread, the gospel preacher who fed the hungry and healed the sick, Jesus, who is for us at Christmas the wordless Word, and the hungering Bread. God has not come to us in this way to leave us unchanged. Rather, we are called to follow his example: Christ's example of what God is like, and how humanity ought to be.

That imitation is shown particularly well in Stephen, not only in his life of service, but also in the manner of his death, which echoes the story of Christ's passion: the false comments about the destruction of the temple, for instance, and both sets of Stephen's dying words. Like Christ, he commends his spirit (only, now to Jesus, not the Father) and prays that God will not hold his killers guilty. Stephen shows us how much it can cost to follow Christ, but also how glorious is its promise. We have a path to follow. 'Lo, we have the infant Christ,' Augustine wrote of the nativity, 'let us grow with Him.'

COLLECT

Gracious Father,
who gave the first martyr Stephen
grace to pray for those who took up stones against him:
grant that in all our sufferings for the truth
we may learn to love even our enemies
and to seek forgiveness for those who desire our hurt,
looking up to heaven to him who was crucified for us,
Jesus Christ, our mediator and advocate,
who is alive and reigns with you,
in the unity of the Holy Spirit,
one God, now and for ever.

Reflection by **Andrew Davison**   33

Monday 28 December

The Holy Innocents

Psalms **36**, 146
Baruch 4.21-27
or Genesis 37.13-20
Matthew 18.1-10

Matthew 18.1-10

'Who is the greatest in the kingdom of heaven?' (v.1)

Questions of greatness and status were clearly a preoccupation for the disciples. But they are following someone so completely uninterested in the idea he was willing to utterly empty himself to come among them. When the question came up again at the Last Supper, Jesus, the greatest among them, took the role of the servant and washed their feet – the action of the least.

Here, Jesus sets a little child before them. Imagine the scene and that child standing under the baffled scrutiny of the disciples. This is greatness, he says. Here is no romantic idealizing of childhood 'innocence'. No stage of life is more vulnerable and dependent. A child had no status or worth in that society. A child was unproductive, powerless, demanding and needy. A child was not looked up to in any sense at all. But in the kingdom, says Jesus, none is greater.

Jesus knew how deadly the pursuit of unredeemed 'greatness' really is. He knew the brutality of a society preoccupied with power, hierarchy and influence where greatness, significance and status are only sustained by oppressing the least. And this explains his fierce judgement on the abuse of the most vulnerable by the powerful. Then and now, his words are designed to shock his disciples and to provoke a deep, penitent reappraisal of the priorities and goals we live by. His teaching and judgements are as relevant as ever.

COLLECT

Heavenly Father,
whose children suffered at the hands of Herod,
though they had done no wrong:
by the suffering of your Son
and by the innocence of our lives
frustrate all evil designs
and establish your reign of justice and peace;
through Jesus Christ your Son our Lord,
who is alive and reigns with you,
in the unity of the Holy Spirit,
one God, now and for ever.

Reflection by **David Runcorn**

Psalms 19, 20
Isaiah 57.15-end
John 1.1-18

Tuesday 29 December

John 1.1-18
'In the beginning was the Word' (v.1)

Woven through the words and images of the famous opening verses of John's Gospel are signs, hints and clues about the incredible story that is about to unfold. If this were a painting, we would be standing well back to take in a huge and detailed landscape. If this were a musical, we would be listening to the overture before the curtain rises. Glimpses of the story surface in these verses like brief extracts of song, dance and narration. The interweaving of these themes offers a foretaste of what will soon be revealed. Already we are being drawn into something as mysterious as it is glorious.

The first verse contains the clue to the big picture. Starting with the same opening phrase as Genesis is bold and deliberate. This will be a creation story or, rather, a *re*-creation story, for all is beginning again. But the first creation story descended all too quickly into loss, grief and exile. Here, 'in the beginning', the music is full of light, energy and hope as the fullness of divine presence appearing in human flesh is revealed among us. Once again, as in the beginning, human life is given – but now in the fullness of grace and truth.

And how can the storyteller possibly know all this? He was there: 'we have seen his glory.'

COLLECT

Almighty God,
who wonderfully created us in your own image
and yet more wonderfully restored us
through your Son Jesus Christ:
grant that, as he came to share in our humanity,
so we may share the life of his divinity;
who is alive and reigns with you,
in the unity of the Holy Spirit,
one God, now and for ever.

Wednesday 30 December

Psalms 111, 112, **113**
Isaiah 59.1-15*a*
John 1.19-28

John 1.19-28
'I am not' (v.20)

There is no way into the presence of Jesus without first meeting the strange, edgy character of John the Baptist. The story itself begins on the edge, in the wilderness, outside all the presumed centres of religious authority and importance. John is a mystery. The authorities want to know who he is. No one can find the file on him. 'Who are you?' he is asked repeatedly. John never answers them. He just keeps saying 'No'. For John, the way of faith begins with knowing who we are *not*. John never names himself at all. They are asking the wrong person the wrong question. He refuses to be known except in relation to Christ. That is all he is there for: to call out and to point people to the one who is to come, the one whom – as yet – 'you do not know'.

So the opening exchanges of this Gospel begin with a series of emphatic, terse negations. Variations on the theme of 'No', 'I am *not*' occur nearly twelve times in this opening chapter. The human side of this story is firmly put in its place. There must be no confusion. 'I am not the Messiah!' But this is a positive negation. He is refusing to be known by the projections and needs of the world around him – and so must we. Who we truly are will be found in the one who is to come.

COLLECT

Almighty God,
who wonderfully created us in your own image
and yet more wonderfully restored us
through your Son Jesus Christ:
grant that, as he came to share in our humanity,
so we may share the life of his divinity;
who is alive and reigns with you,
in the unity of the Holy Spirit,
one God, now and for ever.

Reflection by **David Runcorn**

Psalm **102**
Isaiah 59.15*b*-end
John 1.29-34

Thursday 31 December

John 1.29-34

'Here is the Lamb of God!' (v.29)

The first precise mention of time occurs in this passage: 'The next day'. Three more such references will now follow in quick succession (1.35, 1.43 and 2.1). Up to this point, no precise chronology has framed the opening narrative and exchanges. We are meant to sense a change in energy and direction. Something is happening. In John's Gospel, specific time reference nearly always signals divine action and initiative. Sure enough, Jesus now appears for the first time. John immediately points to him and declares him. 'Behold!' After all those unresolved questions and denials – 'I am *not*' – the one who alone can truly say 'I Am' is revealed. The story now begins.

The most common image of the Lamb of God is of a trussed sacrificial lamb lying passively on the altar. But while it is true that John links Jesus, the Lamb of God, to the taking away of sin, there is some suggestion that a lamb on the altar is not the immediate image John has in mind here. Even today in the Middle East, leading flocks and guiding sheep is not the work of dogs; instead, a young ram takes this role. So although this story will end in the sacrifice, Jesus is revealed here as one who leads. Behold the *Ram* of God.

God in Trinity,
eternal unity of perfect love:
gather the nations to be one family,
and draw us into your holy life
through the birth of Emmanuel,
our Lord Jesus Christ.

COLLECT

Friday 1 January
Naming and Circumcision of Jesus

Psalms **103**, 150
Genesis 17.1-13
Romans 2.17-end

Romans 2.17-end

'... you then, that teach others, will you not teach yourself?' (v.21)

Context is all-important. Jewish/gentile tensions were apparent in Rome as elsewhere in the New Testament churches. There seems to have been a strong and vocal conservative minority of Jewish believers. This entire letter is an attempt to establish an understanding of the gospel where deeply divided groups honour each other as fellow heirs of the gospel first promised by God through Abraham.

Paul has just used his formidable rhetorical skills to offer his famous critique of the godless gentile world of Rome (Romans 1.18-32). We can imagine conservative Jewish believers cheering in the pews. But suddenly, without warning, his rhetorical focus shifts. He has suddenly turned his attack on them – the ones so sure of their own purity and rightness. In every way, he says, you stand judged even as you condemn others. Jesus had warned people about presuming to judge small errors of others while unaware how blinded they are by their own significant failings.

There are issues within our churches today that attract the same kind of entrenched divisions and presumptions of right and wrong. It is increasingly difficult to conduct genuine debate on the issues that matter deeply. The Church of England calls this 'good disagreement'. If we, as a Church, are to model a different way of being community in the midst of diversity and difference, Paul warns us that the first people we need to be teaching are ourselves.

COLLECT | Almighty God,
whose blessed Son was circumcised
in obedience to the law for our sake
and given the Name that is above every name:
give us grace faithfully to bear his Name,
to worship him in the freedom of the Spirit,
and to proclaim him as the Saviour of the world;
who is alive and reigns with you,
in the unity of the Holy Spirit,
one God, now and for ever.

| *Reflection by* **David Runcorn**

Psalm **18.1-30**
Isaiah 60.1-12
John 1.35-42

Saturday 2 January

John 1.35-42

'What are you looking for?' (v.38)

Another 'day' is declared again and, once again, Jesus appears, walking past John and his disciples. John immediately points him out – 'Look, he is the one all this is about'. Compelled by John's words, two of his own disciples promptly leave him and start to follow Jesus. The Ram of God is beginning to gather and lead his new flock. They give every impression of having no real idea who they are following or why. They may not even know who Jesus is at this point. Jesus turns and asks them what they are looking for. Their response – 'where are you staying?' – is not the most obvious reply. It perhaps reflects their awkwardness and confusion. But John always chooses his words very carefully. A better translation would be: 'Where is your abiding?' Jesus welcomes them: 'Come and see'.

I reflect that I have stayed in many places in my life, but abiding describes only a few. The word suggests a quality of depth, indwelling and true home. As so often, Jesus responds by taking words to a different level. For in John's Gospel, the Son only abides in the love and will of the Father. Jesus turns to us too. 'You want to know where I abide? Follow me. I will show you where true home is. It will be yours as well.'

Almighty God,
who wonderfully created us in your own image
and yet more wonderfully restored us
through your Son Jesus Christ:
grant that, as he came to share in our humanity,
so we may share the life of his divinity;
who is alive and reigns with you,
in the unity of the Holy Spirit,
one God, now and for ever.

COLLECT

Reflection by **David Runcorn**

39

Monday 4 January

John 2.1-12

'On the third day there was a wedding' (v.1)

The wedding that happens on the third day is also, with a little detective work, on the seventh day since John's Gospel began. The day of resurrection joins the day when creation is celebrated whole and this forms the climax to the opening section of John's Gospel. The miracle of water into wine is called the first sign. But this is not one sign among many; it is the premier sign – the key to interpreting all that follows.

Coming to a community where celebration has run dry and is powerless to renew itself, Jesus is revealed as the one who fills up and transforms what is empty. We can imagine the bewilderment of the steward and the utter confusion of the groom on being congratulated for suddenly producing such exceptional wine.

But it may just dawn on us that this is a story of *two* weddings. The Master of Ceremonies was right to go to the bridegroom – but he went to the wrong one! Jesus did this.

Alongside the blessing of a village wedding with that anonymous, extravagant gift of God, a greater celebration is beginning, not revealed 'until *now*'.

John the Baptist will shortly be describing Jesus as the bridegroom and himself as the best man. The wedding celebrations are ready to begin. Glory is revealed. The disciples believe. This is the marriage of heaven and earth. The world is a wedding and we are all invited.

COLLECT

Almighty God,
in the birth of your Son
you have poured on us the new light of your incarnate Word,
and shown us the fullness of your love:
help us to walk in his light and dwell in his love
that we may know the fullness of his joy;
who is alive and reigns with you,
in the unity of the Holy Spirit,
one God, now and for ever.

Reflection by **David Runcorn**

Tuesday 5 January

John 2.13-end

'Stop making my Father's house a market-place!' (v.16)

All four Gospels record this highly dramatic event in the temple. All agree in emphasizing the presence of the Passover festival in the background. But in the other three Gospels, this story happens late in the ministry of Jesus. It comes immediately after his triumphal entry into Jerusalem and clearly accelerates the events leading to his arrest and crucifixion. In terms of strict chronology, this sequence probably makes the most sense. But John places this story at the very beginning of his Gospel. It comes immediately after the miracle at Cana where he 'revealed his glory; and his disciples believed in him' (John 2.11). But that revelation was behind the scenes.

So in John's account, Jesus' first public appearance is when he suddenly bursts into the temple in Jerusalem and violently trashes and cleans out the religious market place faith has become. It could not be more dramatic.

John's narrative style is always more a theological reflection than a chronological biography. The importance lies in the meaning, not the fact, of the event.

It may be that John had in mind the prophecy of Malachi. 'See, ... the Lord whom you seek will suddenly come to his temple ... But who can endure the day of his coming, and who can stand when he appears? For he is like a refiner's fire ... and purifier of silver.' (Malachi 3.1-3)

God our Father,
in love you sent your Son
that the world may have life:
lead us to seek him among the outcast
and to find him in those in need,
for Jesus Christ's sake.

COLLECT

Wednesday 6 January

Epiphany

Psalms **132**, 113
Jeremiah 31.7-14
John 1.29-34

Jeremiah 31.7-14

*'See, I am going to ... gather them from the farthest parts
of the earth' (v.8)*

There are millions of people living in our world today who are
longing to hear a promise like this. Even more moving is the
prominence given to the most vulnerable – the blind, the lame, those
with child and even those in labour have special mention. These
words come as a moment of epiphany to a people in far exile, living
under the shadow of a foreign nation and gods. But Jeremiah was
always clear that the deepest crisis for his people was not the military
or political disaster that had overtaken them. The primary crisis was
God. Before Jeremiah could prophecy the people's return, he was
charged with confronting them over their loss of faith. A breaking-
down had to precede the building-up that these words foretell.

The New Testament writers quote and allude to the exile and exodus
years more than any other parts of the Old Testament. Among the
names the first Christians gave themselves were 'sojourners' and
'exiles'. Perhaps today's Church needs a deeper identification with
these stories. The theologian Elaine Heath insists the Church in our
own times is going through deep experiences of exile – 'a dark night
... a divinely initiated process of loss ... a process of purgation and
de-selfing'. She argues that the Church will persevere not because of
church programmes, 'but because God's love has kept it'.

The greatest crisis in any age – and its greatest hope – is always God.

COLLECT

O God,
who by the leading of a star
manifested your only Son to the peoples of the earth:
mercifully grant that we,
who know you now by faith,
may at last behold your glory face to face;
through Jesus Christ your Son our Lord,
who is alive and reigns with you,
in the unity of the Holy Spirit,
one God, now and for ever.

| *Reflection by* **David Runcorn**

Psalms **99**, 147.1-12 *or* **78.1-39***
Isaiah 63.7-end
1 John 3

Thursday 7 January

1 John 3

'See what love the Father has given us' (v.1)

The New Testament breathes an air of wonder and astonishment. In this passage, it is summarized as gift, mystery and promise.

First, our life in Christ continues, as it first began, as a gratuitous *gift* of love from the Father. (Gratuitous: done without good reason; uncalled for; with no cause). All is gift. One translation says love is 'lavished on us' (NIV). Little in this world prepares us to be loved like that.

Secondly, although receiving this gift moment by moment, our journey of faith is lived out in *mystery* for 'what we will be has not yet been revealed'. We are always becomers – part of a story that is out of sight, beyond imagining, and that often feels frankly improbable. We just do not look like the 'real thing' most of the time. Christian living has a limitless capacity for provoking guilt and condemnation on that score. Living as a mystery requires us to be reconciled to being always unfinished and unseen.

Thirdly, what is given and sustained in extravagant gift, and lived in mystery, is held in *promise* for us: 'when he is revealed, we shall be like him.' Christian faith involves trusting to Christ the secret of who we are becoming and the gift of our true self. The promise is secure, hidden in Christ. What more could we want?

Creator of the heavens,
who led the Magi by a star
to worship the Christ-child:
guide and sustain us,
that we may find our journey's end
in Jesus Christ our Lord.

COLLECT

Reflection by **David Runcorn** | 43

Friday 8 January

Psalms **46**, 147.13-end *or* **55**
Isaiah 64
1 John 4.7-end

1 John 4.7-end

'We love because he first loved us' (v.19)

Love that is offered first is offered before anything else. It is fore-given. Love that is offered first is therefore outside of any language of deserving. It is not based on reward or achievement. Love offered first needs no reason to exist. It is unconditional, without measure or purpose. Indeed, there is only one reason why it is present at all – God is love. But a fore-giving love is vulnerable, for it is offered without any guarantee it will be received. The cross warns there is no certainty such a love is welcome at all.

What if our greatest struggle is not with sin and our capacity for messing up (though they are not for minimizing)? For here in our flesh is revealed a way of loving so 'other' that it renders all our familiar techniques for winning and knowing ourselves loved and desirable completely useless. Love offered first is simply not interested.

So perhaps our greatest struggle is to accept the love with which God chooses to love us. What prepares us to love and be loved like that? It utterly dismantles all our carefully chosen strategies, our defences and our well-practised attempts at status, image and deserving. Instead we are called to love with the love that has been fore-given us.

So let us love one another – for no reason at all.

COLLECT

O God,
who by the leading of a star
manifested your only Son to the peoples of the earth:
mercifully grant that we,
who know you now by faith,
may at last behold your glory face to face;
through Jesus Christ your Son our Lord,
who is alive and reigns with you,
in the unity of the Holy Spirit,
one God, now and for ever.

| *Reflection by* **David Runcorn**

Psalms 2, **148** *or* **76**, 79
Isaiah 65.1-16
1 John 5.1-12

Saturday 9 January

1 John 5.1-12

'... whatever is born of God conquers the world' (v.4)

When I say that 'my faith is in Christ', I might mean 'this is my decision and what I believe'. Or I could be saying 'it is Christ who holds my faith'. The former can easily suggest that the business of having faith is my responsibility to sustain. The latter puts divine love at the centre. The stress is on Christ. Someone far more reliable both holds me and my fragile offerings. I am held safe in him.

But it is much more than that. In Christ we are drawn into a life of extraordinary, transforming vitality where all things are possible. 'Love is or it ain't. Thin love ain't love at all,' wrote novelist Toni Morrison. The love in John's Epistle is anything but thin. It conquers the world! It changes everything. Through it anything becomes possible.

Can we believe this? Is love really that powerful? It is much easier to be convinced by the powers that hate and destroy. The ability to imagine a love that is up to this task of transformation is not easy. Perhaps the first response is to let the sheer scale of John's vision and its bold confidence challenge us. What if we suspend disbelief and imagine, just for a moment, that this is true. Love conquers the world. Let the imagination go play. After all, our faith is in Christ.

Creator of the heavens,
who led the Magi by a star
to worship the Christ-child:
guide and sustain us,
that we may find our journey's end
in Jesus Christ our Lord.

COLLECT

Reflection by **David Runcorn** | 45

Monday 11 January

Psalms **2**, 110 *or* **80**, 82
Amos 1
1 Corinthians 1.1-17

Amos 1

'For three transgression ... and for four' (vv. 3,6,9,11,13)

I recently started a new job in Manchester, in the north of England. My colleagues have been very welcoming, but the truth is that I'm inherently suspect. You see, I'm from The south – London. Actually, it's even worse than that – I'm Australian and therefore the ultimate southerner. I'm quite used to this kind of geographic nicety, because as a child my clergyman father moved to a parish in Perth, Western Australia, and it took a long time for people to stop referring to him as a 'wise man from the East'.

There are few things that people appreciate less, I think, than a person coming from Somewhere Else and telling them what to do.

That, however, is precisely what Amos was called to do. He was a southerner, having spent most of his life in the southern kingdom, Judah, but he did his prophetic work in the northern kingdom, Israel. Were the Samarians likely to be happy about having a southerner come and give them a right good telling off? Absolutely not.

Amos, however, was bright. He began by denouncing the surrounding nations. He called them out for their violence and military excesses. He said that God would never forgive them. What a way to lull an audience into a false sense of security! There was a sting in the tail for the Israelites, however, as we'll see tomorrow.

COLLECT

Eternal Father,
who at the baptism of Jesus
revealed him to be your Son,
anointing him with the Holy Spirit:
grant to us, who are born again by water and the Spirit,
that we may be faithful to our calling as your adopted children;
through Jesus Christ your Son our Lord,
who is alive and reigns with you,
in the unity of the Holy Spirit,
one God, now and for ever.

| *Reflection by* **Meg Warner**

Psalms 8, **9** *or* 87, **89.1-18**
Amos 2
1 Corinthians 1.18-end

Tuesday 12 January

Amos 2

'... because they sell the righteous for silver' (v.6)

If you were to trace, in an atlas of the ancient world, the targets of Amos' righteous attacks, you would be able to see the extent of his cunning. He didn't just denounce a random set of nations, but directed his invective at Israel's closest neighbours: Damascus, Gaza, Ashdod and Tyre, Edom, Ammon and Moab.

You might remember the constant prayer of God's people – 'Lord, when will you punish our enemies?' You might even feel like praying something of the kind yourself from time to time. Amos must have seemed to the Israelites – for a short time anyway – like an answer to those prayers.

The best part would have been when Amos began to focus his criticism on Israel's southern neighbour, Judah. I imagine that residents of Manchester might feel something similar, were their civic leaders to criticize London. Do you feel like this sometimes, when your 'closest enemies' find themselves in the firing line?

Israel's smugness would not have lasted long, however, because Israel had been Amos' real target all along. Further, while Amos was proclaiming precisely the same punishment for Israel as for her violent, militaristic neighbours, Israel's 'crimes' were exclusively failures of social justice: Israel had been selfish, indulgent and exploitative, but she was to be punished as a war criminal.

If we are honest, Amos' prophecy hits home for us too, because the crimes of Israel are also our crimes.

Heavenly Father,
at the Jordan you revealed Jesus as your Son:
may we recognize him as our Lord
and know ourselves to be your beloved children;
through Jesus Christ our Saviour.

COLLECT

Reflection by **Meg Warner**   47

Wednesday 13 January

Amos 3

'You only have I known' (v.2)

When you read the Hebrew scriptures, with whom do you tend to identify? Do you see yourself as the descendant of the Israelites – one of God's chosen people? Or do you imagine yourself more as a descendant of their neighbours – waiting to come into the light that the New Testament shines upon the gentiles?

I suspect that most of us see ourselves as sometimes one and sometimes the other. We want to style ourselves God's 'chosen people', but we also sometimes feel excluded, and wonder why God singled out one particular nation for special favour.

For the Israelites, hearing Amos' messages would have felt less like being singled out for God's special favour than for God's special punishment. Actually, that is exactly the message that Amos means to send. For Amos, being God's chosen nation was not so much about special privilege as special responsibility. The invidious task of God's prophets was to tell the chosen people, in words they could understand, that they had failed to carry out their responsibilities.

This would not have been an easy message for Amos to proclaim. It would have been even less easy for Israel to hear. How easy do we find it to hear God's message for us? Does it sometimes seem to come from unlikely mouths? How do we respond to those awkward people whose fate it is to tell us hard truths that we don't wish to hear?

COLLECT

Eternal Father,
who at the baptism of Jesus
revealed him to be your Son,
anointing him with the Holy Spirit:
grant to us, who are born again by water and the Spirit,
that we may be faithful to our calling as your adopted children;
through Jesus Christ your Son our Lord,
who is alive and reigns with you,
in the unity of the Holy Spirit,
one God, now and for ever.

Reflection by **Meg Warner**

Psalms **21**, 24 *or* 90, **92**
Amos 4
1 Corinthians 3

Thursday 14 January

Amos 4

'... prepare to meet your God, O Israel!' (v.12)

Christians often think that prophecy is all about telling the future. In fact, Old Testament prophecy was more about 'telling the present'. One of the responsibilities of the prophets was to 'tell it how it is' to those with authority and wealth. This included telling the privileged about the likely, or inevitable, future consequences of their present actions.

In this chapter, we begin to get a hint of what the heart of Amos' prophecy might be: the hypocrisy of those who, on the one hand, love to attend worship and make impressive sacrifices, but who, at other times, casually oppress the needy and abuse their own authority.

Amos proclaims that the consequence of this kind of hypocrisy will be painful exile from the land. God has done everything possible to avoid this final, catastrophic punishment – by subjecting the Israelites to a series of escalating punishments and injustices – but nothing has been effective in rousing Israel from her complacency and prompting her to return to her God.

Thus God has no option, proclaims Amos, but to expel Israel from her land, in the most painful of ways. She will be dragged by fishhooks, says Amos, through holes in her walls. Amos is predicting the defeat of Israel by the Assyrians and her ignominious expulsion from her lands.

What has God been doing to get your attention? Has it worked?

Heavenly Father,
at the Jordan you revealed Jesus as your Son:
may we recognize him as our Lord
and know ourselves to be your beloved children;
through Jesus Christ our Saviour.

COLLECT

Reflection by **Meg Warner** | 49

Friday 15 January

Psalms **67**, 72 *or* **88** (95)
Amos 5.1-17
I Corinthians 4

Amos 5.1-17

'Seek good and not evil, that you may live' (v.14)

Despite God's escalating cycle of punishments, and Amos' insistence in chapters 1 and 2 that forgiveness is impossible, here Amos tells the Israelites that there is still time to repent and for God to relent from casting Israel out: 'It may be that the Lord, the God of Hosts, will be gracious to the remnant of Joseph.'

For all of Israel's failings, God does not want to banish her from her land. 'Seek me and live', says God. God, moreover, is stronger than Israel's enemies, and her neighbours. God can be trusted and relied upon to be Israel's source of safety and of life. Indeed, God is the source of all life. Amos reminds the Israelites that their God is not merely a territorial, national god, subject to the rise and fall of empires, but the very creator of the world, who turns dark into light and light to dark, who gives orders to the seas and who brings the forces of destruction against the strong.

Although the Israelites might hate to be confronted with the truth of their failings, and although God knows all those failings (so that any speech at all might be considered unwise), nevertheless, says Amos, Israel should seek good and not evil: Israel should do the one thing that might cause God to soften and relent – she should 'establish justice in the gate'.

Being confronted with the truth of your failings is never a comfortable experience – for us as much as for the ancient Israelites. The question, now as then, is how we respond. What can we do to 'establish justice in the gate'?

COLLECT

Eternal Father,
who at the baptism of Jesus
revealed him to be your Son,
anointing him with the Holy Spirit:
grant to us, who are born again by water and the Spirit,
that we may be faithful to our calling as your adopted children;
through Jesus Christ your Son our Lord,
who is alive and reigns with you,
in the unity of the Holy Spirit,
one God, now and for ever.

| *Reflection by* **Meg Warner**

Psalms 29, **33** *or* 96, **97**, 100
Amos 5.18-end
1 Corinthians 5

Saturday 16 January

Amos 5.18-end

'But let justice roll down like waters' (v.24)

In your worship community or church tradition, are you aware of a particular focus on worship, ritual and liturgy, or on action, justice and evangelism? Or to put the question another way: are you aware of a *suspicion* of worship, ritual and liturgy, or of action, justice and evangelism? Most congregations tend to have a preference for one, and many also have a corresponding suspicion of the other. This is not a new tension. In what is probably the best-known passage in all of Amos, Amos steps right into it.

'Why do you long for the Day of the Lord?', Amos asks the Israelites. He tells them they've got God entirely wrong! The day they long for will not bring them more luxury and privileges, but darkness and persecution. What's more, Amos goes on, their solemn festivals, sacrifices and lavish displays of worship do not impress God. The things that God loves are justice and righteousness.

Here, Amos certainly appears to come down strongly on one side of this divide. The call for 'justice and righteousness' is a regular feature of Old Testament prophecy, and it is not unusual for these virtues to be proclaimed over against sacrificial worship.

However, Amos isn't really attacking worship ritual and liturgy here. His real target was the hypocrisy of those who indulged in pretentious and self-satisfied displays of piety, while ignoring the plight of others, or even actively exploiting them. Ostentatious worship, without ethical behaviour, Amos was saying, was not only pointless, but offensive to God. That message hasn't dated.

Heavenly Father,
at the Jordan you revealed Jesus as your Son:
may we recognize him as our Lord
and know ourselves to be your beloved children;
through Jesus Christ our Saviour.

COLLECT

Reflection by **Meg Warner** | 51

Monday 18 January

Amos 6

'... you have turned justice into poison' (v.12)

We begin this new week pretty much where we ended the old one – with Amos continuing to rail against the indulgence of the citizens of the northern kingdom. It is not just the luxury enjoyed by the northerners that Amos objects to, but the complacency that allows leaders and the privileged to carry on enjoying the good life while around them 'Joseph' (a shorthand name for the northern kingdom) experiences ruin.

We, too, are outraged by this kind of behaviour – for example, when we see the directors of struggling companies laying off large numbers of unskilled workers while at the same time awarding themselves obscene bonuses.

We may not be so quick to recognize the same behaviour in ourselves, however – for example, when we continue enjoying the convenience of air travel, take-away coffee cups and single-use plastic containers, despite knowing that each of these contributes to global warming, which impacts disproportionately on precisely those populations that do not have the wealth and privilege to enjoy such conveniences.

Amos moves his rhetoric up a notch in this chapter, becoming clearer about the consequences of this behaviour continuing unchecked: 'they shall now be the first to go into exile, and the revelry of the loungers shall pass away.' God is at this very moment raising up a nation to deliver to 'the loungers' the punishment that they are bringing upon themselves.

COLLECT

Almighty God,
in Christ you make all things new:
transform the poverty of our nature by the riches of your grace,
and in the renewal of our lives
make known your heavenly glory;
through Jesus Christ your Son our Lord,
who is alive and reigns with you,
in the unity of the Holy Spirit,
one God, now and for ever.

Reflection by **Meg Warner**

Psalms **132**, 147.1-12 *or* **106*** (*or* 103) **Tuesday 19 January**
Amos 7
1 Corinthians 6.12-end

Amos 7

'I will rise against the house of Jeroboam with the sword' (v.9)

What does a good leader do when presented with an uncomfortable or inconvenient point of view? Generally, we want our leaders to listen when somebody close to them takes it upon themselves to 'speak truth to power'.

But are there some people you'd prefer our leaders *didn't* listen to? When the people giving advice have vested interests we are suspicious of – professional lobbyists or unelected 'special advisers', multinationals seeking to use their financial leverage, the vocal gun lobby in the USA – we might perhaps wish that our leaders didn't listen quite so carefully.

The question of to whom one should listen was a difficult one in the ancient world. Which prophets could be trusted? Unfortunately, the real test of a true prophet was the prophecy coming true. That made it awkward for prophets just starting out!

Amos dealt with this problem by claiming not to be a prophet at all – distancing himself from other transient preachers. Although his claim to be a herder and dresser of sycamore trees doesn't sound terrifically impressive to our ears, in fact Amos was signalling to King Jeroboam that he was a well-to-do man who had been taken away from his normal life and given a special message by God. The message was a devastating one, predicting disaster if not heeded. Still, Jeroboam didn't listen.

How do you decide which messages, and which messengers, to listen to? Have you ever wished you'd listened more closely?

Eternal Lord,
our beginning and our end:
bring us with the whole creation
to your glory, hidden through past ages
and made known
in Jesus Christ our Lord.

COLLECT

Reflection by **Meg Warner** | 53

Wednesday 20 January

Amos 8

'The end has come upon my people Israel' (v.2)

Amos now reports the fourth in a series of visions. The previous visions have predicted disaster and suffering. This time the vision is of a basket of summer fruits, which seems rather tame after the first three visions of plagues and disasters, and hardly calculated to strike fear into the hearts of the people!

This is indeed a strange chapter – unless you know something about biblical Hebrew. The vision is constructed around a pair of words that sound similar but that have very different meanings. The word 'fruit' as it appears in verses 1 and 2 is, in Hebrew, *qayits*. The word 'end', in verse 2, is, in Hebrew, *qayts*. It is typical of biblical Hebrew to build rhetoric around two similar sounding, but opposing, words, and the tactic is used here to great effect, as an image of warm ripeness morphs into an announcement of disaster and death.

The text doesn't, to be fair, dwell on the picture it implicitly conjures – of overripe fruit decaying and rotting as the late summer slides, inevitably, into autumn and winter, but that is the general idea.

The glamorous and self-important Israelites, who can't wait for the Sabbath to be over so that they can go back to selling the poor for silver, will find themselves entering God's Day of darkness, in which they will encounter mourning, lamentation, hunger and aimless wandering. God will turn Israel upside-down.

COLLECT

Almighty God,
in Christ you make all things new:
transform the poverty of our nature by the riches of your grace,
and in the renewal of our lives
make known your heavenly glory;
through Jesus Christ your Son our Lord,
who is alive and reigns with you,
in the unity of the Holy Spirit,
one God, now and for ever.

| *Reflection by* **Meg Warner**

Psalms **76**, 148 *or* 113, **115**
Amos 9
1 Corinthians 7.25-end

Thursday 21 January

Amos 9

'Are you not like the Ethiopians to me, O people of Israel?' (v.7)

Are you a sucker for a happy ending? Or do you find yourself feeling let down when all the tension and drama of a good story is resolved too easily and the characters wander off, arm in arm, into a golden sunset?

Until about halfway through this final chapter of the Book of Amos the picture is unremittingly bleak. Try reading just up to half-way through verse 8 and stopping there. How does the whole book feel to you? What is its overall message?

Now read again, but this time keep going. Does the change in tone seem abrupt to you? Amos pronounces that Israel will be re-established. All will be as it was previously, and even the throne of David will be re-established. This latter idea is curious, because the eventual fall of Israel to the Assyrians didn't spell the end of the Davidic monarchy, which persisted in Judah until the Judeans, in turn, succumbed to the Babylonians and experienced their own exile.

How do you account for the sudden change? And how do you now understand the book as a whole? There are at least a couple of different ways of doing this. One is to read the ending as later prophecy addressed not to the North, but to the South languishing in Babylon. Another is to understand the ending as a glorious hymn to hope, and to the faithful steadfastness of our God, who may punish, but who will never entirely forsake.

Eternal Lord,
our beginning and our end:
bring us with the whole creation
to your glory, hidden through past ages
and made known
in Jesus Christ our Lord.

COLLECT

Reflection by **Meg Warner** | 55

Friday 22 January

Hosea 1.1 – 2.1

'... take for yourself a wife of whoredom' (1.2)

Hosea is another eighth-century prophet, like Amos, and like Amos, Hosea probably did his prophetic work in the northern kingdom, of which, *unlike* Amos, he was a native.

If Amos' message was unpalatable to the people of the northern kingdom, then Hosea's message (and especially the first few chapters of the book) is unpalatable to many Christians today. Hosea begins within an extended, elaborate marriage metaphor, in which a chronically unfaithful woman represents the nation of Israel, God's own chronically unfaithful spouse. A significant part of the problem for today's readers, and women especially, is that God arguably sets up the 'whoring' woman, Gomer, to fail. God does this to make Hosea's prophecy more potent. This problematic portrait – of a God who uses people for inscrutable purposes – is not unlike the portrait in 2 Samuel 24, in which God instructs David to carry out a census, only to punish the people once David does so, or in the book of Job, in which God puts Job's fate into the hands of Satan. Here, in Hosea, the problem of God's character and relationship with evil, is compounded by a utilitarian (even abusive) portrayal of the principal female character and of her children.

At the same time, for many Christians, the book of Hosea speaks movingly and uniquely of God's faithfulness and fidelity, even in the face of the struggling and failures of God's people.

COLLECT

Almighty God,
in Christ you make all things new:
transform the poverty of our nature by the riches of your grace,
and in the renewal of our lives
make known your heavenly glory;
through Jesus Christ your Son our Lord,
who is alive and reigns with you,
in the unity of the Holy Spirit,
one God, now and for ever.

| *Reflection by* **Meg Warner**

Psalms **122**, 128, 150
or 120, **121**, 122
Hosea 2.2-17
1 Corinthians 9.1-14

Saturday 23 January

Hosea 2.2-17

'I will remove the names of the Baals from her mouth' (v.17)

The metaphor of the unfaithful wife continues in today's passage.

You may have got a sense yesterday that how you respond to a piece of Scripture can depend enormously on the personal experience that you bring to your reading. How might a woman, a man, a person who has experienced a woman's infidelity, a sex-worker, a survivor of sexual abuse, a person who has experienced a man's infidelity, or a trans or non-binary person all read, and respond to, this chapter differently? And how might any differences be magnified further if some of these people lived in the first world, and others in the third world?

How do the experiences you bring shape the way you respond to the portrayal of God here? What insights might you gain by reading together with others who bring different experiences from your own?

Marriage is used often in the Old Testament as a metaphor to represent the relationship between Israel and God, but nowhere more graphically than here. Whether you see God as a faithful or abusive husband in these opening chapters of Hosea will depend in part on the experiences you bring to your reading. Whatever those are, and however you respond to the metaphor of the unfaithful wife, don't give up – this is not the whole story; there are other, very beautiful, family metaphors still to come in Hosea.

Eternal Lord,
our beginning and our end:
bring us with the whole creation
to your glory, hidden through past ages
and made known
in Jesus Christ our Lord.

COLLECT

Monday 25 January

Conversion of Paul

Psalms 66, 147.13-end
Ezekiel 3.22-end
Philippians 3.1-14

Philippians 3.1-14

'... Christ Jesus has made me his own' (v.12)

Paul has always been a passionate character – right back to when he was a young man named Saul. What changes is the focal point of his desire. Quick flashback to Acts 7.58: Saul minding the coats of the furious mob who stone Stephen. Holy, beautiful, Stephen, an early Christian, battered by rocks hurled by bigots, applauded by young Saul. Saul desires approval, belonging and identity through Pharisaical perfection, bent on exterminating the fledgling Church he finds so threatening. It is remarkable that this same human being later writes these startling words: 'Christ Jesus has made me his own.'

The older Paul understands that God alone is the true goal of all human desire. Religious pedigree, the right background, whatever gains we can accrue in life, none of them will ever satisfy our existential hunger for God. Paul goes further and grasps the remarkable truth that God's fierce desire is for us. God wants us. How easily we forget this. It's as though we close the shades and huddle around a feeble fire of our own making, enormously proud of its weak warmth. God whispers, 'Draw back the curtains and stand in my light.' Do we opt for a dying heat source when God offers the sun? Paul presses on because he knows his purpose and direction, he understands the goal of his desires. 'Christ Jesus has made me his own.'

COLLECT

Almighty God,
who caused the light of the gospel
to shine throughout the world
through the preaching of your servant Saint Paul:
grant that we who celebrate his wonderful conversion
may follow him in bearing witness to your truth;
through Jesus Christ your Son our Lord,
who is alive and reigns with you,
in the unity of the Holy Spirit,
one God, now and for ever.

| *Reflection by* **Kate Bruce**

Psalms 34, **36** *or* **132**, 133
Hosea 4.1-16
1 Corinthians 10.1-13

Tuesday 26 January

Hosea 4.1-16

'... no knowledge of God in the land' (v.1)

Judgement. Not a popular theme. When did you last hear Hosea preached from start to finish? When referenced at all, it is usually through the 'nicer' verses, excised from the general tone of God's incandescent rage. If you stick with these readings from Hosea, expect to wince. God's fury is palpable. The temptation is to dismiss this as the angry, judgy old God of yesteryear. This would be a grave error. God's anger is ignited by his people's faithlessness. Wilfully, they abandon their creator to worship a lump of wood. This disordered spirituality cashes out in disorder throughout creation: 'even the fish of the sea are perishing'.

Hosea's description resonates with contemporary themes: corruption in society, betrayal in relationships and environmental disaster all around. Professional religious people come in for special censure for rejecting the knowledge of God. In failing to offer any spiritual corrective to the rabid iniquity in the land, they are culpable. Hosea offers a spirit level against which to measure our own character and context.

Do we expect God to sit aside and smile wistfully at his errant offspring? 'There, there. Just my people doing what they please. No matter to me.' Judgement is an expression of the desire of God, rooted in love. A God who doesn't judge, doesn't care. Judgement is not the opposite of love; it is the expression of it.

COLLECT

Almighty God,
whose Son revealed in signs and miracles
the wonder of your saving presence:
renew your people with your heavenly grace,
and in all our weakness
sustain us by your mighty power;
through Jesus Christ your Son our Lord,
who is alive and reigns with you,
in the unity of the Holy Spirit,
one God, now and for ever.

Reflection by **Kate Bruce** | 59

Wednesday 27 January

Psalms 45, **46** *or* **119.153-end**
Hosea 5.1-7
1 Corinthians 10.14 – 11.1

Hosea 5.1-7

'I know Ephraim' (v.3)

Mizpah and Tabor mean 'watchtower' and 'lofty place'; places from which to watch over the land. The high places of leadership, spiritual and political, come with a duty of care for people. Hosea castigates leaders for failure that will bring dire spiritual consequences. Into this mess, God declares 'I know Ephraim'. Ephraim, the leading tribe in the Northern Kingdom, sets a toxic example that corrupts Israel, and Judah will stumble too. God is fully aware of this.

God's knowing is intimate and total. This knowing is deeply comforting – or profoundly threatening. For the humble of heart, to be known by God offers deep assurance. To reach out and receive forgiveness when we have slipped up in stupidity is the source of all solace. However, if we spurn God, the same fact of God's knowledge is terrifying; hence the need to dig deep into resistance. Barricaded by pride, we entertain the illusion that all is fine. God is denied, ignored, or treated as just another player in the game, rather than the maker of all things. It's ironic that whilst entertaining idols, the people also seek God. Religious practice and spiritual resistance can, and often do, go hand in hand. Israel's version of clubby religiosity, involves taking the flocks, seeking the Lord, doing the done thing. What is our version of this? God knows us. Do we know ourselves?

COLLECT

Almighty God,
whose Son revealed in signs and miracles
the wonder of your saving presence:
renew your people with your heavenly grace,
and in all our weakness
sustain us by your mighty power;
through Jesus Christ your Son our Lord,
who is alive and reigns with you,
in the unity of the Holy Spirit,
one God, now and for ever.

Reflection by **Kate Bruce**

Psalms **47**, 48 *or* **143**, 146
Hosea 5.8 – 6.6
1 Corinthians 11.2-16

Thursday 28 January

Hosea 5.8 – 6.6

'In their distress they will beg my favour' (5.15)

Judgement has a purpose: to bring people back to the one who heals. Woven into Hosea's expression of divine anger is a longing born of deep pain. The wounds of the people afflict God. He desires that they face into their reality, acknowledge they are at rock bottom and turn back, trusting that the one who has torn in judgement will restore, revive and raise up. Cast into a darkness of their own making, the people are not doomed to stay there forever. Judgement offers a reality check. Judgement comes as a light into shadowy places. Judgement holds out map and compass: 'here you are, here is where you need to be'. Move from the place of outer appearance – the rote offerings of sacrifice – to the deep place of encounter with God. From here, steadfast love flows and the dawn of new hope will arise.

Judgement is not the killjoy rantings of an eternally grumpy deity, but a roar from the divine heart. It is the longing that the hearer wakes up from the stupor of selfishness and sin that promised so much but delivered ashes. It is the longing for the prodigal to turn from the pig sty. 'Come home, my beloved. Come home and stay home.' Judgement has a beautiful purpose.

God of all mercy,
your Son proclaimed good news to the poor,
release to the captives,
and freedom to the oppressed:
anoint us with your Holy Spirit
and set all your people free
to praise you in Christ our Lord.

COLLECT

Friday 29 January

Psalms 61, **65** *or* 142, **144**
Hosea 6.7 – 7.2
I Corinthians 11.17-end

Hosea 6.7 – 7.2

'... there they dealt faithlessly with me' (6.7)

Like Adam in the garden, Israel has broken faith with God. The 'there' of verse 7 refers to every high place, every hill and altar offered to an idol. 'There' is every petty-minded attitude serving at the altar of self, every unkindness, every act of abuse and neglect: politically, socially and environmentally. We break faith with God whenever we act without thought of God. We *sin* 'through negligence through weakness, through our own deliberate fault.' All of our sin is against God: 'Against you, you alone, have I sinned, and done what is evil in your sight' (Psalm 51.4). Both the psalmist and Hosea see that such sin is ever before God's sight.

Humanity seems hooked on pleasing ourselves and hanging the consequences. Even when we try to flee the folly and trap of sin, we still end up doing the very things we try to avoid, willing what is right but being unable to do it. We might well cry out with St Paul: 'Who will rescue me from this body of death?' (Romans 7.24). For those with ears to hear, the judgement in Hosea draw us to the forgiveness and new life in Jesus, who comes not to call the righteous, but sinners (Mark 2.17). This is great news for those of us who can point to countless examples of dealing faithlessly with God, there, there and there.

C O L L E C T

Almighty God,
whose Son revealed in signs and miracles
the wonder of your saving presence:
renew your people with your heavenly grace,
and in all our weakness
sustain us by your mighty power;
through Jesus Christ your Son our Lord,
who is alive and reigns with you,
in the unity of the Holy Spirit,
one God, now and for ever.

| *Reflection by* **Kate Bruce**

Psalm **68** *or* **147**
Hosea 8
1 Corinthians 12.1-11

Saturday 30 January

Hosea 8

'Israel has forgotten his Maker' (v.14)

'Israel has spurned the good' that is the will of God. Politically, they behave as if God is irrelevant. Spiritually, they engage in religious DIY, creating and worshipping ornately decorated lumps of wood. All this is happening against the backdrop of the Assyrian conquest of much of Israel in 733 BC. In verse 1, Assyria is pictured as a vulture hovering over Israel as a consequence of their faithlessness. What might be seen as a purely secular event is declared to be an act of God.

If we take God seriously, we cannot divide the world into sacred and secular, excising God from public life as though God is somehow separate from politics, economics, social policy and cultural perspective, as though God neither sees nor cares. We cannot lock God up in a Victorian box pew and let him out for an hour on Sunday. It is imperative that the Church does not forget that God is active in the world. In societies that, at best, often banish God to the margins, the Church must be robust in praying for our politicians, civic leaders, military heads and business directors, praying into all areas of public life – and allowing our intercessions to shape our subsequent actions. As the psalmist puts it: 'The earth is the Lord's and all that is in it, the world, and those who live in it' (Psalm 24.1).

God of all mercy,
your Son proclaimed good news to the poor,
release to the captives,
and freedom to the oppressed:
anoint us with your Holy Spirit
and set all your people free
to praise you in Christ our Lord.

COLLECT

Reflection by **Kate Bruce**   63

Monday 1 February

Psalms **57**, 96 *or* 1, 2, 3
Hosea 9
1 Corinthians 12.12-end

Hosea 9

'The prophet is a fool' (v.7)

Speaking truth to power, Hosea places himself in a vulnerable position. He knows that because Israel is so invested in iniquity, the nation is deeply hostile to Yahweh's challenge and call. God's sentinel, the prophet called to look out for the people and speak God's word to them, is recast as a fool and a madman. Fake news and media spin are nothing new. Hosea is imaged in such a way as to discredit and undermine his word. A fool can be written off, marginalized and ignored, leaving Israel to continue her self-determined path unhindered.

It is not difficult to see this strategy at work in public life today where a fair question or a just challenge can be shot down through character assassination and ridicule.

The more biting challenge is to identify this kind of spin in our personal attitudes. When another person challenges us over an opinion or behaviour, particularly one that we have long held, or that suits our self-interest, do we listen for the voice of God in the word of the other – after all, prophets come in many guises – or do we burn them in an online rant or a back-stabbing comment? When I am called out for an attitude or behaviour that is at odds with God's love and calling, do I listen to the sentinel or do I shove them off a cliff?

COLLECT

God our creator,
who in the beginning
commanded the light to shine out of darkness:
we pray that the light of the glorious gospel of Christ
may dispel the darkness of ignorance and unbelief,
shine into the hearts of all your people,
and reveal the knowledge of your glory
in the face of Jesus Christ your Son our Lord,
who is alive and reigns with you,
in the unity of the Holy Spirit,
one God, now and for ever.

| *Reflection by* **Kate Bruce**

Psalms **48**, 146
Exodus 13.1-16
Romans 12.1-5

Tuesday 2 February
Presentation of Christ
in the Temple

Exodus 13.1-16

'Remember this day on which you came out of Egypt' (v.3)

Remembering matters. Israel is instructed to remember that God rescued them from Egypt. The Festival of Unleavened Bread reminds them of leaving that 'house of slavery' so quickly their dough remained unleavened (Exodus 12.34). The festival culminates in the ritual storytelling of Passover. Divine action is imprinted in memory in the practice of the sacrifice of first-born animals and the redemption of first-born sons. Such remembrance is not about living in the past but about being shaped as a community in the present, and orientated to future expectation of God's action.

Standing in the stream of this tradition, Mary and Joseph present Jesus in the temple, as a redeemed first son, symbolic of God's redemption of his people from slavery. In this story we meet Simeon, a man 'righteous and devout, looking forward to the consolation of Israel' (Luke 2.25). Simeon is steeped in the tradition of remembering God through ritual. This practice shapes his vision and, like Anna, he is looking forward expectantly and so recognizes that Jesus, the symbolic redeemed first born, is the Redeemer of all born.

What we see is dependent on what we expect to see. We need to remember what God has done, through ritual and practice, in order to have eyes open to God's redemptive action now. Remembering matters.

Almighty and ever-living God,
clothed in majesty,
whose beloved Son was this day presented in the Temple,
in substance of our flesh:
grant that we may be presented to you
with pure and clean hearts,
by your Son Jesus Christ our Lord,
who is alive and reigns with you,
in the unity of the Holy Spirit,
one God, now and for ever.

COLLECT

Reflection by **Kate Bruce**   65

Wednesday 3 February

Psalm 119.1-32
Hosea 11.1-11
1 Corinthians 14.1-19

Hosea 11.1-11

'How can I give you up, Ephraim?' (v.8)

Picture a drug-addled youth, sprawled on a stained mattress in a grotty squat. The child had been persuaded home, only to steal and score and run away again. The parent scrolls through old pictures – learning to walk, a kiss on the check, the first solo bike ride. What happened? All that promise vanished like the morning mist. Anger and frustration boil up, 'Why do I bother?'

In this vignette there lies a flavour of the pain and frustration Yahweh experiences with wayward Israel – addicted to the Baals. In spite of provocation and rejection, God's love bursts out: 'How can I give you up, Ephraim?' God's anger is justified, but his love is not satisfied with rejecting Israel. Hosea offers us a picture of divine reasoning 'for I am God and no mortal, the Holy one in your midst, and I will not come in wrath'. The themes of divine love and compassion shine out from this text: 'the dawn from on high will break upon us' (Luke 1.78).

God will roar for his children to return, not the roar of fury, but the roar of loving desire. This is the love that will not let us go. This is love stronger than death, love that bursts the bounds of the grave. Nothing deathly can hem this love in. Here is hope – singing out from Hosea's prophecy: 'How can I give you up?'

COLLECT

Almighty God,
by whose grace alone we are accepted and called to your service:
strengthen us by your Holy Spirit
and make us worthy of our calling;
through Jesus Christ your Son our Lord,
who is alive and reigns with you,
in the unity of the Holy Spirit,
one God, now and for ever.

| *Reflection by* **Kate Bruce**

Psalms 14, **15**, 16
Hosea 11.12 – end of 12
1 Corinthians 14.20-end

Thursday 4 February

Hosea 11.12 – end of 12

'Ah, I am rich. I have gained wealth for myself' (12.8)

Under Jeroboam II, the Northern Kingdom enriched its coffers on the backs of the poor. Hosea turns the laser beam of his prophetic judgement onto such business practices, putting Ephraim in the dock to face God's indictment. There are echoes here of the prophet Amos, who condemned the corruption of sharp practice with false balances (Amos 8.5). Israel stands exposed as corrupt, just like their deceitful ancestor Jacob. Worse still is the assumption that in getting rich through oppression they have done nothing wrong. A second charge against Israel is that of idolatry. Both charges reflect a failure to trust God.

Israel is like the rich man in Luke 12, self-reliant and self-satisfied, storing up treasures for himself in ever bigger barns, unaware that the sands of his time are running out. Jesus calls his disciples to a different perspective: trusting in the provision of God (Luke 12.22-31). Hosea speaks the same language in his call to 'hold fast to love and justice, and wait continually for your God'.

Here's the challenge. Does my use of money express love, embody justice and reflect my hope in God? To the wealthy, the question is: 'Have I become self-satisfied, arrogant in my prosperity?' Trust in God brings the freedom to be radically generous, using resources to worship God by investing in the things that do not rot or rust.

God of our salvation,
help us to turn away from those habits
which harm our bodies and poison our minds
and to choose again your gift of life,
revealed to us in Jesus Christ our Lord.

COLLECT

Reflection by **Kate Bruce** | 67

Friday 5 February

Psalms 17, **19**
Hosea 13.1-14
1 Corinthians 16.1-9

Hosea 13.1-14

'People are kissing calves!' (v.2)

The incredulity of the prophet in the face of idolatry screams off the page: 'People are kissing calves!' Part of the ritual of Baal worship involved kissing the idol, probably a small image reminiscent of the bull of Bethel (Hosea 8.5, 10.5). They have replaced God with a piece of shop-bought tat, hammered by human hands. They have forgotten God, who brought them out of Egypt. They have erased their knowledge of Yahweh, who fed them in the wilderness and watered them in the land of drought. They have forgotten their God. Meanwhile, 'people are kissing calves!'

God is the ultimate power over all nations, before whom every knee shall bow. God holds the destiny of Israel and controls the future of Egypt, that same country Israel hoped would offer support against Assyria. This enemy is an instrument of judgement in the hand of God, imprisoning Israel's rulers (2 Kings 17.4), and invading, destroying and taking captive with ferocious energy (2 Kings 17.5-6, 18, 24). If Assyria is a steamroller, God is in the driving seat. Meanwhile, 'people are kissing calves!'

The authority of God is further underscored: God rules on a cosmic stage; life and death are in his hands. Thrones, dominions, rulers, powers, earth, heaven, life and death, *and* images covered in gold, are *all* in God's hands. Meanwhile, 'people are kissing calves'.

Sometimes we all need a reality check.

C O L L E C T

Almighty God,
by whose grace alone we are accepted and called to your service:
strengthen us by your Holy Spirit
and make us worthy of our calling;
through Jesus Christ your Son our Lord,
who is alive and reigns with you,
in the unity of the Holy Spirit,
one God, now and for ever.

| *Reflection by* **Kate Bruce**

Psalms 20, 21, **23**
Hosea 14
1 Corinthians 16.10-end

Saturday 6 February

Hosea 14
'I will heal their disloyalty; I will love them freely' (v.4)

God promises to do for Israel what they cannot do for themselves. Israel is helpless, in bondage to their deeds (Hosea 5.4). Hosea gives them words to say to God, but they are only able to turn to God because he acts first, freeing them from their addiction to reliance on foreign agents, military might, or puny godlets. Wooed by Yahweh, Israel will flourish and be fertile under the divine protective shadow. All of this is because God will act for Israel.

Matthew sees this hope fulfilled in Jesus when he links the return of the Holy family from Egypt with Hosea 11.1: 'Out of Egypt I have called my son' (Matthew 2.15). In Jesus, God is doing the new thing he promised through Hosea.

When the shackles of sin rattle with every move, God comes with bolt cutters. When our worship of that which is not God leads us beside fetid waters, God comes with rod and staff to lead us home. When we turn to God, owning our failures and frailties, it is because God works within us to enable this. Ignatius of Loyola, founder of the Jesuit order, called this consolation, when God aligns our spirits with his will, enabling us to make the journey from the pigsty to the fireside. This is wonderful, glorious, tremendous, overwhelming truth. This is the hope of all nations: Jesus Christ.

God of our salvation,
help us to turn away from those habits
which harm our bodies and poison our minds
and to choose again your gift of life,
revealed to us in Jesus Christ our Lord.

COLLECT

Monday 8 February

John 19.1-16

'Take him yourselves and crucify him' (v.6)

The poet W. H. Auden was once asked why he was a Christian instead of a follower of one of the other religions of the world. He answered that it was because Jesus Christ is the exact opposite of what he himself would have come up with if left to his own devices to describe God. He went on to say that it was Jesus who made every part of his being want to cry 'crucify him!' because so much of his selfish heart resists the love Christ embodies. The crowd shouting at Pilate agrees.

Pilate appears tense. We are told that 'he was more afraid than ever'. Not only does he have a baying crowd outside, and a report to write to the emperor about his strategy for dealing with local troubles, but the man brought before him troubles him. Whereas the soldiers think it funny to dress Jesus up as a king, perhaps Pilate can see that it is the clothes and baubles placed on him that are exposed for what they really are. It is not Jesus who is ridiculed but the life we have made for ourselves, full of deference, showing off and competitive power. The taunts at him come back at us.

When Pilate says 'Here is the man!' not only are we made to wonder with confusion whether, at last, this is the Son of Man coming in his glory, but we are also asked to see the man, laden with the costume of human folly and oppressed by human cruelty, so that we might begin to see ourselves and, of course, God, the loving victim of his own love.

COLLECT

Almighty God,
you have created the heavens and the earth
and made us in your own image:
teach us to discern your hand in all your works
and your likeness in all your children;
through Jesus Christ your Son our Lord,
who with you and the Holy Spirit reigns supreme over all things,
now and for ever.

| *Reflection by* **Mark Oakley**

Psalms 32, **36**
Ecclesiastes 7.15-end
John 19.17-30

Tuesday 9 February

John 19.17-30
'It is finished' (v.30)

At the beginning of John's Gospel, John the Baptist says that he saw the Spirit of God descend on Jesus (1.32). The whole of Jesus' life and ministry is infused and guided by this Spirit and now, as he bows his head in this public execution, he gives his own spirit back to God, his work complete.

One of the great ironies in this narrative is that, at the very moment when God seems most silent, distant or even absent, in reality God was never closer to this world than when Christ hung helpless on pieces of wood surrounded by those who had always loved and believed in him.

We are not told much about what is happening. A bit of imperially painted wood is the only sign to hand. It becomes important to Christian spirituality to understand that God's silence is God's last defence against our idolatry. Whereas we work quickly to apply our concepts to describe God and size him up, God's silence resists it all; we are left looking at a man who loved the poor and wanted God's justice for them, a man who saw human hypocrisy and the inhumane inventions of religion, a man crushed and murdered, to get him out of our way.

Pulitzer Prize-winning novelist Marilynne Robinson has commented that nothing true can be said about God from a posture of defence. Here at Golgotha is God, undefended, speaking his beautiful truth in the body language of Christ.

COLLECT

Almighty God,
give us reverence for all creation
and respect for every person,
that we may mirror your likeness
in Jesus Christ our Lord.

Reflection by **Mark Oakley**

71

Wednesday 10 February

John 19.31-end

'They took the body of Jesus and wrapped it with the spices' (v.40)

We know that, for the early Christians, the account of Jesus' burial was very important. All four Gospels tell the story, each with their own take on it, and John says that Nicodemus was involved. Nicodemus was the man who came to see Jesus by night and ended up having a conversation about birth, from the womb and from heaven. Now we find him helping out after a death – but his presence may intimate that a new life is on the horizon.

Jesus had been mocked as a king by the soldiers and by the sign over his cross. Those who believe in him still acclaim him as such in their hearts, their love for him is undiminished, and so a hundred pounds (about 45 kg) of 'myrrh and aloes' is brought, a very impressive amount, to give Jesus the kingly burial he deserves.

There is something very beautiful and touching in the fact that after Jesus has been endlessly handed over to various people, authorities, cruel soldiers and a Roman leader, at the end of his life Jesus is once again placed in the hands of those who love him. The 'body of Christ' is placed still in the hands of his followers today, but it is a body of life not death, and it is their reception of him, and their embodiment of his life and ministry, that potentially transforms relationships, communities and individual hopes in our own day.

COLLECT

Almighty God,
you have created the heavens and the earth
and made us in your own image:
teach us to discern your hand in all your works
and your likeness in all your children;
through Jesus Christ your Son our Lord,
who with you and the Holy Spirit reigns supreme over all things,
now and for ever.

| *Reflection by* **Mark Oakley**

Psalm **37***
Ecclesiastes 9
John 20.1-10

Thursday 11 February

John 20.1-10
'Early on the first day of the week' (v.1)

It is easy to forget that John and those faithful and imaginative people who first wrote down the resurrection stories, as well as those who first shared them, passed them on and put them down on parchment, were all making themselves, in the world's terms, less powerful, not more. They were walking out into an unmapped territory, away from the safe places of political and religious influence, away from traditional religion, at odds with Roman society and the law.

They were putting their lives, and those of the people they loved, in danger, at risk of losing everything, even life itself. These stories, for them, were not made-up tales, not something to have on in the background for an hour on Anglican FM on a nice Spring morning. These stories were a matter of life and death – and they took the risk, the risk of being the story keepers.

They do not hide the fact that the disciples were imperfect. Peter rushes in, sees but doesn't seem to understand. The more tentative disciple with him eventually goes in, and he, we are told, believed. It is not always our enthusiasm that creates our fidelity and wisdom but our rootedness in the love we share with God and our openness to have our first impressions changed by him.

It says they went back to their homes. The truth they had been exposed to had to be domesticated and furnished in them before it could be talked about, reflected on and shared.

Almighty God,
give us reverence for all creation
and respect for every person,
that we may mirror your likeness
in Jesus Christ our Lord.

COLLECT

Reflection by **Mark Oakley** | 73

Friday 12 February

Psalm 31
Ecclesiastes 11.1-8
John 20.11-18

John 20.11-18

'... why are you weeping?' (v.15)

There are tears in this story. Mary is crying. She is there for all of us, for there is so much to weep about. Where do we begin? For the beauty of the world groaning under pollution and plastic? For those whose life will end in parts of the world most of us will never see? Or are they tears of anger for the demise of truth in public debate; tears for those seeking refuge who are more like us than we like to admit; tears for the minorities who suffer the projections of hate? Or are they tears for our own life? Mary stands weeping. She understands. Good things often begin when we let ourselves cry. The question of Jesus begins the spiritual life: tell me, why are you weeping?

The early morning begins a new day. The garden recalls the beginning of creation. Mary's tears irrigate a new hope within. Everything points to a re-creation, a freshness born in love's faithfulness. Although the disciples had betrayed him and his enemies had hurt him and then slaughtered him as he if were a lamb, Jesus comes to them all to show them that hope is found in his fidelity not in theirs. It is in the light of this deathless loyalty that the old world defrosts and the new begins to take shape. In the early morning, in a strange but inviting light, we must pick ourselves up and follow him again.

COLLECT

Almighty God,
you have created the heavens and the earth
and made us in your own image:
teach us to discern your hand in all your works
and your likeness in all your children;
through Jesus Christ your Son our Lord,
who with you and the Holy Spirit reigns supreme over all things,
now and for ever.

| *Reflection by* **Mark Oakley**

Psalms 41, **42**, 43
Ecclesiastes 11.9 – end of 12
John 20.19-end

Saturday 13 February

John 20.19-end
'Peace be with you' (v.21)

We often forget that when Jesus greeted the disciples with the words 'peace be with you', it was less like the half-hearted response of an early morning liturgy than a person just saying 'hi'. Jesus was not being a churchgoer; he was being a friend, and he greeted the family of his friends with 'shalom'. So much had happened, so much fear, hurt and despair. Jesus comes through it all and says 'Hi. I'm still here and I'm your friend – and for always'.

Thomas sometimes gets a bad press because of his doubts. I sometimes wonder if he should be known as 'Honest Thomas'. The spiritual adventure of following Christ means trying to think critically but live faithfully. This means being open about our questions and scrutiny. Faith is not certainty. It is a relationship and it knows that our flickering communion with God so often deepens through things that unravel us and our securities. Faith works by questioning our answers as much as answering our questions.

John tells us at the end that believing in Christ gives life. Those of us who get bogged down in administration and ecclesiastical politics can forget this and completely lose sight of the fact that our faith should enlarge our hearts and imagination, our capacity to love and understand others, as well as stand up for what is right and just – and all in the name of a life that is worthy of the name. 'Christianity is either fire or it is nothing at all' (Mother Maria Skobtsova).

Almighty God,
give us reverence for all creation
and respect for every person,
that we may mirror your likeness
in Jesus Christ our Lord.

COLLECT

Reflection by **Mark Oakley**   75

Monday 15 February

John 3.1-21

'God did not send the Son into the world to condemn the world'
(v.17)

If you really want to test the character and strength of someone, you don't give them difficulties and trials, you give them leadership. It seems it had made Nicodemus think – about himself? About life? About what? We don't know, but he's invested a lot in getting himself to where he's got and he doesn't want to compromise it all at this stage, so he goes to see Jesus by night. It's dark outside and inside. It's always exhausting not to live in the outside world what you are inside. He's wanting a conversation, but he doesn't want to be seen having it. Still, it turns to the subjects of birth, living a life and re-living a life. Nicodemus asks a question that he may well have been thinking about for a while: 'How can anyone be born after having grown old?' How can I start again after I've got here?

Jesus tells Nicodemus about the water that drowns the past and bids us dive deeper into the future, the water of baptism. He talks of the freshness of the Spirit to guide this new life. We hear about Nicodemus again in the Gospel. He comes along with 45 kg of spices to anoint the dead body of Jesus and this time he doesn't care who sees him. He has learned at last it is better to live in the light and he comes to care for the discarded body of the man who taught him one night how to live again. Now, he wants everyone to know it.

COLLECT

Almighty Father,
whose Son was revealed in majesty
before he suffered death upon the cross:
give us grace to perceive his glory,
that we may be strengthened to suffer with him
and be changed into his likeness, from glory to glory;
who is alive and reigns with you,
in the unity of the Holy Spirit,
one God, now and for ever.

76 | *Reflection by* **Mark Oakley**

Psalms **48**, 52
Jeremiah 2.1-13
John 3.22-end

Tuesday 16 February

John 3.22-end

'He must increase, but I must decrease' (v.30)

John the Baptist is a good model for the Church. He states that Christ must increase while he must decrease. Christian history reveals that the Church hasn't always tried to follow suit, preferring its own control and power to the new Spirit-filled life that Jesus preaches and prepares people for by baptism.

We live at a time when there are too many voices coming at us from every direction about how to live life, find meaning and be a successful human being. As Jesus pushes those who come to him under the water, all these voices are drowned out just for a few seconds. His new friends emerge and take a fresh breath of a new life when the only voice that matters now is the one that comes from heaven, telling them they are children of God, loved and for always. Life is now the adventure of trying to live up to this voice each and every day and not live down to the old voices that make a life like the pancakes that will be cooked tonight – fat and flat.

We in the West can be bloated by ego-chat and too much stuff or food. We end up feeling flat and stuck to the surface of existence. The heart is drawn and intrigued by an invitation to 'eternal life', something, at last, born from above.

Holy God,
you know the disorder of our sinful lives:
set straight our crooked hearts,
and bend our wills to love your goodness
and your glory
in Jesus Christ our Lord.

COLLECT

Wednesday 17 February
Ash Wednesday

Psalm **38**
Daniel 9.3-6, 17-19
1 Timothy 6.6-19

1 Timothy 6.6-19

'... pursue righteousness, godliness, faith, love, endurance, gentleness' (v.11)

Lent is a snowfall in the soul. Just as snow makes us see our landscape in a different light, making us renavigate our environment and wonder at the sight of our own breath, so Lent invites us to distil, reimagine and remember the fragile miracle of our own self.

We are reminded here that we brought nothing into the world and will take nothing out. As ash is placed on our head today, the cross is placed on the heads that house our brains, the centres of our will power and decision-making. These are being called back to life, to a balanced sense and a proportionate understanding of ourselves. Along with Timothy, we are encouraged to pursue love, gentleness and what is right. This letter, like Lent, asks us to stop being indifferent, cautious and compromised. It speaks of the 'life that really is life', the one that is activated and sustained by love of God and our neighbour.

Time presses upon us and tells us we're too busy to be reflective, but our souls know better. Souls die from lack of reflection. Unawareness, like money, is a root of all evil too. Responsibilities distract us and tell us we're too involved with the 'real' world to be concerned about the spiritual questions. But it is always spiritual questions that make the difference in the way we go about our public and day-to-day lives.

COLLECT

Almighty and everlasting God,
you hate nothing that you have made
and forgive the sins of all those who are penitent:
create and make in us new and contrite hearts
that we, worthily lamenting our sins
and acknowledging our wretchedness,
may receive from you, the God of all mercy,
perfect remission and forgiveness;
through Jesus Christ your Son our Lord,
who is alive and reigns with you,
in the unity of the Holy Spirit,
one God, now and for ever.

Reflection by **Mark Oakley**

Psalm **77** *or* 56, **57** (63*)
Jeremiah 2.14-32
John 4.1-26

Thursday 18 February

John 4.1-26

'God is spirit, and those who worship him must worship in spirit and truth' (v.24)

As a Jewish male, Jesus is in a position of advantage over this woman, but as a thirsty traveller, he is obviously at a disadvantage. Jesus invites the dialogue by becoming vulnerable ('Give me a drink') and by allowing the woman to exercise some power over him. The scene is paradoxical. Here is the giver of living water, thirsty himself. A thirsty Messiah and a resourceful woman will find out that they need each other. It is a beautiful metaphor for how God and humanity are intimately interconnected.

Their conversation is one for a parched society. The Victorian poet and priest Gerard Manley Hopkins prayed that our roots would be sent rain, and similarly here we understand that the dryness of life needs the water, the teaching and the Spirit of Christ if anything is to grow in us.

Jesus says that God is spirit and that we must worship in truth. It is said that the Church talks a lot about truth but finds honesty difficult. Maybe being truthful is one sure way of worshipping God and might be more acceptable to God than half-hearted pieties and self-proclaiming certainties?

Holy God,
our lives are laid open before you:
rescue us from the chaos of sin
and through the death of your Son
bring us healing and make us whole
in Jesus Christ our Lord.

COLLECT

Friday 19 February

Psalms **3**, 7 *or* **51**, 54
Jeremiah 3.6-22
John 4.27-42

John 4.27-42

'Come and see a man who told me everything I have ever done!'
(v.29)

St John's Gospel has an emphasis on Jesus as light, and we here find the Samaritan woman celebrating the fact with her friends that Jesus has told her everything that she's done in life. I'm not quite sure that's something I'd be very comfortable with! The woman, on the other hand, wants others to see how light thrown on you changes your life.

There is talk of judgement in the Christian faith and some reference to it in John's Gospel. We often have in mind the medieval pictures of torment as wicked souls are tossed into hell. In this encounter, though, we find a very different truth. Here judgement is liberating. The woman, at last, has confronted who she is and has done it with her new friend who took the time to value her and even seek her help. We often fear God not because God is angry but because God is real and we aren't. We are hidden in masks and disguises, deceitful even to ourselves. The judgement of the gospel is ultimately a relief as all this is taken off us and we stand before God as we are, in all our beauty and need.

The Samaritan woman's cause for evangelism is that she has nothing to hide any longer thanks to her encounter with Jesus at a well. What she is has been valued and loved, and now the living water will start, we don't doubt, to make her grow in spirit even more.

COLLECT

Almighty and everlasting God,
you hate nothing that you have made
and forgive the sins of all those who are penitent:
create and make in us new and contrite hearts
that we, worthily lamenting our sins
and acknowledging our wretchedness,
may receive from you, the God of all mercy,
perfect remission and forgiveness;
through Jesus Christ your Son our Lord,
who is alive and reigns with you,
in the unity of the Holy Spirit,
one God, now and for ever.

Reflection by **Mark Oakley**

Saturday 20 February

John 4.43-end

'Unless you see signs and wonders you will not believe' (v.48)

Throughout his Gospel, John shares seven signs that Jesus performs, each revealing something significant about Jesus' identity and mission. Early in the story, Jesus turns water into wine – and not just wine, but the best wine in vast quantities – revealing the profound abundance of God in Jesus, what is earlier described as 'grace upon grace' (1.16). In this scene, Jesus heals the son of a royal official revealing his opposition to those things that keep abundant life from the children of God and his ability to restore health and life.

The official is a man used to giving orders, but here he comes begging for Jesus to save the life of his child. Jesus seems irritated that miracles and signs are needed before people believe, but the man doesn't seem to hear and just wants help. Such open love and honest raw need is the path that leads to healing. He doesn't enter doctrinal or language games with Jesus in order to get a miracle and have his faith confirmed.

The Gospel of John is a book of signs pointing to the recklessly loving grace of God. Like the Bible, life itself is to be read by us with attentiveness so we can read the love between the lines and find ourselves full of gratitude, which, when it comes, is not only a miracle in itself but allows us to see so many more.

Holy God,
our lives are laid open before you:
rescue us from the chaos of sin
and through the death of your Son
bring us healing and make us whole
in Jesus Christ our Lord.

COLLECT

Reflection by **Mark Oakley** | 81

Monday 22 February

John 5.1-18

'Do you want to be made well?' (v.6)

Jesus performs another mighty work. The scene shifts to a healing sanctuary in Jerusalem, where many unfortunates gather around the miraculous pool. Between them they represent every kind of malady – 'blind, lame, and paralysed'. As often in the Gospel stories, the reader is alert to deeper allusions. This group of invalids stands for all that is wanting in human vision, motivation and strength.

Among them, Jesus singles out one man lying on a pallet. He is scarcely a sympathetic character, perhaps one of those people who make your heart sink, who has lain in a piteous state for decades. Complaining that no one will help him, we sense that he is as passive spiritually as he is impotent physically. Jesus' invitation is direct and incisive: 'Do you want to be made well?'

Like a swirling kaleidoscope, the story reflects layers of symbolic meaning, unfolding a rich significance in Jesus' mighty works. This man has been weak and sickly for 38 years, the same length of time the Jews wandered helplessly in the wilderness, waiting for God's promise to be fulfilled (Deuteronomy 2.14).

We notice the detail that this healing takes place on a sabbath: the day when God's people and the whole creation are restored and renewed. Far from resting idle at such a time, Jesus speaks out to challenge the enervating faithlessness in both individuals and nations. 'Stand up, take your mat and walk!'

COLLECT

Almighty God,
whose Son Jesus Christ fasted forty days in the wilderness,
and was tempted as we are, yet without sin:
give us grace to discipline ourselves in obedience to your Spirit;
and, as you know our weakness,
so may we know your power to save;
through Jesus Christ your Son our Lord,
who is alive and reigns with you,
in the unity of the Holy Spirit,
one God, now and for ever.

| *Reflection by* **Margaret Whipp**

Psalm **44** *or* **73**
Jeremiah 5.1-19
John 5.19-29

Tuesday 23 February

John 5.19-29

'... whatever the Father does, the Son does likewise' (v.19)

After the mighty work comes a reaction. Jesus' audacious behaviour provokes fury among those who fear for the sanctity of the sabbath. Just who does this man think he is?

'Amen, Amen,' responds Jesus. The Greek phrase translated as 'very truly' introduces a solemn pronouncement, as Jesus speaks of the holy and intimate relationship with his Father God.

The evangelist's theology at this point is reverent and very carefully weighed. Far from the casual blasphemy alleged by his pious critics, Jesus' speech does not set himself up to subvert God's authority. His stance is, in fact, the very opposite of a rebellious child. All that Jesus seeks to be and to do sits in humble relationship with his Father; he seeks no autonomous status or will. This is his staggering claim of a kind of sonship, which is at once both radically empowering and profoundly submissive.

At the heart of this filial relationship is love. The God who 'so loved the world' (John 3.16) now entrusts his beloved Son with the knowledge of his purpose and the priceless gift of eternal life.

Jesus is determined to do 'only what he sees the Father doing'. When we reflect on our own place in God's loving mission here on earth, how much do we reflect the same faithfulness and intimate dependence?

COLLECT

Heavenly Father,
your Son battled with the powers of darkness,
and grew closer to you in the desert:
help us to use these days to grow in wisdom and prayer
that we may witness to your saving love
in Jesus Christ our Lord.

Wednesday 24 February

John 5.30-end

'I do not accept glory from human beings' (v.41)

The polemical debate is ratcheting up. Jesus' enemies, in a foretaste of the trial to come, question the source of his bold authority. How can he make such claims for himself? Where is the evidence; and who are his witnesses?

Ironically, it is Jesus' accusers who are really on trial. They are the ones who protect their privilege through cosy structures of human approval, 'for they loved human glory more than the glory that comes from God' (John 12.43). Jesus has no time for 'old-boy' networks. His one concern is to be fully faithful to his divine calling. For those with eyes to see, it is self-evident that Jesus reflects his Father's glory – 'glory as of a father's only son, full of grace and truth' (John 1.14).

How tragic it is when religious leaders, picking zealously over scriptural niceties, entirely miss their main thrust. It is culpable blindness to reject the burning evidence of authority in Jesus' life, to which those scriptures, along with the Baptist's testimony, bear eloquent witness.

The very best of religion can be perverted by self-seeking power. When we seek glory from one another, in our mutual back-slapping and tribalism, our churches become closed and self-sufficient with no appetite for the true glory that comes from God. Could our own religious networks be corrupted through such smugness?

COLLECT

Almighty God,
whose Son Jesus Christ fasted forty days in the wilderness,
and was tempted as we are, yet without sin:
give us grace to discipline ourselves in obedience to your Spirit;
and, as you know our weakness,
so may we know your power to save;
through Jesus Christ your Son our Lord,
who is alive and reigns with you,
in the unity of the Holy Spirit,
one God, now and for ever.

| *Reflection by* **Margaret Whipp**

Psalms **42**, 43 *or* **78.1-39***
Jeremiah 6.9-21
John 6.1-15

Thursday 25 February

John 6.1-15

'Now the Passover ... was near' (v.4)

We know this story very well. All four Gospels present an account of the miraculous feeding of a multitude. Typically, the fourth Gospel provides a distinctively theological reading of the event. It is one of the great 'signs' that will introduce a profound reflection on Jesus, the living Bread of Life.

Why mention the small detail of the approaching Passover festival? This incidental fact earths the timing of the miracle in the spring season, when the grass is abundant and green. But, more suggestively, it also points forward to the ultimate sign of Jesus' glory revealed in his Passover sacrifice for the sins of the world.

The story is wonderfully told, to be relished at every level. We can smile at the cluelessness of the disciples, and the ludicrously meagre resources snatched from the hands of a little lad. We are hushed as Jesus gives thanks over the bread – the Greek verb denotes our word for Eucharist. And we are heartened by the Lord's insistence that all the scattered fragments will be gloriously gathered up.

Week by week, believers across the world celebrate the Eucharist as a foretaste of the heavenly banquet prepared for all peoples. Still taking nothing grander than our small, perishable offerings, Christ satisfies our deepest hunger for eternal and imperishable food. People who first saw this sign began to appreciate its phenomenal significance. Do we?

Heavenly Father,
your Son battled with the powers of darkness,
and grew closer to you in the desert:
help us to use these days to grow in wisdom and prayer
that we may witness to your saving love
in Jesus Christ our Lord.

COLLECT

Reflection by **Margaret Whipp**   85

Friday 26 February

John 6.16-27

'It is I; do not be afraid' (v.20)

Four words, in the vivid Greek narration of this drama, tell us everything we need to know about Jesus. 'I AM; FEAR NOT.' Into the midst of the storm, Jesus comes, bearing divine reassurance and peace.

Hebrew literature is full of dark stories about the raging of the sea. In graphic detail, Psalm 77 describes one of those elemental storms: 'the clouds poured out water, the skies thundered; your arrows flashed on every side' (Psalm 77.17). Meditating on God's power to redeem, the psalm recalls how the Lord strode through mighty waters, making a path through the heaving seas. The imagery is unforgettable and the meaning unambiguous: the one who walks through stormy seas is none other than the almighty Lord himself.

Did the disciples begin to grasp this? The story tells how, as they crossed the sea in their small boat, it grew dark, such that they could not see Jesus. Surprised by the ferocity of the storm, they became suddenly aware of the nearness of the Lord; yet, even then, they were terrified and hesitated to take him into the boat.

Buffeted by anxious times, all Christians know these archetypal fears. When we are overwhelmed by forces too strong for us, even in the pitch of night, Christ comes close – to reassure, to speak peace, to step right into our lives, to guide us to our safe haven.

'It is I; do not be afraid.'

COLLECT

Almighty God,
whose Son Jesus Christ fasted forty days in the wilderness,
and was tempted as we are, yet without sin:
give us grace to discipline ourselves in obedience to your Spirit;
and, as you know our weakness,
so may we know your power to save;
through Jesus Christ your Son our Lord,
who is alive and reigns with you,
in the unity of the Holy Spirit,
one God, now and for ever.

| *Reflection by* **Margaret Whipp**

Psalms 59, **63** or **76**, 79
Jeremiah 7.1-20
John 6.27-40

Saturday 27 February

John 6.27-40
'I am the bread of life' (v.35)

Little by little, the glorious vision of the Fourth Gospel continues to unfold. Jesus first utters the majestic phrase, 'I am', at the calming of the tempest earlier in the chapter. Now we begin to glimpse the vast depth of meaning set forth in those words.

'I am' is nothing less than an emphatic expression of divine origin, and of personal union with God. Moses, trembling before the burning bush, was the first to receive the revelation of the Lord's name in mysterious terms. Translators, quite naturally, struggle to render the enormity of this designation, which concentrates all the energy of the verb 'to be'. How can human thought or language begin to apprehend the truth of a name that is given as 'I AM WHO I AM', or simply 'I AM'? (Exodus 3.14-15).

Here in the gospel of Jesus, we begin to see with our own eyes and grasp with our own hands the electrifying immanence of this divine aliveness. Step by step, the evangelist will take us deeper into this mystery, through seven momentous sayings on the lips of Jesus.

'I AM the bread of life.' Like manna in the wilderness, yet so much more, Jesus satisfies our aching hunger. His gift is as earthy as bread, and as heavenly as life eternal: it is the gift of his own self.

'Lord, give us this bread always!'

Heavenly Father,
your Son battled with the powers of darkness,
and grew closer to you in the desert:
help us to use these days to grow in wisdom and prayer
that we may witness to your saving love
in Jesus Christ our Lord.

COLLECT

Reflection by **Margaret Whipp** |

Monday 1 March

Psalms 26, **32** or **80**, 82
Jeremiah 7.21-end
John 6.41-51

John 6.41-51

'Is not this ... the son of Joseph?' (v.42)

Here come the objections! Bold claims on the lips of Jesus provoke outrage and bewilderment in his hearers. He talks about coming down from heaven; but many of those listening know very well the earthly context of his family and upbringing. Their disdainful attitude shows how familiarity breeds contempt.

The evangelist notes their 'murmuring' (KJV). The word is reminiscent of the fault-finding attitude of the Israelites in the wilderness who were dissatisfied with God's generous provision for their physical needs (Exodus 16.2,7-12). Now something far greater than manna is set forth for God's people – if only they have eyes to see.

'I am the bread of life.' Jesus repeats the startling revelation. Unlike the lifeless manna of the desert, Jesus stands before them in all the fullness of life. And, unlike our mundane food that must perish and be replaced from day to day, the food that Jesus offers will endure for ever.

The whole mystery of the incarnation is contained in these words. Jesus is always lifting our gaze from the earthly plane to heavenly realities. For the cynic, it is laughable that this ordinary man from Nazareth should present himself as coming down from heaven. But for those whose hearts are open to the grace of God, this 'son of Joseph' is the very embodiment of life eternal – here, now, and dwelling among us.

COLLECT

Almighty God,
you show to those who are in error the light of your truth,
that they may return to the way of righteousness:
grant to all those who are admitted
    into the fellowship of Christ's religion,
that they may reject those things
    that are contrary to their profession,
and follow all such things as are agreeable to the same;
through our Lord Jesus Christ,
who is alive and reigns with you,
in the unity of the Holy Spirit,
one God, now and for ever.

| *Reflection by* **Margaret Whipp**

Psalm **50** *or* 87, **89.1-18**
Jeremiah 8.1-15
John 6.52-59

Tuesday 2 March

John 6.52-59

'Those who eat my flesh and drink my blood' (v.56)

We have come a long way from the picnic on the hillside. Through rich layers of figurative language, the evangelist draws our attention ever deeper into the full meaning of Jesus' life and death. Today's reflection carries a profound message for contemporary Christians who, like the first gospel readers, still meet Jesus in the Eucharist.

'How can this man give us his flesh to eat?' It is a shocking image, one that forces us to face the connections between death and life, sacrifice and self-giving. The only way that Jesus' flesh can become life-giving food for others will be through his death. His blood, which in Jewish thinking was such a sacred life-force, will be released only through brutal sacrifice. These everyday metaphors of eating and drinking are radically disrupted and transcended.

The invitation to believers is to partake. We must eat and drink if we are to know eternal life. Jesus insists on this act of most intimate communion: it is through his own indwelling that we will share in the divine union itself.

Such daring theology invites argument and mocking disbelief. Then as now, there are many who find it all, quite literally, too much to swallow. Yet still Jesus calls to the table those who have much faith and those who can only seek a little more: to feed on him in our hearts with thanksgiving.

COLLECT

Almighty God,
by the prayer and discipline of Lent
may we enter into the mystery of Christ's sufferings,
and by following in his Way
come to share in his glory;
through Jesus Christ our Lord.

Reflection by **Margaret Whipp**   89

Wednesday 3 March

Psalm **35** *or* **119.105-128**
Jeremiah 8.18 – 9.11
John 6.60-end

John 6.60-end

'Lord, to whom can we go?' (v.68)

We reach a watershed moment for the disciples. Following this Jesus is no longer easy, or consoling, or pretty. His stark language provokes a disturbing response, a sifting of commitment. Not for the first time, we encounter Jesus as a figure of division. Large crowds may be eager to follow him for as long as he remains a popular miracle-worker. But, when it is no longer convenient or fashionable, we read that many 'turned back and no longer went about with him'.

Jesus applies no coercion or emotional pressure to these lukewarm adherents: he simply lets them go. But to his inner Twelve, Jesus puts the haunting question: 'Do you also wish to go away?' He cuts straight to the heart. Times of ambivalence and confusion are unavoidable, but Jesus' challenge touches the core of motivation and will.

Simon Peter's agonized response is heartening to any later disciple who experiences their faith, at times, to be horribly uncertain, conflicted, or downright painful. 'To whom can we go?' These words, dredged from the depths of Peter's soul, tell how completely he has come to trust in this Jesus. He speaks for all of us who have found nowhere else such life-giving purpose and peace.

Times of crisis will test our faith to the marrow. For Peter, his wavering faith grew stronger, bearing witness as never before: 'you are the Holy One of God!'

COLLECT

Almighty God,
you show to those who are in error the light of your truth,
that they may return to the way of righteousness:
grant to all those who are admitted
    into the fellowship of Christ's religion,
that they may reject those things
    that are contrary to their profession,
and follow all such things as are agreeable to the same;
through our Lord Jesus Christ,
who is alive and reigns with you,
in the unity of the Holy Spirit,
one God, now and for ever.

| *Reflection by* **Margaret Whipp**

Psalm **34** *or* 90, **92**
Jeremiah 9.12-24
John 7.1-13

Thursday 4 March

John 7.1-13

'My time has not yet come' (v.6)

Tension and danger now surround Jesus and his disciples. Their movements are being watched. Jesus is a subversive figure of close interest to the authorities, and we know it is no exaggeration that they are seeking an opportunity to kill him.

How will Jesus respond? Here, as in other parts of the Gospel, his family are keen to come forward with advice. A great festival is approaching when Jerusalem will be packed out with pilgrims. Why not play to the crowds, and take the limelight through a very public display of signs and miracles?

Jesus is unmoved by this fallacious strategy. He is not a populist leader seeking fame and following for his cause. He keeps his counsel, choosing instead to proceed to the festival in his own way and his own time.

Once again, we are astonished at the clear-sighted calm with which Jesus makes his decisions. He is not pushed back and forth, whether by fear or by fortune, but presses steadily forward to fulfil his divine vocation. His overriding concern is to be faithful to God's timing and purpose, even though his path to glory must bring a uniquely personal cost.

In a fearful world, where leaders and influencers jostle for the slightest tactical advantage, such poise and discernment are very rare qualities indeed.

Almighty God,
by the prayer and discipline of Lent
may we enter into the mystery of Christ's sufferings,
and by following in his Way
come to share in his glory;
through Jesus Christ our Lord.

COLLECT

Friday 5 March

John 7.14-24

'Jesus went up into the temple and began to teach' (v.14)

If Jesus is trying to avoid a confrontation in Jerusalem, this is not the most sensible way to proceed. Perhaps influenced by the prophetic image (Malachi 3.1), the evangelist describes Jesus' sudden appearance in the temple, where he brings his message home to the very nerve centre of Jewish religious identity. It is a challenge that seems calculated to court controversy. Amid the teeming crowds and the heightened atmosphere of a major festival, this assertive move provokes both astonishment and fury.

The polemical debate that follows does not make for easy reading. On one level, we might imagine a witty and good-natured intellectual exchange between traditionalist and radical exponents of the law. But there is a darker and more threatening level of argument that Jesus does not flinch from naming: 'Why are you looking for an opportunity to kill me?'

It can be deeply shocking to recognize the violent undercurrents that crackle beneath the surface of seemingly polite religious debate. Anyone who is bold enough, when necessary, to challenge vested interests of prestige and power must learn to expect some ferocious reactions. Jesus steps forward as someone who is willing to speak truth to power. He is not afraid to own his God-given authority. Nor is he naïve about the conflict that will inevitably ensue. Do we share his courage?

COLLECT

Almighty God,
you show to those who are in error the light of your truth,
that they may return to the way of righteousness:
grant to all those who are admitted
    into the fellowship of Christ's religion,
that they may reject those things
    that are contrary to their profession,
and follow all such things as are agreeable to the same;
through our Lord Jesus Christ,
who is alive and reigns with you,
in the unity of the Holy Spirit,
one God, now and for ever.

Reflection by **Margaret Whipp**

Saturday 6 March

John 7.25-36
'I know him' (v.29)

Most modern languages use different words to describe forms of knowledge. There is an objective knowledge, *knowing about* someone or something, which is quite different from the intimate, subjective *knowledge of* someone through personal relationship.

Jesus takes his opponents to task over their woefully shallow knowledge of God. They murmur and quibble over points of abstruse interpretation, whilst failing to recognize the embodiment of grace and truth that stands right before their eyes. Page after page, the evangelist attests to Jesus' intimate relationship with God. Though no one has seen God directly, Jesus is 'the only Son, who is close to the Father's heart, who has made him known' (John 1.18).

All true knowledge is based on relationship. Jesus is secure in this personal knowledge of the Father. We may project all our fears and prejudices onto a distorted, idolatrous image of God. But genuine knowledge comes through humble seeking, and loving, and serving. This was the source of Jesus' radical freedom: and it can be ours as well.

A great prayer by Saint Augustine addresses God as 'the light of the minds that know thee, the life of the souls that love thee, and the strength of the wills that serve thee'. Through Jesus, we too can pray St Augustine's words: 'Help us so to know thee that we may truly love thee, so to love thee that we may fully serve thee, whose service is perfect freedom.'

Almighty God,
by the prayer and discipline of Lent
may we enter into the mystery of Christ's sufferings,
and by following in his Way
come to share in his glory;
through Jesus Christ our Lord.

COLLECT

Reflection by **Margaret Whipp** | 93

Monday 8 March

John 7.37-52

'Let anyone who is thirsty come to me' (v.37)

The Festival of Booths (or Tabernacles) was a sort of Harvest Thanksgiving since it celebrated the gathering in of the crops and fruit. It went on a long time. Huts were built made of branches (the booths or tabernacles of the title), recalling the temporary dwellings of the Israelites in their 40 years in the wilderness.

John doesn't explain any of this. Nor does he tell us about the custom of pouring water over the altar, a sign of God's promise that he would pour out his Spirit on his people. When Jesus speaks of quenching the thirst of the spiritually parched, he indicates that the promise at the heart of this great festival was being fulfilled in him, from whom would flow 'rivers of living water'.

Most readers of John's Gospel down the centuries would not have known the connection between these words of Jesus and customs at the Feast of Booths. It isn't necessary to know it. The reader of the Gospel only needs to recognize what it is to be spiritually dry and parched. Without that recognition, there is not much that Jesus can do for us. The human body cannot live long without water. Spiritual lifelessness is the consequence of not seeking the streams of living water Jesus promises us. This may be a particular danger for those of us well established in the faith who may neglect gradually the source of a healthy spiritual life.

COLLECT

Almighty God,
whose most dear Son went not up to joy
    but first he suffered pain,
and entered not into glory before he was crucified:
mercifully grant that we, walking in the way of the cross,
may find it none other than the way of life and peace;
through Jesus Christ your Son our Lord,
who is alive and reigns with you,
in the unity of the Holy Spirit,
one God, now and for ever.

Reflection by **Graham James**

Psalms 6, **9** *or* **106*** (*or* 103)
Jeremiah 11.18 – 12.6
John 7.53 – 8.11

Tuesday 9 March

John 7.53 – 8.11
'Neither do I condemn you' (v.11)

This famous encounter between Jesus and the woman taken in adultery is not primarily about sexual infidelity. Any temptation to cast Jesus as a twenty-first-century liberal on sexual matters is a mistake. It's his refusal to condemn this woman who has sinned against the law of Moses that is the focus of the story.

A great crowd has gathered, keen to hear Jesus. We are probably in the outer Court of the Women in the Temple since that was where anyone could listen to religious teachers. Scribes and Pharisees arrive with the presumably distraught and dishevelled woman in tow. (There's no mention of the man involved.) She is being used (and abused) to set a trap for Jesus. If he fails to condemn her to be stoned, he would be denying the Mosaic law. But if he does so, he would be usurping the Roman authorities' exclusive right to impose a death penalty.

Instead of debating the issue, Jesus simply invites anyone who is without sin to cast the first stone. The whole crowd gradually dissolves. No one has condemned her, and neither does Jesus. He has not come to condemn but to save the world (John 3.17).

Even the briefest review of the tabloid press or social media shows that condemnation remains commonplace today. Condemnation is eternal death. The gospel is a protest against such ready condemnation. Are we able to rid ourselves of this deadly error?

Eternal God,
give us insight
to discern your will for us,
to give up what harms us,
and to seek the perfection we are promised
in Jesus Christ our Lord.

COLLECT

Reflection by **Graham James** | 95

Wednesday 10 March

Psalm **38** *or* 110, **111**, 112
Jeremiah 13.1-11
John 8.12-30

John 8.12-30
'I am the light of the world' (v.12)

At the Feast of Booths (or Tabernacles), four great lamps were lit in the temple, in the Court of the Women. The blaze on the Temple Mount could be seen for miles. In the Psalms, both the law ('a lamp to my feet' Psalm 119) and the Lord himself ('my light and my salvation' Psalm 27) were sources of illumination. The imagery was familiar and powerful.

For Jesus to speak of himself as 'the light of the world' was thus the boldest of claims. He was claiming to be sent from the Father to lead the people of God out of darkness, and also to be the authentic interpreter of the law and the prophets. From this point in John's Gospel, the enemies of Jesus become more vocal. What seems to us a gentle and attractive 'I am' saying of Jesus was, for his accusers, one of the most pernicious.

Lights have been used in most forms of Christian worship down the centuries, particularly candles. The symbolism of candles has never lost its attraction even in the age of electricity. Perhaps it's because a candle is a living flame. A living flame needs oxygen, just like human beings. As it burns, a candle is gradually dying. The light of the world, drawing the same air as the people he comes to save, is on the way to his death.

COLLECT

Almighty God,
whose most dear Son went not up to joy
    but first he suffered pain,
and entered not into glory before he was crucified:
mercifully grant that we, walking in the way of the cross,
may find it none other than the way of life and peace;
through Jesus Christ your Son our Lord,
who is alive and reigns with you,
in the unity of the Holy Spirit,
one God, now and for ever.

| *Reflection by* **Graham James**

Psalms **56**, 57 *or* 113, **115**
Jeremiah 14
John 8.31-47

Thursday 11 March

John 8.31-47

'... he [the devil] is a liar and the father of lies' (v.44)

Jesus charges some of his fellow Jews with not following Abraham
but doing the bidding of the devil and father of lies. His words were
employed by the Nazis to demonize all Jews. Yet John's Gospel is
clear that there were many Jews who believed in Jesus. Jesus declares
that his real opponent is the devil, the great deceiver who appears
to be telling the truth when he is lying and leads people to perdition.

The Greek word for devil, *diabolos*, means 'slanderer'. The law of
slander in most countries applies at the most serious end of false
accusation. The alternative translation 'backbiter' brings it a bit closer
to our own behaviours. Once I heard someone render *diabolos* as
'fault-finding spirit'. Few of us seem to avoid fault-finding. We tend
to find fault behind people's backs – a very different thing from
constructive criticism. Sometimes we do it to make ourselves feel
superior, but it is destructive of trust and truth. We are much more
likely to see the speck of dust in someone else's eye while ignoring
the boulders in our own.

Jesus speaks of the devil as the father of lies. He also speaks about
the truth setting us free. What about making this a day – or even a
week – free of fault-finding? If we escape the clutches of the father
of lies, we will travel on the way to the truth which sets us free.

Eternal God,
give us insight
to discern your will for us,
to give up what harms us,
and to seek the perfection we are promised
in Jesus Christ our Lord.

COLLECT

Friday 12 March

Psalm **22** *or* **139**
Jeremiah 15.10-end
John 8.48-end

John 8.48-end

'... before Abraham was, I am' (v.58)

The idea that our identity is not fixed but discovered is a relatively recent one. In relation to gender, there are new possibilities for change, at least for some people. But there is nothing new in questions of identity proving controversial, especially when they relate to our parentage. It was through DNA that Justin Welby, the Archbishop of Canterbury, discovered his father was Anthony Montague-Browne, once Winston Churchill's private secretary. Without downplaying the significance of this discovery, the Archbishop used the opportunity to say that his genetic make-up was not the primary factor in the person he believed himself to be. 'My identity is founded in who I am in Christ', he said.

Our identity is shaped by a range of characteristics – gender, race, family, nationality, culture and belief among them. In today's passage from John's Gospel, Jesus claims to have existed before Abraham, identifying himself with the God of heaven and earth in his eternal being. His words seem an unmistakeable allusion to God's own self-description in Exodus 3: 'I am who I am.' Thus, Jesus reveals his own identity. If what he is saying is not true, he has committed the greatest blasphemy. What gives us our identity? When we are in Christ, we do not throw off the complete range of characteristics that make each of us unique. But what weight do we give them? Would we agree with the words of the Archbishop?

COLLECT

Almighty God,
whose most dear Son went not up to joy
    but first he suffered pain,
and entered not into glory before he was crucified:
mercifully grant that we, walking in the way of the cross,
may find it none other than the way of life and peace;
through Jesus Christ your Son our Lord,
who is alive and reigns with you,
in the unity of the Holy Spirit,
one God, now and for ever.

| *Reflection by* **Graham James**

Psalm **31** *or* 120, **121**, 122
Jeremiah 16.10 – 17.4
John 9.1-17

Saturday 13 March

John 9.1-17

'Go, wash in the pool of Siloam' (v.7)

Jesus, 'the light of the world', now gives sight to a man born blind. More than that, the previously blind man, gradually comes to see who Jesus is. He sees more than many who have never wanted for sight.

My maternal grandmother became blind from glaucoma shortly before I was born. She was a faithful follower of Jesus Christ. Sometimes she heard the preachers in her chapel suggest that the healing miracles of Jesus, including when he gave sight to the blind, depended on the faith and trust of the one who was healed. And yet she, who had no shortage of faith and trust, had become blind. What did she lack? It was certainly not spiritual sight.

This chapter of John's Gospel was a comfort to her. The blind man doesn't even ask to be given sight. Jesus heals him before they exchange a word. He does so by mixing the dust of the earth (out of which we are all created) with his saliva (thought to be a precious source of life in the ancient world). And then the man washes in the pool of Siloam – in water from well beyond Jerusalem, thanks to Hezekiah's long tunnel. The creator of all, the light of the world, the fount of living water – they all give the blind man his spiritual as well as physical sight. What signs of God will we be able to see today?

COLLECT

Eternal God,
give us insight
to discern your will for us,
to give up what harms us,
and to seek the perfection we are promised
in Jesus Christ our Lord.

Reflection by **Graham James**   99

Monday 15 March   Psalms 70, **77** *or* 123, 124, 125, **126**
Jeremiah 17.5-18
John 9.18-end

John 9.18-end
'His parents … were afraid' (v.22)

The blind man's parents make an appearance as their son is being questioned about Jesus. What do they know about how he received his sight? They are evasive, claiming they don't know who opened their son's eyes. They don't want to get involved. Their boy is old enough to speak for himself, so they prefer to keep out of the controversy that surrounds him. The Gospel writer suggests they feared expulsion from the synagogue and the community if they testified to Jesus as someone working with God's authority.

This encounter with the blind man's parents may seem a minor detail in a bigger story, but it probably had significance for some of the first readers of John's Gospel. Jews who followed Christ knew what it was to be expelled from their synagogues for believing Jesus was the Messiah. Some of them experienced their families standing aside or even betraying them. Those whose eyes were opened to see the truth about Jesus found the cost of discipleship meant being cast out from their community, and sometimes from their family as well.

Many Christians today know what it is to experience indifference or hostility from their families. Some are excluded and even betrayed. Discipleship can be a lonely experience.

What's been the greatest cost you have experienced in following Jesus Christ?

C O L L E C T	Merciful Lord,
	absolve your people from their offences,
	that through your bountiful goodness
	we may all be delivered from the chains of those sins
	which by our frailty we have committed;
	grant this, heavenly Father,
	for Jesus Christ's sake, our blessed Lord and Saviour,
	who is alive and reigns with you,
	in the unity of the Holy Spirit,
	one God, now and for ever.

| *Reflection by* **Graham James**

Psalms 54, **79** *or* **132**, 133
Jeremiah 18.1-12
John 10.1-10

Tuesday 16 March

John 10.1-10

'... the shepherd of the sheep' (v.2)

Pope Francis has said that the shepherds of the Roman Catholic Church should have 'the smell of the sheep' about them. He calls his bishops and clergy to immerse themselves in the lives of the people they serve.

Shepherds live closely with their sheep. In recent years, James Rebanks, a shepherd in the Lake District in the UK, has attracted tens of thousands of followers to his Twitter account describing his daily life and work. His book *The Shepherd's Life* was an unexpected bestseller. He is the son of a shepherd, and his father was the son of a shepherd too. It's in his bones. His descriptions of the lambing season and the hard work of winter months show that he smells of his sheep.

Few people have direct experience of shepherding, but it does not take much imagination to understand this imagery. Even so, the Gospel writer suggests that those listening to Jesus were slow to catch on. That's surprising, since the relationship between God and his people was frequently expressed in ancient Israel as one of sheep and shepherd, as in Psalm 23, 'The Lord is my shepherd'.

Sometimes pastoral imagery is used in the Church almost exclusively in relation to official ministers. They should certainly smell of the sheep. But most of us have others who fall within our care, and should know our voice and our concern for them. To whom will we be shepherds today?

Merciful Lord,
you know our struggle to serve you:
when sin spoils our lives
and overshadows our hearts,
come to our aid
and turn us back to you again;
through Jesus Christ our Lord.

COLLECT

Wednesday 17 March
Psalms 63, **90** *or* **119.153-end**
Jeremiah 18.13-end
John 10.11-21

John 10.11-21

'... there will be one flock, one shepherd' (v.16)

This vision of the good shepherd drawing everyone into one flock comes after we have been told that the blind man to whom Jesus gave sight was driven out of his community (John 9.34). He was expelled because he would not condemn Jesus for giving him his sight on the sabbath. (Even a mighty work done on the sabbath contravened the law of Moses, so the scribes and Pharisees claimed.)

Jesus draws a contrast between religious teachers concerned to keep the purity of their group, whatever the human casualties, and his own desire to draw in 'other sheep who do not belong to this fold'. He does not say who these other sheep are, but early readers of John's Gospel would have included many gentiles, who may have applied these words to themselves. It's likely, however, that the words of the prophet Ezekiel provide the context here. The prophet condemns the religious leaders of his day. God himself will have to come and be the people's shepherd. 'I myself will be the shepherd of my sheep ... I will seek the lost ... bring back the strayed ... bind up the injured .... strengthen the weak' (Ezekiel 34.15,16). The whole course of the ministry of Jesus has been shaped by these priorities. It has brought vehement opposition. The question John poses his readers is 'Whose side are you on?', though he is too subtle to put it quite so crudely.

COLLECT

Merciful Lord,
absolve your people from their offences,
that through your bountiful goodness
we may all be delivered from the chains of those sins
which by our frailty we have committed;
grant this, heavenly Father,
for Jesus Christ's sake, our blessed Lord and Saviour,
who is alive and reigns with you,
in the unity of the Holy Spirit,
one God, now and for ever.

| *Reflection by* **Graham James**

Psalms 53, **86** *or* **143**, 146
Jeremiah 19.1-13
John 10.22-end

Thursday 18 March

John 10.22-end

'If you are the Messiah, tell us plainly' (v.24)

Some people see God in many places – in the dawn of a new day, a forgiving word, the birth of a child, an act of self-sacrifice or being in love. Others experience the very same things but see no evidence that God exists at all.

A similar dynamic is found here when Jesus is asked to say plainly if he is the Messiah. He has already claimed to be the light of the world, the good shepherd and the bread of life. Jesus has given sight to the blind, fed five thousand people, healed the son of a royal official, and cured a lame man at the pool of Bethesda. If they do not believe his words, he says, then surely his works speak for themselves. How could he have spoken and acted more plainly?

John notes, almost in passing, that it is the Festival of Dedication, known also as the Festival of Lights. It celebrates the rededication of the temple a century and a half earlier following its desecration. It's a time when many lamps are lit. In Jesus, the light of the world has come and is in plain sight. And yet many refuse to see.

The accusers of Jesus may not want to see who he is, perhaps because he confounds their expectations of who the Messiah should be or what he should do. What expectations may blind us to seeing God plainly in our lives today?

Merciful Lord,
you know our struggle to serve you:
when sin spoils our lives
and overshadows our hearts,
come to our aid
and turn us back to you again;
through Jesus Christ our Lord.

COLLECT

Reflection by **Graham James**   103

Friday 19 March
Joseph of Nazareth

Psalms 25, 147.1-12
Isaiah 11.1-10
Matthew 13.54-end

Isaiah 11.1-10
'A shoot shall come out from the stock of Jesse' (v.1)

Isaiah 11 begins with an eloquent vision of a kingdom of justice, righteousness and wisdom, with a ruler whose 'delight will be in the fear of the Lord'. The people of Israel have been faithless and have lost their king. Isaiah expects renewal to come when a new shoot emerges from the line of Jesse, the father of King David.

Centuries later, Matthew's Gospel begins by recalling how the lineage of Joseph, the husband of Mary, can be traced back to David and Jesse and even to Abraham. Despite the belief in the virgin birth and Joseph's status as guardian or foster-father of Jesus, Joseph's ancestry is treated as highly significant. He has his own place in enabling Jesus to proclaim the kingdom of peace anticipated in Isaiah's vision.

Joseph's support for Mary and protection of his son are central to the birth narratives and the early life of Jesus. Yet he fades from the story and has not always been given the profile he deserves in the Church. For example, it was only in 1962 that his name was added to the long list of saints mentioned in the Canon of the Mass in the Roman Catholic Church. Perhaps this makes Joseph a suitable saint for our own age when in Western societies the role of fathers is sometimes contested, unclear or undervalued.

COLLECT

God our Father,
who from the family of your servant David
raised up Joseph the carpenter
to be the guardian of your incarnate Son
and husband of the Blessed Virgin Mary:
give us grace to follow him
in faithful obedience to your commands;
through Jesus Christ your Son our Lord,
who is alive and reigns with you,
in the unity of the Holy Spirit,
one God, now and for ever.

| *Reflection by* **Graham James**

Psalm **32** *or* **147**
Jeremiah 20.7-end
John 11.17-27

Saturday 20 March

John 11.17-27

'... if you had been here my brother would not have died' (v.21)

I once visited a priest whose wife had died two days previously. He told me he had already worked through the stages of bereavement and come to acceptance. It seemed unlikely in 48 hours. Then his wife's sister arrived. He told her that if she had come earlier, his wife might not have died. I felt rather relieved that his grief was still so raw. The tears flowed.

Martha's grief is raw too. We know her and Mary from Luke's Gospel where Mary is the one who sits listening to Jesus while Martha rushes around doing the household chores. Here we learn they have a brother Lazarus who has died. Mary sits at home mourning. Martha, by contrast, is out to greet Jesus. She blames him for not being there to prevent Lazarus' death. But Martha still hopes Jesus can do something. She believes in the resurrection on the last day. That was common enough in Judaism at the time. Jesus tells her, 'I am the resurrection and the life'. The light of the world is also life for all eternity. Through him anyone can discover what it is to live abundantly. It's with her bereavement still raw that Martha makes the fullest profession of faith found in John's Gospel: 'You are the Messiah, the Son of God, the one coming into the world.' If she had suppressed her grief, would she have made this life-changing discovery?

COLLECT

Merciful Lord,
absolve your people from their offences,
that through your bountiful goodness
we may all be delivered from the chains of those sins
which by our frailty we have committed;
grant this, heavenly Father,
for Jesus Christ's sake, our blessed Lord and Saviour,
who is alive and reigns with you,
in the unity of the Holy Spirit,
one God, now and for ever.

Reflection by **Graham James** | 105

Monday 22 March

Psalms **73**, 121 *or* **1**, 2, 3
Jeremiah 21.1-10
John 11.28-44

John 11.28-44
'Did I not tell you ...' (v.40)

Today's passage is charged with emotional intensity. Echoes of Martha's remarkable declaration that Jesus is the Messiah in verse 27 mingle with grief following Lazarus' death. His sisters are deeply distressed, and angry with Jesus for arriving late. Their loss is heightened by the presence of other mourners, and we sense the gentle bustle of activity that often accompanies major life events. Into this mix Jesus' own anguish spills over and he begins to weep. Then there is talk of opening the tomb, Martha's anxiety about the body's decomposition and finally the dramatic emergence of Lazarus.

Throughout, the ordinary and extraordinary are held side by side. Jesus' divinity and humanity are present in equal measure. Mary and Martha's touching faith in Jesus doesn't diminish their frustration. Jesus himself is overcome with the sadness of loss, and perhaps his own imminent suffering and death, just moments before he calls Lazarus out.

Life and death are both in the balance as we are reminded that the holding together of apparently impossible contradictions is so often the way of faith. In the Persian calendar, yesterday was Nowruz – New Year. I remember as a child growing up in Iran how it wasn't unusual for the Church community to celebrate the Nowruz season at the start of each Spring, with its promise of new life and renewal, while at the same time marking a solemn event in the Christian calendar, such as Good Friday. The experience was and is a permanent reminder that in life there is always death and in times of greatest sorrow there is always hope of resurrection.

COLLECT

Most merciful God,
who by the death and resurrection of your Son Jesus Christ
delivered and saved the world:
grant that by faith in him who suffered on the cross
we may triumph in the power of his victory;
through Jesus Christ your Son our Lord,
who is alive and reigns with you,
in the unity of the Holy Spirit,
one God, now and for ever.

| *Reflection by* **Guli Francis-Dehqani**

Psalms **35**, 123 *or* **5**, 6 (8)   **Tuesday 23 March**
Jeremiah 22.1-5, 13-19
John 11.45-end

John 11.45-end
'... and he remained there with the disciples' (v.54)

The chief priests and Pharisees are fearful of Jesus' impact on the crowds and of potential political consequences. Caiaphas is frightened for his own status and position. Even Jesus, it seems, experiences fear; he's lying low, refusing to emerge in public, not yet ready to face the end.

Fear is a healthy human instinct. It acts as a warning against imminent dangers, ensuring we protect ourselves and others. We teach children to be wary of fire, careful chopping vegetables, mindful crossing the road – a gentle instilling of fear in the face of possible dangers. Talking with my teenage son recently about what he might do if he were mugged, my advice was, 'don't be brave, give them your wallet and run'. In other words, be sensibly fearful and act accordingly.

Yet sometimes we must rise above our fears with unwavering determination. In some parts of the world, Christians face physical danger and persecution, which many meet with extraordinary courage and bravery. In other parts of the world, fear emerges from the Church's increasing marginalization. This is the fear of loss of influence, of irrelevance and eventual extinction. This kind of fear corrodes and creates the illusion that the future of the Church is dependent on us. In reality, the future is in God's hands. Our calling, whatever our context, is to resist fear, be faithful in the knowledge of God's constant presence, and to love without ceasing.

Gracious Father,
you gave up your Son
out of love for the world:
lead us to ponder the mysteries of his passion,
that we may know eternal peace
through the shedding of our Saviour's blood,
Jesus Christ our Lord.

COLLECT

Reflection by **Guli Francis-Dehqani**   107

Wednesday 24 March

John 12.1-11

'The house was filled with the fragrance of the perfume' (v.3)

I imagine Mary's actions in anointing Jesus' feet to have been entirely spontaneous – an outpouring of great love – feelings of the heart overwhelming logic of the head. This shocking yet exquisitely beautiful offering is in direct contrast to Judas' self-righteous anger, justified with perfectly reasonable arguments about how the money could have been spent on the poor. The story is a reminder that the realm of faith is never fully explainable by the intellect but demands a response, beyond mere reason, from the very core of our soul.

But this story also confronts our sometimes comfortable complacency. It challenges us to take risks and to stand up for others. Mary took a monumental risk. What she did was not only wastefully extravagant but well beyond conventional behaviour for a woman. It would hardly have been surprising had Jesus himself chastised her. And yet she took a risk to show how much she loved him.

Then, in a wonderful gesture of solidarity, Jesus *stood up for Mary.* 'Leave her alone', he said in response to Judas' reprimand. Mary was accused unfairly, and Jesus, who could so easily have remained silent, came to her defence.

When was the last time you took a risk for your faith, doing what was right instead of what was easiest? When was the last time you spoke up for someone else, when it would have been so much easier to bow your head in silence?

COLLECT | Most merciful God,
who by the death and resurrection of your Son Jesus Christ
delivered and saved the world:
grant that by faith in him who suffered on the cross
we may triumph in the power of his victory;
through Jesus Christ your Son our Lord,
who is alive and reigns with you,
in the unity of the Holy Spirit,
one God, now and for ever.

| *Reflection by* **Guli Francis-Dehqani**

Psalms 111, 113
1 Samuel 2.1-10
Romans 5.12-end

Thursday 25 March
Annunciation of Our Lord to the Blessed Virgin Mary

Romans 5.12-end

'... the many will be made righteous' (v.19)

Today, we celebrate the feast of the Annunciation – a foretelling of the incarnation and the announcement by Angel Gabriel to Mary that she would give birth to God's son. The Bible passage is Paul's theological underpinning of why Christ's coming was necessary. With the events of Holy Week just around the corner, these verses provide a link between the birth narratives and those that tell of Jesus' death.

Paul's is a dense thesis in which Adam and Christ are compared, one bringing sin to the world through disobedience and the other reconciliation through righteousness. Adam and Christ represent choices about what kind of existence we desire: one that ends in death or one that leads to eternal life. If it is the latter, we must journey into next week when Christ's obedience will take him to the cross, from where he will transform violence to gentleness, hatred to love and death to life.

The gift of life, Paul stresses, is free and for the taking. It is an invitation that we can only accept in trust and faith, and it doesn't promise an easy path. Gabriel's message to Mary was also an invitation to which she responded 'yes'. Her journey was full of suffering, but still today Mary is a reminder of how often we encounter Christ most forcefully when we are most wounded and it is then we discover the true value of the new life he offers.

COLLECT

We beseech you, O Lord,
pour your grace into our hearts,
that as we have known the incarnation of your Son Jesus Christ
by the message of an angel,
so by his cross and passion
we may be brought to the glory of his resurrection;
through Jesus Christ your Son our Lord,
who is alive and reigns with you,
in the unity of the Holy Spirit,
one God, now and for ever.

Reflection by **Guli Francis-Dehqani**

Friday 26 March

Psalms **22**, 126 *or* 17, **19**
Jeremiah 24
John 12.20-36*a*

John 12.20-36*a*

'... it is for this reason that I have come to this hour' (v.27)

Jesus associates his impending death with glory: 'The hour has come for the Son of Man to be glorified' – an odd juxtaposition, underscoring the upside-down world of God's economy where failure and suffering are redeemed. Christ's moment of greatest suffering is to be his moment of greatest glory as love and gentleness overcome hatred and violence.

Approaching his death, Jesus doesn't speak of how to ensure his legacy continues. He talks instead of a seed dying before it bears fruit. This reminds me of the words of the early Christian author Tertullian: 'the blood of the martyrs is the seed of the Church' – death leading to new growth. Let's not romanticize the reality, but this often seems to be the experience of the persecuted Church – that through times of trial and suffering comes a deepening of faith, new insights into the meaning of the cross and hope for the future.

There is much talk at present, in the West especially, of how to safeguard the future of a shrinking Church. It is right and proper that we take seriously our calling to proclaim the faith afresh in each generation and pass it on to the next. But in the process there is a danger that we might just miss something profound about fruit coming only once the seed has died. It is a painful truth to contemplate, but what might you in your context need to allow to die in order that something new might blossom?

COLLECT

Most merciful God,
who by the death and resurrection of your Son Jesus Christ
delivered and saved the world:
grant that by faith in him who suffered on the cross
we may triumph in the power of his victory;
through Jesus Christ your Son our Lord,
who is alive and reigns with you,
in the unity of the Holy Spirit,
one God, now and for ever.

| *Reflection by* **Guli Francis-Dehqani**

Psalms **23**, 127 *or* 20, 21, **23**
Jeremiah 25.1-14
John 12.36b-end

Saturday 27 March

John 12.36*b*-end

'... for they loved human glory more than the glory that comes from God' (v.43)

John marks the end of Jesus' public ministry with the brief statement that 'he departed and hid from them'. The time for telling stories and parables, for teaching and performing miracles is over, and the people won't see Jesus again until after his arrest. In human terms, his efforts had failed. After all he'd said and done, the people did not believe in him. It must have hurt. There must have been a part of Jesus that had hoped the suffering wouldn't be needed. That through skill and effort and commitment he would manage to convince people of the need to repent and believe.

If Jesus was, as we believe, fully human (as well as fully God), then his need for worldly affirmation will have been real and strong. Most of us are familiar with the feeling; we look for it again and again – to be noticed, successful, wealthy, influential. We may tell ourselves it's because we want to do good, and at our best there may be something of that. But in truth, this craving for human affirmation comes from a need to prove ourselves – to convince others, and ourselves, that we are worthwhile, valued and, ultimately, loved. Jesus' acceptance of his calling demonstrates that all we really need is to embrace our ultimate identity as beloved of God – those who are loved not because of what we achieve but simply because of who we are.

COLLECT

Gracious Father,
you gave up your Son
out of love for the world:
lead us to ponder the mysteries of his passion,
that we may know eternal peace
through the shedding of our Saviour's blood,
Jesus Christ our Lord.

Reflection by **Guli Francis-Dehqani**   111

Monday 29 March
Monday of Holy Week

Psalm 41
Lamentations 1.1-12*a*
Luke 22.1-23

Luke 22.1-23

'When the hour came ...' (v.14)

Fear, betrayal and conspiracy are themes that set the mood in today's passage as we begin the journey through Holy Week. Jesus must have sensed that events were overtaking him, that things had moved to the point of no return and the final outcome was looking grim. I know when my anxieties are really heightened, normal routines escape me. I struggle to think straight or make good decisions. The idea of eating, never mind preparing a meal to share with others, is appalling. Yet that's exactly what Jesus does. He calmly carries on with his plans, arranges a meal with his disciples and prepares them for what is to come by establishing the central act of remembrance whereby we still encounter him centuries on every time we partake in Holy Communion.

What is so striking about these verses is that although people are closing in and Jesus appears to be at the mercy of others, he in fact remains in charge, totally in control, setting the agenda and the pace. The point is, of course, that he wasn't entering this phase unprepared. Jesus' entire life was founded on securing his relationship with his heavenly father. And this gave him confidence to focus his thinking and steadily follow his calling.

For us to enter our times of trial with composure, we too need to have done the groundwork, establishing a life based on prayer and reliance on God.

COLLECT

Almighty and everlasting God,
who in your tender love towards the human race
   sent your Son our Saviour Jesus Christ
to take upon him our flesh
and to suffer death upon the cross:
grant that we may follow the example of his patience and humility,
and also be made partakers of his resurrection;
through Jesus Christ your Son our Lord,
who is alive and reigns with you,
in the unity of the Holy Spirit,
one God, now and for ever.

Reflection by **Guli Francis-Dehqani**

Psalm 27
Lamentations 3.1-18
Luke 22. [24-38] 39-53

Tuesday 30 March

Tuesday of Holy Week

Luke 22. [24-38] 39-53

'Pray that you may not come into the time of trial' (v.40)

Today, we begin to get a proper sense of the extent of Jesus' agony. As doubt creeps in and fear grips him, he descends to the depths of despair. 'Remove this cup from me', he implores and, as he prays earnestly, sweat pours off him like droplets of blood. It's a vivid picture of dread and terror. And then ... they come to arrest him. How tempting it must have been to allow the disciples to protect him with their swords and to flee to a place of safety under the cover of darkness. Instead, Jesus embraces the suffering that lies ahead, admonishes the disciple who has struck the slave and heals his ear.

It's not until an orange is squeezed that you know if the juice is sweet or sour. It's not until any of us is gravely tested that we'll know the extent of our faithfulness and obedience. It is sobering to think of the host of martyrs down the centuries who have remained true, refusing to deny their faith, even to the point of death; those who have refused to flee but bravely stood up for truth in the face of injustice.

As we give thanks for those who have gone before, we pray for Christians persecuted around the world today and we pause to consider for a moment: 'What would I do if they came for me?'

True and humble king,
hailed by the crowd as Messiah:
grant us the faith to know you and love you,
that we may be found beside you
on the way of the cross,
which is the path of glory.

COLLECT

Reflection by **Guli Francis-Dehqani**   113

Wednesday 31 March
Wednesday of Holy Week

Psalm 102 [*or* 102.1-18]
Wisdom 1.16 – 2.1; 2.12-22
or Jeremiah 11.18-20
Luke 22.54-end

Luke 22.54-end
'Then Peter remembered' (v.61)

The night before writing this, I visited a prison in my area where inmates were performing their own poetry and music following a rehabilitation workshop. A line from one of the pieces has remained with me: 'I've stolen, I've lied, I've been deceitful; I've done all these things but I've never lost hope'. A touching portrayal of what it's like to recognize when we've sunk to our lowest while knowing too that it doesn't need to be the end; that it can be a turning point and the beginning of the path to renewal.

That's how we meet Peter today. The crowing cockerel and a look from Jesus trigger the memory of his brash confidence just days before, and with it comes the devastating realization of how badly he's failed. This could have been the end for Peter. He might well have walked away – fled and returned to his fishing nets and the safety of his old life. Instead, the incident becomes a defining moment, which brought him eventually to the reassertion of his loyalty, his restoration by the risen Jesus and the calling to become shepherd of the flock.

And there is the challenge for each of us. After we fail (as we surely will) and after weeping bitter tears of regret, which direction will we choose to travel? The short road to self-pity and defeatism or the long road through forgiveness to healing and recovery?

COLLECT

Almighty and everlasting God,
who in your tender love towards the human race
    sent your Son our Saviour Jesus Christ
to take upon him our flesh
and to suffer death upon the cross:
grant that we may follow the example of his patience and humility,
and also be made partakers of his resurrection;
through Jesus Christ your Son our Lord,
who is alive and reigns with you,
in the unity of the Holy Spirit,
one God, now and for ever.

| *Reflection by* **Guli Francis-Dehqani**

Psalms 42, 43
Leviticus 16.2-24
Luke 23.1-25

Thursday 1 April

Maundy Thursday

Luke 23.1-25

'... but Jesus gave him no answer' (v.9)

One of the things I find most difficult to deal with in life is when I feel I've been treated unfairly. I'm talking here about the everyday small injustices we encounter, often over relatively insignificant matters that nonetheless, in the moment, leave us feeling powerless, hurt and humiliated. Times when we've been misrepresented, wrongly accused or just treated a little shoddily and every fibre of our being is bristling with anger and our instinct is to lash out in response.

Now, I'm a passionate advocate of Christians speaking out and acting for justice in situations of abuse and persecution or where a crime is being committed. And yet there is also something in the Christian story (and at the heart of today's reading) about the place of humility – of knowing that sometimes the better response is to remain undefended, acknowledge the pain, find it in our heart to forgive and move on – to mend relationships rather than damage them further.

Jesus, who not long ago had angrily cast out the moneylenders from the temple, now stands silent before Pilate and Herod. And as he does so, he demonstrates the extraordinary courage and conviction needed to take this stance. In his demeanour we don't see weakness but rather a profound show of strength. May God grant us the wisdom to know when to take action against the injustices we experience and when to remain silent.

COLLECT

True and humble king,
hailed by the crowd as Messiah:
grant us the faith to know you and love you,
that we may be found beside you
on the way of the cross,
which is the path of glory.

Reflection by **Guli Francis-Dehqani**   115

Friday 2 April

Good Friday

Psalm 69
Genesis 22.1-18
John 19.38-end
or Hebrews 10.1-10

Hebrews 10.1-10

'... make perfect those who approach' (v.1)

I'm eternally grateful to my parents for their gift of unconditional love. However guilty I was at times of behaving badly or causing them hurt, I never doubted that I was loved; I never had to prove myself worthy of their devotion. Despite my many failings, their love helped form and shape me, giving me security, confidence and, perhaps most importantly, insights into forgiveness and compassion.

And in the language of faith, that is what Paul reminds us of in today's reading, and it is what lies at the heart of Good Friday. Today, guilt is overcome by love. Jesus' unswerving obedience and faithfulness even to death on a cross releases us from perpetual guilt (which required regular sacrifices), and instead we are embraced by unconditional love. Today, the law makes way for grace. Jesus becomes the *final sacrifice* – once and for all – and we are beckoned towards freedom. No more guilt, no more sacrifices and no more need to prove ourselves worthy of God's love. That is the extraordinary message of Good Friday that our wounded world is in such great need of hearing.

As we stand at the foot of the cross, so we discover our true identity as children of God, loved unconditionally, soaked in grace, no longer burdened by sin and guilt. Here, in the outstretched arms of Christ, we find healing for our pain and, despite the darkness, the glimmer of new beginnings.

COLLECT

Almighty Father,
look with mercy on this your family
for which our Lord Jesus Christ was content to be betrayed
    and given up into the hands of sinners
    and to suffer death upon the cross;
who is alive and glorified with you and the Holy Spirit,
one God, now and for ever.

| *Reflection by* **Guli Francis-Dehqani**

Psalm 142
Hosea 6.1-6
John 2.18-22

Saturday 3 April

Easter Eve

John 2.18-22

'... in three days I will raise it up' (v.19)

Today's verses follow on from Jesus' cleansing of the temple. The people are demanding an explanation about his actions and his reply comes in the form both of a riddle and a parable. In Jewish tradition, 'after three days' or 'on the third day' was a phrase used to indicate a length of time before God would deliver the people from their troubles. Three days denotes a turning point towards something new and better. It suggests, also, a period of waiting – it isn't now or tomorrow, but after three days. There is need for patience and fortitude.

In this passage, God is relocated from a place to a person – from being present in the temple to being present in the body of Jesus. We know that our access to God is now through a *relationship* with the person of Christ and that we cannot restrict God to a place or building. But however much we *believe* this to be true, sometimes we struggle to *feel* it. Sometimes God feels very far and we are swamped by darkness and silence. Sometimes we are powerless to change circumstances as we would like. Well, today is the day when our doubt and emptiness and helplessness is honoured in the Church calendar; when we sit with our pain and dwell with our uncertainty, unable to fix things or speed them up, but instead clinging on until 'the third day' when all we will revealed.

Grant, Lord,
that we who are baptized into the death
of your Son our Saviour Jesus Christ
may continually put to death our evil desires
and be buried with him;
and that through the grave and gate of death
we may pass to our joyful resurrection;
through his merits,
who died and was buried and rose again for us,
your Son Jesus Christ our Lord.

COLLECT

Reflection by **Guli Francis-Dehqani** | 117

Monday 5 April

Monday of Easter Week

Psalms 111, 117, 146
Song of Solomon 1.9 – 2.7
Mark 16.1-8

Mark 16.1-8

'... and they said nothing to anyone, for they were afraid' (v. 8)

There is an unnerving lack of resolution in today's text, which is thought to form the original ending of Mark's Gospel. The text has given rise to some disquiet right from the Gospel's earliest years. The NRSV offers two alternative 'happy' endings (a shorter and a longer, both to be found in some of the oldest manuscripts), both of which conclude with the continuing work of the risen Christ through the disciples he had commissioned.

Tempting though it may be to follow the example of these ancient writers, we may miss something vital if we skim over the discomfort created by this passage. What must it have *felt* like? We have the benefit of hindsight – and we sometimes assume that what was happening must have been obvious – but what those closest to Jesus were experiencing was unprecedented. In reality, after Jesus' death it must have seemed that there were no grounds for hope, no possible way forward. With this original ending to his Gospel, Mark makes no attempt to 'sugar the pill'. In *Feasting on the Gospels*, the theologian Mary Luti applauds Mark's reticence, declaring that he 'clears a space for us to feel whatever we feel when confronted with the Easter proclamation'. There is a mystery here beyond our human understanding, and Mark's ending allows that mystery an honoured place, inviting us to enter into it.

Yes, Lord, we believe ... but what does it all *mean*?

COLLECT

Lord of all life and power,
who through the mighty resurrection of your Son
overcame the old order of sin and death
to make all things new in him:
grant that we, being dead to sin
and alive to you in Jesus Christ,
may reign with him in glory;
to whom with you and the Holy Spirit
be praise and honour, glory and might,
now and in all eternity.

| *Reflection by* **Barbara Mosse**

Psalms 112, 147.1-12
Song of Solomon 2.8-end
Luke 24.1-12

Tuesday 6 April
Tuesday of Easter Week

Luke 24.1-12

'Why do you look for the living amongst the dead?' (v.5)

The themes of terror and amazement run, thread-like, through the biblical reports of the immediate aftermath of Jesus' resurrection. In Luke's account, the women demonstrate the same fear as in the passage from Mark we considered yesterday, but Luke has them telling the disciples what they have experienced. The men don't believe them, but Peter at least goes to the tomb to check for himself.

We needn't be too concerned about the differences between these accounts. It wasn't unusual for writers to add or extract elements to the biblical narratives. We know, historically, that the crucifixion happened, but the authors were primarily writing from a faith perspective, rather than that of history. Faith, by its very definition, can't be pinned down and 'proved' in a science laboratory. In *Feasting on the Gospels*, the American minister Shannon Michael Pater reminds us that 'faith is lived; it is alive. Even in times of death and doubt, it is a seed hidden in the soil, waiting for fruition'.

The angels' question to the women raises a corresponding one for us: where do *we* look for the living Christ? Do we perhaps hark back to earlier times, whether good or bad, when we were especially aware of Christ's presence? We can be thankful for this – but it is in the past. The challenge is to look for the living Christ *now*, whatever our circumstances; whether bleak and despairing, or joyful and full of hope.

God of glory,
by the raising of your Son
you have broken the chains of death and hell:
fill your Church with faith and hope;
for a new day has dawned
and the way to life stands open
in our Saviour Jesus Christ.

COLLECT

Reflection by **Barbara Mosse** | 119

Easter Season

Wednesday 7 April
Wednesday of Easter Week

Psalms 113, 147.13-end
Song of Solomon 3
Matthew 28.16-end

Matthew 28.16-end
'I am with you always' (v. 20)

From the time of Moses onwards, mountains in scripture have been places of divine revelation and encounter. Old Testament examples include Moses' first meeting with the angel of the Lord who spoke out of a burning bush; his meeting with God in the darkness on the summit of Mount Sinai; Elijah's unexpected mountain-top encounter with God in the 'still, small voice'. The tradition continues in the New Testament with the devil's temptation of Jesus on 'a very high mountain' (Matthew 4.8), and his transfiguration on a mountain witnessed by Peter, James and John. In each case, the person, or people, experiencing these mountain-top epiphanies has their experience of God challenged, deepened, driven into another dimension.

And in today's reading, the post-resurrection Jesus has a final meeting with his disciples, on an unnamed mountain in Galilee. The many resurrection appearances recorded in the Gospels come to a climax here. Matthew doesn't record Jesus' ascension itself, but his words clearly represent his final instructions and reassurances. Reassurances, yes – but also the disciples' greatest challenge. Up to this time they have had Jesus physically present with them; they have been able to see, hear and touch him. In what sense can Jesus continue to be with them, when he is no longer physically present?

In what sense do *we* experience Jesus with us, having never known his physical presence?

COLLECT

Lord of all life and power,
who through the mighty resurrection of your Son
overcame the old order of sin and death
to make all things new in him:
grant that we, being dead to sin
and alive to you in Jesus Christ,
may reign with him in glory;
to whom with you and the Holy Spirit
be praise and honour, glory and might,
now and in all eternity.

120 | *Reflection by* **Barbara Mosse**

Psalms 114, 148
Song of Solomon 5.2 – 6.3
Luke 7.11-17

Thursday 8 April
Thursday of Easter Week

Luke 7.11-17

'He was his mother's only son, and she was a widow' (v. 12)

The theme of God's power to bring life out of death through Jesus continues. Today, we are taken back to an event earlier in Jesus' ministry: his raising to life of a widow's only son. Along with the grief accompanying her double bereavement, the woman's plight is all too clear: with the deaths of her husband and her only son she was left completely alone, with no male relative to give her a secure place in a patriarchal culture. Her future looked bleak indeed.

As Jesus brought the young man back to life, his power as a miracle worker – one able to bring life out of death – is made explicit. But it is not primarily as a demonstration of power that Jesus did this; he acted rather out of compassion for the woman and her grief, and the desperate situation she found herself in.

The work of Jesus through his public ministry was well known, and the crowd were used to miraculous healings. But what Jesus accomplished here went far beyond anything they had experienced before, and they reacted with fear.

When we face our own situations of grief and loss of hope, how do we react? Do we trust Jesus to touch us with his compassion, or do we close in on our own sense of hopelessness? The question with which we ended Monday's reflection remains relevant here: yes, Lord, we believe ... but what does it all mean?

COLLECT

God of glory,
by the raising of your Son
you have broken the chains of death and hell:
fill your Church with faith and hope;
for a new day has dawned
and the way to life stands open
in our Saviour Jesus Christ.

Reflection by **Barbara Mosse** | 121

Friday 9 April
Friday of Easter Week

Psalms **115**, 149
Song of Solomon 7.10 – 8.4
Luke 8.41-end

Luke 8.41-end

'Your daughter is dead; do not trouble the teacher any longer' (v. 49)

We have here two miracles. Jairus pleads with Jesus to come and heal his sick daughter, but while Jesus is on the way to Jairus' house, he is side-tracked by a woman with a haemorrhage whom Jesus involuntarily heals when she touches the hem of his cloak. During the delay, Jairus' daughter dies, and a member of his household tells Jairus bluntly and with a seeming lack of compassion.

What, I wonder, did Jairus think about the delay? Fear, extreme anxiety, despair; impatience with both Jesus and with the woman who had diverted him away from the urgency of his daughter's situation? All this and more, perhaps. Maybe there have been times when we too have sought Jesus' help, then feared all was lost when that help seemed – from our perspective – to be delayed. But Jesus forestalls Jairus' likely reaction with reassurance: 'Do not fear. Only believe, and she will be saved.'

Given the sheer number of people in our world, today and across time, it challenges and stretches our faith to accept that God is able to respond *personally* to everyone who seeks God's help. But God's ways are not our ways, and they will always outstretch the bounds of human possibility. In today's reading, both the nameless woman and Jairus' nameless daughter receive the healing and restoration to life that they need.

COLLECT

Lord of all life and power,
who through the mighty resurrection of your Son
overcame the old order of sin and death
to make all things new in him:
grant that we, being dead to sin
and alive to you in Jesus Christ,
may reign with him in glory;
to whom with you and the Holy Spirit
be praise and honour, glory and might,
now and in all eternity.

| *Reflection by* **Barbara Mosse**

Psalms 116, 150
Song of Solomon 8.5-7
John 11.17-44

Saturday 10 April
Saturday of Easter Week

John 11.17-44

'... Lazarus had already been in the tomb for four days' (v. 17)

The sequence of events we have followed over the last few days finds its climax here in Jesus' raising of Lazarus from the dead. When Jesus and his disciples arrive, Lazarus has been dead and buried for four days; there is no room for any suspicion that maybe Lazarus wasn't *really* dead. The certainty of Lazarus' death is emphasized too in other ways. 'Lord, if you had been here, my brother would not have died' is the accusation voiced by each of the sisters; and when Jesus orders the stone to be removed from the tomb, Martha complains: 'Lord, already there is a stench because he has been dead for four days.'

The journey from death to life is a theme that has run through all this week's readings. In gospel chronology, these events anticipate the great event of Easter; in their placing in the Church's liturgical calendar, they echo the experience of the Easter narrative as seen in the lives of ordinary people. Jesus himself taught that a seed must first fall into the earth and die, so that it may 'rise again' and bear much fruit (John 12.24). We will each experience many 'mini-deaths' in our lives – bereavement, job loss, depression – before our final physical death. Jesus invites us to accept the patterning of the Easter narrative into our own lives and to allow him to bring new life out of the ashes of the old.

God of glory,
by the raising of your Son
you have broken the chains of death and hell:
fill your Church with faith and hope;
for a new day has dawned
and the way to life stands open
in our Saviour Jesus Christ.

COLLECT

Monday 12 April

Psalms 2, **19** *or* **1**, 2, 3
Deuteronomy 1.3-18
John 20.1-10

Deuteronomy 1.3-18

'... how can I bear the heavy burden of your disputes all by myself?'
(v.12)

The Book of Deuteronomy is the fifth book of the Jewish Torah. Chapters 1–30 of the book consist of three sermons or speeches delivered to the Israelites by Moses on the plains of Moab, shortly before they enter the Promised Land. The first sermon recounts the 40 years of wilderness wanderings that had led to that moment, and ends with an exhortation to observe the law and to ponder how it should shape the character, attitudes and conduct of those who do.

It is remarkable that Moses highlights how 'wise, discerning, and reputable' folk are to be chosen by the people to be leaders and judges over disputes. They are to hear without partiality and to be fair to the poor and to the great alike. It is a system of law that seeks to be just to the resident and to the foreigner and to ensure justice is upheld for the very lowest in society.

People of faith today often find compassion easier than justice. However, our tradition is clear. Nothing that is morally wrong can be politically right. Justice is the social response to the commandment to love our neighbour. These are important lessons at a time of increasing inequality and forms of Christianity that seem indifferent to the poor or to justice and prefer to focus on their own wealth and success.

COLLECT

Almighty Father,
you have given your only Son to die for our sins
and to rise again for our justification:
grant us so to put away the leaven of malice and wickedness
that we may always serve you
in pureness of living and truth;
through the merits of your Son Jesus Christ our Lord,
who is alive and reigns with you,
in the unity of the Holy Spirit,
one God, now and for ever.

Reflection by **Mark Oakley**

Psalms **8**, 20, 21 *or* **5**, 6 (8)
Deuteronomy 1.19-40
John 20.11-18

Tuesday 13 April

Deuteronomy 1.19-40

'... journey back into the wilderness' (v.40)

This narrative is a retrospective look at why, after the Exodus, the Israelites did not conquer the Promised Land west of the Jordan from its southern border. We learn that it was the people's disobedience and lack of faith that led to God's frustration and anger. This begins the long journey back into the wilderness and the confirmation that Moses won't himself enter the land but only lead the people to it.

It sounds rather familiar – the community of faith 'grumbling in their tents'. It is very easy for us to get jaundiced and spiritually akin to Eeyore in the Winnie the Pooh stories. The spiritual lesson here, though, is that such moaning and self-affirming complaining about others leads to paralysis. Martin Luther King Jr. never said, 'I have a nightmare'. He preached that he had a dream and the hope of this dream was the motivation towards its fulfilment. The energy and bile we foolishly use up in churchy disputes is not only a travesty but, suggests this story, a spiritual failure with long-term consequences.

The other reminder here is that many of us are asked to help people in their spiritual lives but maybe at the cost to our own. A woman once told me that she wanted to become a priest so she could help others have the relationship with God that she only wished she had herself. Moses saw the others reach the Promised Land, and his work was done.

COLLECT

Risen Christ,
for whom no door is locked, no entrance barred:
open the doors of our hearts,
that we may seek the good of others
and walk the joyful road of sacrifice and peace,
to the praise of God the Father.

Reflection by **Mark Oakley** | 125

Wednesday 14 April

Psalms 16, **30** *or* 119.1-32
Deuteronomy 3.18-end
John 20.19-end

Deuteronomy 3.18-end

'Look well, for you shall not cross over this Jordan' (v.27)

Moses wants to cross over into the land and see it, but he is only to see it from afar as Joshua is the one who is finally to cross over. Moses is to bear the consequences of the people's lack of faith.

This passage shows us Moses praying to God but having his request turned down. It is a reminder that 'no' is as legitimate an answer to prayer as 'yes'. This is one of the sources of doubt, of course, in our day – just what is prayer supposed to achieve and why do so many prayers go unanswered? C. S. Lewis commented that we shall probably spend eternity thanking God for the prayers he didn't answer, so selfish and limited is our perspective. Aside from that, it may be helpful to remember that the ancient Assyrian's word for prayer was the same as they used for the opening up of clenched fists.

Prayer is not an attempt to change God's mind by demand but to be changed by God in an opening of life and gratitude. For some, the purpose of prayer is for the person who prays to become what they pray for – or the answer to it. For others, prayer is more akin to looking out for a kingfisher at a stream. There's a lot of waiting and boredom, but when the flash of colour comes, it exceeds expectations and lights up our landscape. However we view prayer, there is no doubting that it is a relationship that understands both love and loss.

COLLECT

Almighty Father,
you have given your only Son to die for our sins
and to rise again for our justification:
grant us so to put away the leaven of malice and wickedness
that we may serve you
in pureness of living and truth;
through the merits of your Son Jesus Christ our Lord,
who is alive and reigns with you,
in the unity of the Holy Spirit,
one God, now and for ever.

| *Reflection by* **Mark Oakley**

Psalms **28**, 29 *or* 14, **15**, 16
Deuteronomy 4.1-14
John 21.1-14

Thursday 15 April

Deuteronomy 4.1-14
'... take care and watch yourselves closely' (v.9)

I remember words from this passage being on the wall of a Holocaust museum I once visited: 'watch yourselves ... so as neither to forget the things that your eyes have seen nor to let them slip from your mind all the days of your life'. It is at the heart of belief in God that memory is the source of inspiration; even so, while the past is full of rich lessons and epiphanies of God, ultimately we are to be loyal to the future more than to the past.

As we journey on, though, we are to 'watch ourselves'. There is nothing harder. Self-scrutiny is something we love to be distracted from and, because we are so immersed in our particular worldviews, we are often unable to be as objective with ourselves as we like to imagine we are about others.

Rowan Williams has said that you can judge a religion on how well it helps you see more. Does faith open your eyes or close them? How open to new truth does it allow you to be? Sin can be a surprisingly conservative thing as we resist God's transformation of our full stops into commas, or, indeed, God's working for greater justice in the world. Faith demands a keener and more honest attention of us. And, as this ancient and wise scripture teaches, it must begin with ourselves. Hurt people tend to hurt people. We can do a lot of damage by our lack of self-awareness.

Risen Christ,
for whom no door is locked, no entrance barred:
open the doors of our hearts,
that we may seek the good of others
and walk the joyful road of sacrifice and peace,
to the praise of God the Father.

COLLECT

Friday 16 April

Deuteronomy 4.15-31

'... you will seek the Lord your God, and you will find him if you search after him with all your heart and soul' (v.29)

It is very clear that the people of God are being warned against idolatry. We like to think that this involves statues of gods and heroes, and so the warnings don't really affect us, but idolatry is as alive as it ever was. Whatever we treat as a god – whether that is money, success, our own ego, sex or possessions – this is what captures our heart and directs it away from the beauty, truth and goodness of the living God. Such addictions can ruin relationships with others and our own self-worth. We must see what it is we are serving in life.

One way to take a quick spiritual check-up is to look at your next bank statement, as where your money goes will tell you clearly where you place your values. Recognition is the first step to salvation, and the passage today reassures that although idols are destructive – that possessions can possess us – we are able to turn life around and return to God because 'the Lord your God is a merciful God, he will neither abandon you nor destroy you'.

It has been quipped that there is nothing more empty than a person full of themselves. But we also know that life can become empty when we are led to place our ultimate hopes in ephemeral things. Such a life becomes restless, as St Augustine knew, and the restless heart has only one true place to find its harbour.

COLLECT

> Almighty Father,
> you have given your only Son to die for our sins
> and to rise again for our justification:
> grant us so to put away the leaven of malice and wickedness
> that we may always serve you
> in pureness of living and truth;
> through the merits of your Son Jesus Christ our Lord,
> who is alive and reigns with you,
> in the unity of the Holy Spirit,
> one God, now and for ever.

128 | *Reflection by* **Mark Oakley**

Psalms 63, **84** *or* 20, 21, **23**
Deuteronomy 4.32-40
John 21.20-end

Saturday 17 April

Deuteronomy 4.32-40

'Keep his statutes and his commandments ... for your own well-being' (v.40)

Here we find the great acclamation of monotheism: that there is only God and no other. Because God is the source of all there is, it is to his laws of love and justice that the human will should be tuned for its own well-being and integrity. Any image of God that does not rest on this is unhealthy, and the more you worship your own image of God, the more unhealthy you will become. Yahweh and his cleansing freshness is the only God worthy of pursuit.

We find God compared to fire, flames that can warm or scorch, help make or destroy. There is no sense that God is a middle-class conscience or a tepid being under our control. Those who speak in his name, proclaim his laws and call people back to his dislocating truth cannot ever be the bland leading the bland. They are to be the thunder that clears the air, that sweeps the wind and spirit of God into human consciences, behaviours and strategies.

Deuteronomy constantly puts the 'odd' back into God, reminding us of God's majesty and power. God is the creator and sustainer but also the guide and heartland of the people he cherishes. This is a God of fire, with a heat and passion in his love and heart. As John Donne, the great seventeenth-century poet and preacher, says: 'All Divinity is either love or wonder!'

Risen Christ,
for whom no door is locked, no entrance barred:
open the doors of our hearts,
that we may seek the good of others
and walk the joyful road of sacrifice and peace,
to the praise of God the Father.

COLLECT

Monday 19 April

Psalms **96**, 97 *or* 27, **30**
Deuteronomy 5.1-22
Ephesians 1.1-14

Deuteronomy 5.1-22

'... he added no more' (v.22)

Although now less prominently displayed and less frequently memorized than in previous generations, the 'Ten Commandments' remain foundational for Christian morality, and this passage reminds us of the scriptural basis for their unique status. Unlike the other commandments delivered at Sinai, which were revealed to Moses and then transmitted by him to the people, these ten were spoken directly to the whole assembly 'face to face'. Their immediacy is underlined by their being couched in the second person singular form: God speaks each of them to each individual.

No other commandments are placed on the same level as these ten. They have a sufficiency ('he added no more') confirmed by their being engraved on tablets of stone. That act of inscription is also a testimony to their permanence and their gravity.

A once-fashionable method of teaching Religious Education invited children to write their own 'ten commandments for today'. This was an attempt to engage them in thinking about the issues that were immediate, lasting and serious in their lives, but it is hard to think of any approach more removed from the biblical understanding of the status of the Ten Commandments. When a man engaged Jesus in a conversation about goodness, the first thing the Lord did was to remind him of these commandments (Mark 10.19). Whatever else God asks of me in my life, he requires that I attend to these. As the Book of Common Prayer says: 'Lord, have mercy upon us, and write all these thy laws in our hearts, we beseech thee'.

COLLECT

Almighty Father,
who in your great mercy gladdened the disciples
    with the sight of the risen Lord:
give us such knowledge of his presence with us,
that we may be strengthened and sustained by his risen life
and serve you continually in righteousness and truth;
through Jesus Christ your Son our Lord,
who is alive and reigns with you,
in the unity of the Holy Spirit,
one God, now and for ever.

| *Reflection by* **Michael Ipgrave**

Psalms **98**, 99, 100 *or* 32, **36**
Deuteronomy 5.22-end
Ephesians 1.15-end

Tuesday 20 April

Deuteronomy 5.22-end

'Today we have seen that God may speak to someone and the person may still live' (v.24)

The majesty of God in the Hebrew Scriptures is often depicted, as here, in terms of fire. It is repeatedly acknowledged that nobody may see God and live. But here the question is not one of seeing, but of hearing: the people recognize with amazement that despite hearing the voice of God out of the fire, they are still alive. However, they are filled with anxiety at the prospect of this experience continuing, and they beg Moses to stand in their place as mediator and interpreter of any further divine message.

The theme is reprised and transformed in the Letter to the Hebrews, whose (Christian) readers are reminded that they have come to another mountain, the city of the living God where Jesus speaks in the midst of a festive gathering (Hebrews 12.18-24). Not only do we hear the word of the living God spoken through the words of Jesus, but in his life we also see the face of the living God. There is a real sense of a new dispensation offered to us here.

Nevertheless, the contrast between old and new is not absolute. On the one hand, the people of Israel do hear the words of God and live, and the law becomes to them a source of blessing. On the other hand, the writer to the Hebrews reminds us not to lose our sense of awe in the presence of the holy one, 'for indeed our God is a consuming fire' (Hebrews 12.29).

Risen Christ,
you filled your disciples with boldness and fresh hope:
strengthen us to proclaim your risen life
and fill us with your peace,
to the glory of God the Father.

COLLECT

Reflection by **Michael Ipgrave** | 131

Wednesday 21 April

Psalm **105** *or* **34**
Deuteronomy 6
Ephesians 2.1-10

Deuteronomy 6

'... write them on the doorposts of your house' (v.9)

If you walk through the old quarters of some European cities, you will sometimes come across a house with a small depression hollowed out towards the top of the doorpost. That is a sign that Jewish people once lived in that house. It marks the place where once there was fixed a *mezuzah*, a small receptacle containing these verses from Deuteronomy that proclaim the unity of God and the command to love him. The Jewish family may have been obliterated, probably in the mass murder of the Holocaust, but there still remains this sign that this was once a place that housed the people of the God of Israel. Contemporary Jewish families continue to follow Deuteronomy's instructions. In a wonderfully compact poem called *Mezuzah*, the American poet Richard Chess calls this 'love nailed to the doorpost': a reminder of the place of God's law in the everyday business of the comings and goings of a family's life.

That reminder is always intensely personal and it is always in the present tense. To fulfil the requirement of Jewish law, the parchment must be handwritten; no artificially printed copy can adequately express the individual commitment of the practising Jew. And the text must be written afresh every few years; faith in God and love for God cannot be taken for granted, but are always in need of renewal.

The *mezuzah* speaks of an everyday witness to the living God of Israel among his people. The space where a *mezuzah* was once placed is itself a silent witness to that same God. Even the horrors of the Holocaust cannot obliterate that witness.

COLLECT

Almighty Father,
who in your great mercy gladdened the disciples
    with the sight of the risen Lord:
give us such knowledge of his presence with us,
that we may be strengthened and sustained by his risen life
and serve you continually in righteousness and truth;
through Jesus Christ your Son our Lord,
who is alive and reigns with you,
in the unity of the Holy Spirit,
one God, now and for ever.

132 | *Reflection by* **Michael Ipgrave**

Psalm **136** *or* **37***
Deuteronomy 7.1-11
Ephesians 2.11-end

Thursday 22 April

Deuteronomy 7.1-11

'... the Hittites, the Girgashites, the Amorites, the Canaanites,
the Perizzites, the Hivites, and the Jebusites' (v.1)

The beginning of this chapter insists in the strongest language that
Israel should utterly destroy the seven nations of Canaan, showing
them no mercy. It is difficult to read these verses without feeling
disquiet, even repulsion. They have been avidly seized upon by
Richard Dawkins (*The God Delusion*) as evidence that the Bible
promotes an ideology of genocide, while some Christians point to
them as evidence of the supposedly bloodthirsty mentality of the Old
Testament compared to the pacific attitude of the New.

There is a long tradition of Jewish commentary on this and similarly
strident passages, and the rabbis have always been well aware of the
problems they raise. One influential reading emphasizes that the
groups of people referred to can no longer be identified, or even
that they no longer exist. That being the case, the 'Law of the Seven
Nations' has in effect become a dead letter, since there is nobody to
whom it can be applied. Even within the Book of Deuteronomy itself,
there will later be given rules of 'normal warfare' (20.1-20), which
are very different from the total extermination urged here. Certainly,
today's verses cannot be read as a policy instruction for the bitterly
contested world of the contemporary Middle East.

Lord, when I come to read the Scriptures, especially those parts that
seem to me alien or unacceptable, give me grace to remember that
I am not their first interpreter, and give me humility to learn from the
wisdom of the ages.

Risen Christ,
you filled your disciples with boldness and fresh hope:
strengthen us to proclaim your risen life
and fill us with your peace,
to the glory of God the Father.

COLLECT

Reflection by **Michael Ipgrave** | 133

Friday 23 April

George, martyr,
patron of England

Psalms 5, 146
Joshua 1.1-9
Ephesians 6.10-20

Joshua 1.1-9

'Be strong and courageous' (v.6)

These words 'Be strong and courageous', occurring three times in this short passage, seem obviously suitable for the feast day of George, the soldier martyr – and rather uncomfortable in the context of the campaign of invasion and dispossession that is about to unfold in Joshua. But they are also closely linked to the Book of the Law: spoken by Moses in Deuteronomy 31.6, when he completes his delivery of Torah, they are now repeated to his chosen successor as the Lord urges the people to remain faithful to that instruction.

'Courage', in Hebrew *chazak*, is of course needed by troops on a military campaign, as here. *'Chazak!'* is also the acclamation shouted in synagogues when the reading of a passage (among Sephardi Jews) or of a book (the Ashkenazi tradition) of the Torah is completed. So en-couragement is given, not so much for external prowess as for the spiritual challenge of learning more and more of God's law.

In his commentary on this passage, John Calvin asked why in verse 8 the command was not that 'this book of the law should not depart *from your eyes*' rather than '*out of your mouth*' as the text actually has. The answer is, that it is constant recitation of the law that makes it part of the people's life, and so gives them courage to go further in its study and application. Joshua was widely seen by the medieval Crusaders as an inspiring role model, but this passage points to a different medieval tradition, that of monastic 'rumination', constant meditation on scripture.

COLLECT

God of hosts,
who so kindled the flame of love
in the heart of your servant George
that he bore witness to the risen Lord
by his life and by his death:
give us the same faith and power of love
that we who rejoice in his triumphs
may come to share with him the fullness of the resurrection;
through Jesus Christ your Son our Lord,
who is alive and reigns with you,
in the unity of the Holy Spirit,
one God, now and for ever.

| *Reflection by* **Michael Ipgrave**

Psalms 108, **110**, 111 *or* 41, **42**, 43
Deuteronomy 8
Ephesians 3.14-end

Saturday 24 April

Deuteronomy 8

'... manna that your ancestors did not know' (v.16)

At two points in this chapter, Moses points out to the Israelites that the provision of manna in the wilderness is an entirely novel experience. As he leads his people on this extraordinary journey through unfamiliar territory into an unseen land, God feeds them with a new kind of food. At other points in the narrative (e.g. Numbers 11), we read that they grow tired of this diet, and long for the familiar remembered provisions of the Egyptian fleshpots. But Israel are called to be a new kind of people, and a new people feeds on new bread.

The strange newness of the manna is underlined in Exodus 16.15 by the interpretation given to its name: *'Ma na?,* What is this?' However, it is not just the ingredients of the manna that are mysterious to the people, but also its provenance. In the Psalms it is described as 'the bread of angels' (Psalm 78.25), the eating of which places the people of Israel in some way in the company of the heaven from which it has been rained down upon them.

Christians from earliest days have seen in the manna a prefiguration of the eucharistic bread, the heavenly provision that Jesus gives to sustain them on their journey through the wilderness of this world. And it is newness of life for which this food prepares us: in the words of St Thomas Aquinas' hymn, *panis angelicus fit panis hominum* – 'bread of angels become bread for humans', given that we may become signs of a new life.

Almighty Father,
who in your great mercy gladdened the disciples
with the sight of the risen Lord:
give us such knowledge of his presence with us,
that we may be strengthened and sustained by his risen life
and serve you continually in righteousness and truth;
through Jesus Christ your Son our Lord,
who is alive and reigns with you,
in the unity of the Holy Spirit,
one God, now and for ever.

COLLECT

Monday 26 April

Mark the Evangelist

Psalms 37.23-end, 148
Isaiah 62.6-10
or Ecclesiasticus 51.13-end
Acts 12.25 – 13.13

Acts 12.25 – 13.13

'John, however, left them' (13.13)

Mark is an elusive figure, both in his identity and in his reported actions. In the New Testament, he has two names, one Hebrew (John) and one Latin (Mark), and both are among the commonest in their respective languages, so the possibilities of confusion of identity are many. Nevertheless, tradition has identified this John Mark with the evangelist of the second gospel, and that identification lies behind the choice of today's reading.

Mark's actions also are elusive. Taken by Paul and Barnabas to Perga in Pamphylia, there he 'left them'. The words are terse, and give no reason for the young man's decision to return to his home city of Jerusalem, but later this episode becomes the cause of a quarrel between Paul and Barnabas. Acts 15.38, expressing Paul's low estimation of Mark, describes his departure as a 'desertion'. The contention between the two apostles over Mark becomes so sharp that they part company.

There are hints in Paul's letters that he may later have become reconciled to Mark. Nevertheless, it is hard not to see him as a slippery character; indeed, he has traditionally been identified with the young man who slips away naked at Jesus' arrest, leaving his linen cloth behind him (Mark 14.52). Perhaps it was an enigmatic, mercurial personality that equipped him so well to be the author of the strangest of all the Gospels. Mark's witness is that of one who does not take centre stage but lives among the footnotes; and that can serve as a vehicle for inspiration and truth.

COLLECT

Almighty God,
who enlightened your holy Church
through the inspired witness of your evangelist Saint Mark:
grant that we, being firmly grounded in the truth of the gospel,
may be faithful to its teaching both in word and deed;
through Jesus Christ your Son our Lord,
who is alive and reigns with you,
in the unity of the Holy Spirit,
one God, now and for ever.

| *Reflection by* **Michael Ipgrave**

Psalm **139** *or* **48**, 52
Deuteronomy 9.23 – 10.5
Ephesians 4.17-end

Tuesday 27 April

Deuteronomy 9.23 – 10.5
'I lay prostrate before the Lord' (9.25)

Deuteronomy 9 includes a dramatic account of Moses' prayer before the Lord on behalf of Israel: for 40 days, in fasting and prostration, he seeks to turn away God's destructive anger. Biblical figures take different attitudes when God threatens judgement. Noah accepts the divine sentence of the Flood without question; Abraham bargains with God over Sodom and Gomorrah up to a point, but then gives way; only Moses argues all the way until he has secured a change in God's purpose. For this reason, he is seen as the model of intercessory prayer in Israel.

But is there a problem here? How can one man, even Moses, stand between human beings and their God? The answer is found earlier in Chapter 9, when God asks Moses to separate himself from sinful Israel. Moses does not do that, insisting instead on his solidarity with his people. So, when he intercedes for Israel, it is as part of them and not merely for others that he prays. As he lies prostrate before the Lord, he carries the people with him, and this gives his prayer authenticity and effect.

In my daily prayers, I use cycles and lists of names for whom I am to pray on particular days, and that degree of organization is needed for all of us in busy lives. But our prayers will mean nothing if we do not know a sense of connection with those for whom we are praying: to intercede is to be in God's presence with another on my heart.

Almighty God,
whose Son Jesus Christ is the resurrection and the life:
raise us, who trust in him,
from the death of sin to the life of righteousness,
that we may seek those things which are above,
where he reigns with you
in the unity of the Holy Spirit,
one God, now and for ever.

COLLECT

Wednesday 28 April

Psalm **135** *or* **119.57-80**
Deuteronomy 10.12-end
Ephesians 5.1-14

Deuteronomy 10.12-end

'... you were strangers' (v.19)

Most of the exhortation in these verses understandably urges the people of God to follow the commandments for the reason that they are authored by the God who has chosen them and loves them. In verse 19, though, a different motivation suddenly appears: Israel is reminded to show kindness to strangers because 'you were strangers in the land of Egypt'. This phrase echoing through the Hebrew Bible, defines the formative experience of the holy people as one of alienation, marginalization and displacement. Later, these themes will be reinforced and deepened by the long years of exile that have so shaped Jewish spirituality and identity.

Our world today is full of refugees, asylum seekers and displaced people; beyond that, there are even more seeking to build their lives, raise their families and establish their communities in lands that are in some sense alien to them. One of the great blessings experienced by Christians in this country today is that in many places those whom our society sees as 'strangers' are part of the worshipping and praying body of our churches. In some places our churches would have disappeared without their presence, and in many they have been revitalized by their participation.

So we can retrieve in our own times the biblical identity of the people of God as 'strangers' in this world. After centuries of taking for granted the Church's place in society, that should renew our sense of mission. But it always comes with a political edge, for there are forces in our society determined to show no kindness to strangers.

COLLECT

Almighty God,
whose Son Jesus Christ is the resurrection and the life:
raise us, who trust in him,
from the death of sin to the life of righteousness,
that we may seek those things which are above,
where he reigns with you
in the unity of the Holy Spirit,
one God, now and for ever.

| *Reflection by* **Michael Ipgrave**

Psalm **118** *or* 56, **57** (63*)
Deuteronomy 11.8-end
Ephesians 5.15-end

Thursday 29 April

Deuteronomy 11.8-end
'... not like the land of Egypt' (v.10)

The *Mappa Mundi* in Hereford Cathedral Library is an object of great beauty and endless fascination, but as a 'map of the world', it is of very little practical use for travelling from A to B. Its purpose rather is to express an overview of the inhabited world. It does that by placing the Holy Land absolutely and unavoidably at the centre of the picture. For the medieval Christians who drew it, the *Mappa Mundi* marked out the incomparable significance of this land in the eyes of their faith.

A much earlier version of such a 'geo-theology' is found in these verses, where Moses describes to the people of Israel the uniqueness of the land they are about to possess. Unlike the Land of Egypt, where hard human effort is needed for irrigation, the landscape and climate of the Promised Land will assure its inhabitants of abundant produce. Yet this is not an automatic consequence of topography and meteorology; it is a sign of the special care that God exercises over this territory, and the tenderness with which he prepares it for his people, provided they keep close to him.

Love for the Land of Israel and longing for it have been abiding themes of Jewish history through centuries of exile. In the twelfth century, the poet Judah Halevi, far away in Spain, wrote: 'My heart is in the East, and I am at the end of the West'. Whatever view I take of the Holy Land as a Christian, I need to recognize its importance for Jewish people.

COLLECT

Risen Christ,
faithful shepherd of your Father's sheep:
teach us to hear your voice
and to follow your command,
that all your people may be gathered into one flock,
to the glory of God the Father.

Reflection by **Michael Ipgrave**   139

Friday 30 April

Psalm **33** *or* **51**, 54
Deuteronomy 12.1-14
Ephesians 6.1-9

Deuteronomy 12.1-14

'... the place that the Lord will choose' (v.14)

This passage begins with a fierce polemic against pagan shrines, but its main point becomes clear in verses 13-14. This is not a matter of Israel's God against others' gods, but of the proper place to worship the God of Israel. Deuteronomy insists that this cannot be a decision for the Israelites but for God. He will himself choose a place 'to put his name there'. Of course, we know this place will be Jerusalem, but the precise location is not spelled out here, as this passage is set in the wilderness before the Israelites enter the Land.

Centralization may seem an unattractive prospect to us. Would it not be better to have locally available worship? And what is so special about one place rather than another for the God of all? But the underlying logic is to underline that this is God's choice. To 'put his name there' implies a real presence of God in the sanctuary of his election, a presence that cannot be indifferently replicated elsewhere.

If presence in this way implies uniqueness, for Christians the unrepeatability is not of place but of person. No one location is specified for the worship of the New Covenant, but Deuteronomy's logic reappears in the insistence that God chooses to dwell in Jesus Christ in a way not found in any others. That personal presence in turn enables worship in a multiplicity of places, as St Francis prayed: 'We adore you, Lord Jesus Christ, here and in all your churches throughout the world'.

COLLECT

Almighty God,
whose Son Jesus Christ is the resurrection and the life:
raise us, who trust in him,
from the death of sin to the life of righteousness,
that we may seek those things which are above,
where he reigns with you
in the unity of the Holy Spirit,
one God, now and for ever.

| *Reflection by* **Michael Ipgrave**

Psalms 139, 146
Proverbs 4.10-18
James 1.1-12

Saturday 1 May
Philip and James, Apostles

Proverbs 4.10-18
'... she is your life' (v.13)

Philip is the apostle who pleads with Jesus at the Last Supper: 'Lord, show us the Father, and we will be satisfied' (John 14.8). He does so in response to Jesus' resonant declaration to Thomas: 'I am the way, and the truth, and the life' (John 14.6).

The themes of way, truth and life are all present in this passage from Proverbs. Verses 10-13 positively commend a specific way of behaviour, which is then contrasted in verses 14-18 with an opposing path, 'the way of evildoers'. The guidance conveyed is described as 'instruction', a body of true wisdom with a specific content that is capable of being taught and learned. And the result of holding on to such instruction is long life – that is how we should interpret verse 13b, which forms the climax of the positive part of this passage.

This book of the Bible, here and in other places, frequently presents these themes as proverbial wisdom conveyed by a father to his son through verbal media: sayings, maxims, analogies, riddles and so forth. In Jesus, Christians believe that the way, the truth and the life are spoken into the world by the Father through the body language of a life lived in the fullness of wisdom. In seeing him, we learn with Philip that we do indeed see the image of the invisible God; in holding on to his truth and walking in his way, we can be assured that we will come through him to the life the Father promises for us. Such is true wisdom.

COLLECT

Almighty Father,
whom truly to know is eternal life:
teach us to know your Son Jesus Christ
as the way, the truth, and the life;
that we may follow the steps of your holy apostles
Philip and James,
and walk steadfastly in the way that leads to your glory;
through Jesus Christ your Son our Lord,
who is alive and reigns with you,
in the unity of the Holy Spirit,
one God, now and for ever.

Reflection by **Michael Ipgrave** | 141

Monday 3 May

Psalm **145** *or* **71**
Deuteronomy 16.1-20
I Peter 1.1-12

Deuteronomy 16.1-20

'... all the days of your life' (v.3)

'Remember' is a word that runs through Deuteronomy, weaving together its different parts and marking its place in the canon of Scripture as a whole. What Moses urges the people to remember is not what is taking place as he speaks to them; instead, we must turn to the preceding books for that history. It is not even primarily what they have experienced in their own lives, for the generation of the exodus has now almost entirely passed away. Yet they are to remember it as happening to them, as their story, their history: 'so that all the days of your life you may remember the day of your departure from the land of Egypt'. Each member of God's people, for all time, is to remember that day as their day, and to remember it every day as the precious truth of their existence.

The Easter season is the most ancient season of the Christian year, but it has not retained the hold on popular imagination of Lent, Advent or Christmas. Why might that be? From early centuries, Christians chose to fill the time between what they continued to call Passover (with 'Easter' serving as our indirect English translation) and the festival of weeks (i.e. Pentecost) with daily celebration of Christ's passing over from death to life, from cross to resurrection. All our days, we are to remember this as the day of our departure, our release, our birth – and rejoice.

COLLECT

Almighty God,
who through your only-begotten Son Jesus Christ
have overcome death and opened to us the gate of everlasting life:
grant that, as by your grace going before us
    you put into our minds good desires,
so by your continual help
we may bring them to good effect;
through Jesus Christ our risen Lord,
who is alive and reigns with you,
in the unity of the Holy Spirit,
one God, now and for ever.

| *Reflection by* **Jeremy Worthen**

Psalms **19**, 147.1-12 *or* **73**
Deuteronomy 17.8-end
1 Peter 1.13-end

Tuesday 4 May

Deuteronomy 17.8-end

'... and he shall read in it' (v.19)

In this passage, we find a remarkable set of constraints upon the institution of kingship – remarkable given the reality of that institution in the ancient Near East generally, and how it is often reflected elsewhere in the Old Testament. Those constraints are rooted in the view that kingship is acceptable and can serve as a means of God's care and providence, but that it is not necessary, originating in the people's decision. The identity of Israel determines the character of its royal rule: called to be holy, this people cannot be ruled by someone forever thirsting for more power, more pleasure, more wealth. Their king must instead be a person who longs for his life and that of his people to conform to God's precious teaching, and therefore is committed to studying it day by day.

Our society is not immune to the idea that responsibility should be rewarded: greater responsibility in many institutional contexts means more pay, more power over others, more freedom about one's daily actions. Nor are churches wholly unaffected by this notion. The temptation remains to use positions of responsibility – great or small – to accumulate such rewards for our own satisfaction, pushing out the purpose of the responsibility given to us, which concerns the good of others. We too need daily disciplines that will keep us on the right path, 'neither exalting' ourselves 'above other members of the community nor turning aside from the commandment'.

Risen Christ,
your wounds declare your love for the world
and the wonder of your risen life:
give us compassion and courage
to risk ourselves for those we serve,
to the glory of God the Father.

COLLECT

Wednesday 5 May

Psalms **30**, 147.13-end *or* **77**
Deuteronomy 18.9-end
1 Peter 2.1-10

Deuteronomy 18.9-end

'You must remain completely loyal' (v.13)

We believe that all that we need to know for our salvation has been revealed in the word that is God's gift. Still, we cannot refrain from inquiring: what should I do in this new situation I am facing – and what is it God would have me do? And we cannot help wondering: where is this situation heading – and could God guide me by showing me what would follow from different choices? We are ready to listen to voices that might help us answer such pressing questions.

Moses does not tell the people that this is always wrong. Yet he also wants them to realize the danger. There are many voices to which they might 'give heed' – some of them pointing to paths that lead away from God, even if at first glance they look like faithfulness. Some voices will say: the word that is God's gift is not enough for you, so let me supply some additional sources of information. Others may claim to be only speaking in God's name, and perhaps believe they are, when they are not.

The word translated 'completely loyal' has as its root meaning whole, complete, full. To remain wholly united to the God who has spoken to us, we need to heed continually the voice of the one in whom the Word, made flesh, never ceases to resound: 'This is my Son, the Beloved; listen to him!' (Mark 9.7).

COLLECT

Almighty God,
who through your only-begotten Son Jesus Christ
have overcome death and opened to us the gate of everlasting life:
grant that, as by your grace going before us
    you put into our minds good desires,
so by your continual help
we may bring them to good effect;
through Jesus Christ our risen Lord,
who is alive and reigns with you,
in the unity of the Holy Spirit,
one God, now and for ever.

Reflection by **Jeremy Worthen**

Deuteronomy 19

'... although a death sentence was not deserved' (v.6)

One reason for the popularity of crime fiction, in literary and visual form, is its capacity for holding together the reality of evil and the affirmation of goodness through the workings of what is sometimes termed temporal justice.

Temporal justice is a recurring concern in this section of Deuteronomy. The promised land is no utopia; God knows that the commandments will be broken, and sinful acts will be committed. Critical to its teaching about 'loving the Lord your God and walking always in his ways' is what happens next. Justice must be vindicated: a response is required that recognizes the wrong that has been done and upholds instead what is right.

It is easy, however, for things to become twisted at this point. One person has killed another – but that does not mean there has been an offence deserving death. If it was an accident, then the execution of the killer would itself become a serious crime. There must be a space, literal and metaphorical, that allows for investigation of motive. A witness comes forward – but witnesses can lie. There must be room for different testimonies to be weighed before a verdict can be reached.

The affirmation of goodness through temporal justice requires patience, wisdom and skill. When punitive action is demanded simply to appease visceral anger, or when judgements of truthfulness are based on perceived allegiance and affinity, it is evil that wins out.

Risen Christ,
your wounds declare your love for the world
and the wonder of your risen life:
give us compassion and courage
to risk ourselves for those we serve,
to the glory of God the Father.

COLLECT

Reflection by **Jeremy Worthen**

Friday 7 May

Psalms **138**, 149 *or* **55**
Deuteronomy 21.22 – 22.8
1 Peter 3.1-12

Deuteronomy 21.22 – 22.8

'You may not withhold your help' (22.3)

What are the limits of our responsibility? In past centuries, knowledge of the lives of others may not have extended much further than the edge of one's own village. Today, we constantly hear of the plight of those thousands of miles away, and an illness that respects no borders makes us realize how closely connected the lives of all human beings on this planet are.

Commandments about how to deal with stray farm animals may look somewhat quaint in this context. Two features of the short section at 22.1–4 are worth reflecting on, however – both at risk of getting lost in translation. The first is that the word rendered 'neighbour' and 'owner' in the NRSV is the Hebrew word for 'brother'. Its repetition emphasizes that relationships are marked by fundamental kinship and mutual belonging. A parallel passage in Exodus 23.4–5 speaks of 'your enemy's ox or donkey'. Even our enemy remains someone with whom we belong before God.

The second feature is that the verb translated 'ignore' and 'withhold help' in the NRSV means literally 'hide yourself'. The point is that you cannot pretend you were not there, or you did not know, any more than you can imagine that the other person, your 'neighbour', is nothing to do with you. This passage does not provide us with neat answers to hard questions about the limits of our responsibility, but it does say we cannot close them down by turning away from our sisters and brothers.

COLLECT

Almighty God,
who through your only-begotten Son Jesus Christ
have overcome death and opened to us the gate of everlasting life:
grant that, as by your grace going before us
    you put into our minds good desires,
so by your continual help
we may bring them to good effect;
through Jesus Christ our risen Lord,
who is alive and reigns with you,
in the unity of the Holy Spirit,
one God, now and for ever.

Reflection by **Jeremy Worthen**

Deuteronomy 24.5-end

'Remember that you were a slave in Egypt' (v.18)

It's an ancient truth, easily forgotten when life is untroubled, that material security can never be taken for granted. What is our response to that consciousness of fragility? Is it to hold onto whatever we can as tightly as we can? Can we imagine what it might be like to live continually at the limits of minimal resources?

The divine teaching that Moses communicates to the Israelites makes a distinction between 'other Israelites' (as the NRSV translates 'your brothers' here) and 'aliens'. They have obligations to both, however, and indeed the commandments concerning people for whom life is especially precarious group the alien with the orphan and the widow. Those who are not Israelites are singled out as among those to be treated with particular care and compassion, 'so that the Lord your God may bless you in all your undertakings'.

Twice in this short passage, Moses reminds the people that they were once slaves in Egypt. Part of the point is what one might call empathy: draw on your own experience of living at the mercy of others in relating to those who need your mercy today.

Alongside that is the truth that you are only here because 'God redeemed you from there': you have no right to the blessings you are about to enjoy. You must not, therefore, let a deceitful sense of luck or entitlement cloud the way you treat those who are most vulnerable.

Risen Christ,
your wounds declare your love for the world
and the wonder of your risen life:
give us compassion and courage
to risk ourselves for those we serve,
to the glory of God the Father.

COLLECT

Monday 10 May

Deuteronomy 26

'... to be his treasured people' (v.18)

The agreement that God seeks with us is so deep that we will never fathom it, yet also perfectly simple: God desires 'to be your God', and us 'to be his treasured people'. The same phrase, literally 'the people of his treasured possession', occurs at Exodus 19.5, while the noun for 'treasured possession' appears on its own in Psalm 135.4 and Malachi 3.17 to describe God's relationship to Israel.

What would you say is your most treasured possession? Such an object is treated with great care: we want it to be preserved, and we want to be able to show it to and share it with others on suitable occasions. That care may mean we have particular habits and even strict disciplines about how it should be handled.

Deuteronomy rehearses again the teaching of God for Israel that was given at Sinai. We may find ourselves feeling bewildered at times by so many statutes, commandments and ordinances. But here is the heart of it: God wants us to be a treasured possession, and therefore to be the recipient of divine care, not just for our preservation but for our 'praise and honour' (v.19). And that means particular habits and even strict disciplines: it means polishing, refining, engraving, that extends to every part of our lives and into the depths of our being, so that God may ever delight in us and we in our God.

COLLECT

God our redeemer,
you have delivered us from the power of darkness
and brought us into the kingdom of your Son:
grant, that as by his death he has recalled us to life,
so by his continual presence in us he may raise us
   to eternal joy;
through Jesus Christ your Son our Lord,
who is alive and reigns with you,
in the unity of the Holy Spirit,
one God, now and for ever.

| *Reflection by* **Jeremy Worthen**

Psalms 124, 125, **126**, 127 *or* 87, **89.1-18**
Deuteronomy 28.1-14
1 Peter 4.12-end

Tuesday 11 May

Deuteronomy 28.1-14

'... the Lord swore to your ancestors to give you' (v.11)

From earliest times, beginning with the New Testament, Christians have understood Christ's death and resurrection in the light of Israel's deliverance from Egypt, as the mystery of God's Passover. They have also drawn repeatedly on Israel's journey through the wilderness in reflecting on the Church's pilgrimage towards the heavenly city. But what of the divine gift of life in the land, that continual refrain we have heard throughout Deuteronomy and find again in this passage, now amplified into a lyrical description of every blessing a farming community might long for? What does that have to do with Christian discipleship?

The journey has an end. In Christ, we are set free from sin and death, so that we might live in God's presence. We walk the pilgrim way, by faith and not by sight, so that we might come to 'the Jerusalem above' (Galatians 4.26). We wait for the end, and yet we are also already touching it, and touched by it, for God in Christ, the anointed one, 'has anointed us, by putting his seal on us and giving us his Spirit in our hearts as a first instalment' (2 Corinthians 1.21-22), whose fruits we now enjoy.

God swore to 'your ancestors' to give this dwelling place to 'you' – and, as often elsewhere in Deuteronomy, it is the singular pronoun here. Each of us, in every generation, needs to know that the promise, like the command, is for me.

Risen Christ,
by the lakeside you renewed your call to your disciples:
help your Church to obey your command
and draw the nations to the fire of your love,
to the glory of God the Father.

COLLECT

Wednesday 12 May

Psalms **132**, 133 *or* **119.105-128**
Deuteronomy 28.58-end
1 Peter 5

Deuteronomy 28.58-end

'The Lord will bring you back in ships to Egypt' (v.68)

Those who devised the Lectionary perhaps thought they were showing kindness in allocating only a short extract from Moses' final warnings for disobedience, which begin at verse 15, and also in omitting the earlier curses in chapter 27 that precede the blessings of obedience we read yesterday. We do not like to dwell too much on suffering.

This final, climactic passage is shocking enough, however. It describes the reversals that must follow as the covenant unravels, if Israel turns away from God. The evils from which Israel was once delivered will return, in still more destructive form. The covenant begins when Abraham 'believed the Lord' (Genesis 15.6); if Israel ceases to place her trust in God, then even 'assurance of your own life' will fade away – 'believed' and 'assurance' being translations of different forms of the same Hebrew word. No alternative security is now possible. Even returning in desperation to the point of departure is futile: Israel can never again find a home in Egypt.

Because the Son of God is faithful, the divine covenant with humanity cannot be dissolved: we trust in him and his righteousness, knowing we can have no confidence in our own. Yet our freedom remains, and therefore so does the space for giving up and turning back. 'If we endure, we will also reign with him; if we deny him, he will also deny us; if we are faithless, he remains faithful – for he cannot deny himself' (2 Timothy 2.12-13).

COLLECT

God our redeemer,
you have delivered us from the power of darkness
and brought us into the kingdom of your Son:
grant, that as by his death he has recalled us to life,
so by his continual presence in us he may raise us
    to eternal joy;
through Jesus Christ your Son our Lord,
who is alive and reigns with you,
in the unity of the Holy Spirit,
one God, now and for ever.

| *Reflection by* **Jeremy Worthen**

Thursday 13 May
Ascension Day

Hebrews 7.[11-25] 26-end
'... this he did once for all' (v.27)

The Church's marking of Ascension Day forty days after Easter follows the chronology we find at the beginning of Acts. Yet it is also clear from the New Testament that the resurrection of Christ cannot be constrained by the habitual parameters of space and time in a creation 'subjected to futility' (Romans 8.20). The relationship between the risen Lord and the witnesses to the resurrection may have changed at this point, but 'Jesus Christ is the same yesterday and today and forever' (Hebrews 13.8).

The exaltation of Jesus to sit at God's right hand is a theme running through this letter (e.g. Hebrews 1.3; 8.1; 12.2), invoked in the passage for today by the phrase 'exalted above the heavens'. Yet it is not as though it marks a point where Jesus begins to do something he has never done before. It is rather about divine recognition that what he did once in dying for our sins on the cross stands for all time and into eternity; that the Son of God, who emptied himself and humbled himself, 'has been made perfect for ever'.

His priestly ministry, therefore, of self-offering and interceding for us, stands eternally. That is what we celebrate in the Ascension: not that the crucifixion can be treated as a temporary setback, a prelude to the hero's final triumph, but that who Jesus is for us on the cross, he is forever.

Grant, we pray, almighty God,
that as we believe your only-begotten Son
our Lord Jesus Christ
to have ascended into the heavens,
so we in heart and mind may also ascend
and with him continually dwell;
who is alive and reigns with you,
in the unity of the Holy Spirit,
one God, now and for ever.

COLLECT

Reflection by **Jeremy Worthen**   151

Friday 14 May

Matthias the Apostle

Psalms 16, 147.1-12
I Samuel 2.27-35
Acts 2.37-end

Acts 2.37-end

'... the apostles' teaching and fellowship' (v.42)

Acts 2.42 has been used on numerous occasions as an abiding outline of the life of the Church: 'They devoted themselves to the apostles' teaching and fellowship, to the breaking of bread and the prayers.' There is, however, a question as to whether it is both the teaching and the fellowship in this sentence that are linked to the apostles, or just the teaching.

Whatever the merits of different translations, it remains the case that receiving the teaching of the apostles and being in fellowship or communion (the same word in Greek) with the apostles cannot be separated. For the teaching with which they were entrusted is the gospel of Christ, and it is in accepting that gospel that we know communion with all those who are in union with him, beginning with the apostles he chose.

Did Jesus also choose Matthias? One might infer this from the use of the drawing of lots in Acts 1.26. When the disciples gathered after witnessing Christ's ascension, they did not conclude the calling of twelve apostles was a temporary phase that might now be set aside for the sake of a more flexible Church structure. It was a gift that had become a given, despite the realities of sin and tragedy that mark all human history and the undertakings that unfold within it. The Church has a texture that is woven for us, and we stitch our new threads within it.

COLLECT

Almighty God,
who in the place of the traitor Judas
chose your faithful servant Matthias
to be of the number of the Twelve:
preserve your Church from false apostles
and, by the ministry of faithful pastors and teachers,
keep us steadfast in your truth;
through Jesus Christ your Son our Lord,
who is alive and reigns with you,
in the unity of the Holy Spirit,
one God, now and for ever.

Reflection by **Jeremy Worthen**

Psalms 21, **47** *or* 96, **97**, 100
Numbers 11.16-17, 24-29
1 Corinthians 2

Saturday 15 May

1 Corinthians 2

'... so that we may understand the gifts bestowed on us' (v.12)

A Christian community is a meeting of disciples. If it is accepted that not all are at the same point in the journey, then presumably some are further ahead than others. If some understand more, then it would make sense that more weight should be given to their views.

Where should we look for the authority of knowledge in the Church? Is it with those appointed to offices of teaching? Is it with those who speak from a great weight of scholarship? Or should we seek out those whose spirituality enables them to 'discern all things' directly?

It is easy to lose our way in the face of such competing claims. This chapter offers us three points of orientation. First, what we want to understand is 'the gifts bestowed on us by God' – not abstract speculation, and not beginning from what is ours by nature and right. Second, it is only by God's Spirit that we can understand the gifts God has bestowed: understanding the gift is itself a gift, and God the giver must be our common teacher. Third, the gifts bestowed are ours in Christ, and therefore to enter this mystery we must know above all else 'Jesus Christ, and him crucified'. Summing all this up at the end of the chapter, Paul reminds us that the source of true understanding is 'the mind of Christ'.

COLLECT

Grant, we pray, almighty God,
that as we believe your only-begotten Son
our Lord Jesus Christ
to have ascended into the heavens,
so we in heart and mind may also ascend
and with him continually dwell;
who is alive and reigns with you,
in the unity of the Holy Spirit,
one God, now and for ever.

Reflection by **Jeremy Worthen**   153

Monday 17 May

1 Corinthians 3

'For all things are yours ...' (v.21)

Do you know how rich you are?

As fallen creatures, part of us is always pulling back towards the poverty of trying to live without God. Paul gives us a very different example, an example of faithful living, one that fully embraces the meaning of Christ's life, death and resurrection for the world. Paul strives passionately for clarity and understanding; he sees a world dawning in the light of Christ and longs to draw us into this fullness of seeing and living.

In today's reading, Paul once again ministers to our littleness and frailty. He heaves us up from the ground where we are tempted to squander our time and talent messing about in the dust, and stands us up squarely on our feet in Christ. 'Your squabbles only show you haven't got it yet,' Paul says. 'Lift up your eyes! See the big picture!' Christ is ascended, and since we are in him, and he is of God, we too are established at a higher level, on a lasting and true and single foundation – this is the source of your works and their growth! Understand this, says Paul, and you'll realize that 'all things are yours'. We can trade in our seemingly vital squabbles over bits of power and security for a life that is anchored elsewhere: at the right hand of God.

Why would we settle for less?

COLLECT

O God the King of glory,
you have exalted your only Son Jesus Christ
with great triumph to your kingdom in heaven:
we beseech you, leave us not comfortless,
but send your Holy Spirit to strengthen us
and exalt us to the place where our Saviour Christ is gone before,
who is alive and reigns with you,
in the unity of the Holy Spirit,
one God, now and for ever.

| *Reflection by* **Donna Lazenby**

Psalms 98, **99**, 100 *or* **106*** (*or* 103)
1 Samuel 10.1-10
1 Corinthians 12.1-13

Tuesday 18 May

1 Corinthians 12.1-13
'Now there are varieties of gifts ...' (v.4)

Today's scripture is a relishing foretaste of the life about to be poured out on God's children at Pentecost. Christ's ascension to the right hand of the Father is good news because from the heart of the Trinity will rush a Spirit that – because of God's work through our human Lord – will minister to reanimate the world. And this Spirit ignites many different ministries and many different gifts. There is a tendency today to associate 'spiritual gifts' with particular denominations, or to reduce our definition of 'spiritual gifts' to one or two of their manifestations. But the life that flows from the heart of God animates the whole life of the Church, and she is rich and diverse in her abundant gifts, which will minister to the many needs of the world.

Which of Paul's 'spiritual gifts' will surprise you today? Offering an insightful contribution at a meeting, perhaps, that steers the group towards a good decision? Or being gifted with the ability to read the signs of the times: such as spotting a resurgence in interest in tattoos among young people, and wondering how this expresses their search for meaning and identity. Or helping others to recognize the false promises of desire-exploiting advertising and to make their way instead towards the wells of life that *actually* quench our thirst.

Which gifts of the Spirit do you believe are needed most urgently in the Church today?

Risen, ascended Lord,
as we rejoice at your triumph,
fill your Church on earth with power and compassion,
that all who are estranged by sin
may find forgiveness and know your peace,
to the glory of God the Father.

COLLECT

Reflection by **Donna Lazenby** | 155

Wednesday 19 May

Psalms 2, **29** *or* 110, **111**, 112
1 Kings 19.1-18
Matthew 3.13-end

Matthew 3.13-end

'I need to be baptised by you, and do you come to me?' (v.14)

John the Baptist is a true prophet, not only in the sense of having the power to make predictions about the future, but also because he is able to read reality in the light of the work and intentions of God. One who can greet the Lord's request to be baptized with the clarity of 'I need to be baptized by you, and do you come to me?' has a strong grasp on the shape of things. What a coming of age in the lives of two who may have been childhood friends – who, as unborn children, leapt at their first acquaintance from within their mothers' wombs! At the scene of his wilderness baptism, I wonder what this momentary exchange with John felt like for Jesus, in the depths of his heart. Was it a relief – a strange and poignant relief – to be face to face with someone who actually saw and got him? Strange because it was desperately unusual, and poignant because pregnant with the knowledge of his personal role in the world-changing events to come.

These prophets will live hauntingly parallel lives: later, Jesus will catch word that John has been imprisoned and beheaded, the price of his enduring faithfulness. This death will prefigure Jesus' own execution. Their journeys will chime as they live lives at right-angles to the currents of violence, selfishness and love-rejection weaving through a turbulent world.

What does John's clarity say to your vision of your Lord?

COLLECT

O God the King of glory,
you have exalted your only Son Jesus Christ
with great triumph to your kingdom in heaven:
we beseech you, leave us not comfortless,
but send your Holy Spirit to strengthen us
and exalt us to the place where our Saviour Christ is gone before,
who is alive and reigns with you,
in the unity of the Holy Spirit,
one God, now and for ever.

| *Reflection by* **Donna Lazenby**

Psalms **24**, 72 *or* 113, **115**   **Thursday 20 May**
Ezekiel 11.14-20
Matthew 9.35 – 10.20

Matthew 9.35 – 10.20

'As you go, proclaim the good news ...' (10.7)

As we celebrate our Lord's ascension, and look forward to the coming of the Spirit on the Church at Pentecost, we are summoned to awareness of the power in which we stand as God's children. As we share the faith and respond to God as our Lord's disciples, we stand in the flow of God's grace to the world. We give freely because we only offer what we have received without merit, and we walk freely because, while we must faithfully witness to Christ, we are not finally responsible for the receptivity of those whom we meet on the road.

We are living lightly, and yet this is dangerous living and calls for a wily tenacity. This is the vivid living of the saints and mystics, people whose lives are especially translucent to the beauty, glory and dependency of being mere creatures who yet live in Christ. St Francis grasped that the same poverty that set him free is the poverty against which the world makes war. The world resists the revelation that life is both all grace and all gift, because that means recognizing both dependence and the need to receive our life – and these come with a Lord. The world seeks, instead, to be its own God, to lodge its heel in some nook of self-sufficiency, and from here to take its stand and make its bargaining with life: a bargaining for self-rule and self-direction.

What power are you walking in? How lightly are you walking?

Risen, ascended Lord,
as we rejoice at your triumph,
fill your Church on earth with power and compassion,
that all who are estranged by sin
may find forgiveness and know your peace,
to the glory of God the Father.

COLLECT

Reflection by **Donna Lazenby**   157

Friday 21 May

Psalms **28**, 30 *or* **139**
Ezekiel 36.22-28
Matthew 12.22-32

Matthew 12.22-32

'... the one who had been mute could speak and see' (v.22)

In today's reading, we see Christ's analytical brilliance in play: once again, confronted with sophisticated efforts to evade the meaning and consequence of his ministry, Jesus leads his witnesses to comprehension of the truth by peeling back the layers of inadequate logic one by one. Having just healed one man of his blindness and muteness, now the crowds and the Pharisees – the gathered inhabitants of the world – are presented with the options of seeing or denying, of discerning or obfuscating, of receiving or renouncing. The consummative words of Jesus' unfolded argument are uncompromising: 'But if it is by the Spirit of God that I cast out demons, then the Kingdom of God has come to you.'

And so the connection is clear between seeing who Christ is and making a decision, between belonging to his life or, in rejecting him, choosing another way, for 'whoever is not with me is against me, and whoever does not gather with me scatters'. Jesus is 'the way', and seeing is believing where faith is actually salvation.

And so the question confronts us too, as in every encounter with the living Christ it must: what of our own blindness and muteness? Our failure to see and our refusal to declare? Which districts of our hearts are with the seeing, believing, healed man? Which are with the wonderingly open-hearted crowd, or the resisting Pharisees? Which parts of us receive with relish the fullness of our Lord's glory, and which remain resistant to full conversion to the One who in his resurrection has bound up Satan and plundered the house of death?

COLLECT

O God the King of glory,
you have exalted your only Son Jesus Christ
with great triumph to your kingdom in heaven:
we beseech you, leave us not comfortless,
but send your Holy Spirit to strengthen us
and exalt us to the place where our Saviour Christ is gone before,
who is alive and reigns with you,
in the unity of the Holy Spirit,
one God, now and for ever.

| *Reflection by* **Donna Lazenby**

Psalms 42, **43** *or* 120, **121**, 122
Micah 3.1-8
Ephesians 6.10-20

Saturday 22 May

Ephesians 6.10-20

'... be strong in the Lord and in the strength of his power' (v.10)

Jesus knows our temptations. He is also the source of the power we have to defeat them. In the wilderness experience preceding his public ministry, we see clearly the various temptations Christ has to confront. Here is, as Paul says, a High Priest who has been tempted in every way that we are. But in the desert we also see the power available and at his disposal, a power available to us as well. We see the power sourced in his knowledge of belonging to God, the power charged in his relationship with his Father. We see the power pulsing through the Scriptures, which he knows by heart and can summon to the moment. We see the power of an accompanying Spirit that has hurled him into the wilderness and resources his response to what would throw him aside from his calling one way or another.

In today's reading, it is the Paul who knows himself securely as 'an apostle of Christ Jesus by the will of God' addressing the Church in Ephesus in this identity. Paul lays before everyday saints like you and me the resplendent garment we can put on in Christ as a mantle of the Spirit. On the eve of Pentecost, let us prayerfully gaze over this precious robe, noticing every aid of the Paraclete-helper in whose life and power we are set up and sustained to live our life to God.

Do we know yet the help we have at hand? For in us is the Spirit who faithfully prays for us, nurturing us in the Christ who holds us eternally before our Father.

Risen, ascended Lord,
as we rejoice at your triumph,
fill your Church on earth with power and compassion,
that all who are estranged by sin
may find forgiveness and know your peace,
to the glory of God the Father.

COLLECT

Reflection by **Donna Lazenby**   159

Monday 24 May

Romans 1.1-17

'Paul, a servant of Jesus Christ …' (v.1)

What is your first word?

As children, we had a first word. There was a moment when we grasped something meaningful in this strange new world around us. We assigned a word to a person, place or thing, staked our signpost, and began to get some orientation, to find a way. Adults likely got excited when our first clear word rang out! It signalled a new and special phase in our growth in understanding. A child's first word can intrigue us; we wonder if it's an insight into their personality or perspective – why *that* word? It can also be a cause for humour – or even shock if they mirror back something less than ideal in the adult world around them!

First words matter. They say something about our priorities, something that we've noticed about the world, something about how we're getting orientated to life. In today's reading, we have Paul's opening address to the Church in Rome. This Church has erupted at the centre of political power. How dearly Paul longs to visit these saints! But all he has for now is words. So he begins with God, and a summary of the gospel, and introducing himself must be done in terms of, and with reference to, that gospel.

What is your first word? With what words and attitudes do you greet the day, do you greet life? What do your words, and your posture towards life, tell others about who you are and who you're serving?

COLLECT

O Lord, from whom all good things come:
grant to us your humble servants,
that by your holy inspiration
we may think those things that are good,
and by your merciful guiding may perform the same;
through our Lord Jesus Christ,
who is alive and reigns with you,
in the unity of the Holy Spirit,
one God, now and for ever.

Reflection by **Donna Lazenby**

Psalms **132**, 133
Job 2
Romans 1.18-end

Tuesday 25 May

Romans 1.18-end

'... but they became futile in their thinking' (v.21)

One of Paul's themes, which recurs through his letters, is the way the world claims wisdom while actually being foolish. Paul was himself an expert student of Judaism, having studied under a master and scholar, and one of the hallmarks of his journey is intellectual conversion. His encounter with Christ on the road to Damascus catalyses a radical re-imagining of the shape and structure of reality. Now Christ must take centre place within a re-conceived picture of 'religious' reality. More than this, because God's work in Christ is about all things, the whole world must now be read in the light of this fully disclosed truth. The result? The world's self-generated theories about life, meaning and what it looks like to live well and purposefully – its best efforts at such philosophy – will be foolishness if made without reference to Christ. Look at the world around you: what is its proffered 'wisdom'? What is its 'best' wisdom? What does the wisdom of God revealed in Christ say to the 'wisdom' of the age? What might it mean for you and your community to begin to unmask this false wisdom, and to offer the gospel's alternative?

Look also into your own heart. Paul gives us here a definition of an idol: idolatry has taken place where people have 'worshipped and served the creature rather than the Creator'. Look carefully and prayerfully. Can you pinpoint your own idols and – specifically – how they appear to offer what is only God's to give?

O Lord, from whom all good things come:
grant to us your humble servants,
that by your holy inspiration
we may think those things that are good,
and by your merciful guiding may perform the same;
through our Lord Jesus Christ,
who is alive and reigns with you,
in the unity of the Holy Spirit,
one God, now and for ever.

COLLECT

Reflection by **Donna Lazenby** | 161

Wednesday 26 May

Psalm 119.153-end
Job 3
Romans 2.1-16

Romans 2.1-16

'Therefore you have no excuse ...' (v.1)

Do you think of judgement as good news?

As Paul continues his letter to those he has not yet met, we may be struck by the straight dive into the deep straits of the judgement of God. His letter flows: first, a joyful proclamation of the gospel, followed by thanksgiving for the existence of these new saints, but now it comes up sharp against the unyielding holiness of God's law. Where there are gentiles – Paul's special commission, a ministry for which he would keenly suffer – he must present with clarity the context without which we cannot grasp the gospel: we are lost in our sin and, because God rightly judges us, the news of his work in Christ is good news for us. Our lives are not neutral, but stand in offence of a sovereign law.

Depending on our culture, these words of 'judgement' can sound harsh to contemporary ears. But isn't it good news that a good judge lives? For there are agonies and evils that we long to see judged, defeated and overturned. The challenge for us is to hear Paul's question: 'Do you not realize that God's kindness is meant to lead you to repentance?' What areas are there in your own, and your community's, life where God's kindness may have tempted you to resign yourself to your faults rather than to resist them? How can you use repentance as something to return to, again and again – an ever-freshening return to the mercy of the Son as our conversion to Christ ever deepens?

COLLECT

O Lord, from whom all good things come:
grant to us your humble servants,
that by your holy inspiration
we may think those things that are good,
and by your merciful guiding may perform the same;
through our Lord Jesus Christ,
who is alive and reigns with you,
in the unity of the Holy Spirit,
one God, now and for ever.

| *Reflection by* **Donna Lazenby**

Psalms **143**, 146
Job 4
Romans 2.17-end

Thursday 27 May

Romans 2.17-end

'... and real circumcision is a matter of the heart' (v.29)

We have just celebrated Pentecost: the Spirit of God poured out on human creatures. God makes flesh to be inhabited by Spirit. This is to be fully human, and the Church is the Holy Spirit's temple. Circumcision – living as God's child in the world, belonging to his people – is a 'spiritual' matter, says Paul; it takes place as one keeps the law of God and is not merely a question of bearing the physical sign. If 'real circumcision is a matter of the heart', then it is such good news that this is precisely where God's Spirit comes to help us. Through our praying, and the Spirit's ceaseless prayer on our behalf, the complex chambers of the heart are enlightened, re-ordered and healed, and our desires chastened and refined. Just as the Holy Spirit empowered the Son of God, Jesus of Nazareth, so the Spirit helps us today as human beings to live for God, and to live true to God. Where are you most longing for the Spirit's help?

Paul writes that a person who is circumcised inwardly 'receives praise not from others but from God'. One test of whether our hearts belong intensely to God is how satisfied we are to do works of love for others that only God along with the receiver will see. Do you know where you tend to draw your sense of reputation, acceptance, affirmation or acclaim from? How comfortable are you and your community with investing in 'obscurity'? As Paul reminds us vividly here, God sees – and blesses – what is done in secret.

COLLECT

O Lord, from whom all good things come:
grant to us your humble servants,
that by your holy inspiration
we may think those things that are good,
and by your merciful guiding may perform the same;
through our Lord Jesus Christ,
who is alive and reigns with you,
in the unity of the Holy Spirit,
one God, now and for ever.

Reflection by **Donna Lazenby** | 163

Friday 28 May

Romans 3.1-20

'By no means!' (vv.4, 6)

In today's reading, we can really feel Paul wrestling – wrestling to express the internal logic of the gospel as it defines and interrelates judgement and grace; wrestling to express the gospel's response to misunderstandings and perversions of the relationship between justice and freedom. As you endeavour to understand more of God, and to live your faith, what do you wrestle with, and why? What would you love more opportunity to explore in the company of fellow saints?

For Paul, as for us, the answer begins with Christ. Christ is the clue, the beginning and the end of the meaning and order of the universe, God's first and final word to us on everything. God's intention is grace, and his fulfilment is grace, and it is this grace alone that saves us. The world is fallen, Paul argues, and if we are playing games with the truth of our need for salvation, games that suggest we can go on sinning or that somehow our fallenness is unserious, then we've missed what an incredible mess we're in.

We have also missed the unfathomable beauty of God's provision in Christ. There has only ever been one righteous man, one person who has truly and fully and consistently lived a life unto God. It is his Spirit who now comes to help us. Let us never forget that this is the power at work in us, the power that helped our Lord live a fully human life, the power that raised a human being from death.

COLLECT

O Lord, from whom all good things come:
grant to us your humble servants,
that by your holy inspiration
we may think those things that are good,
and by your merciful guiding may perform the same;
through our Lord Jesus Christ,
who is alive and reigns with you,
in the unity of the Holy Spirit,
one God, now and for ever.

| *Reflection by* **Donna Lazenby**

Psalm 147
Job 6
Romans 3.21-end

Saturday 29 May

Romans 3.21-end

'... all have sinned and fall short of the glory of God; they are now justified' (v.23)

Paul has had a mighty revelation. For this scrupulously observant Jewish scholar to say 'But now, irrespective of law, the righteousness of God has been disclosed' shows that he has received something extraordinary: the insight that one man, Jesus Christ, has become the law's fulfilment and has presented the grounds for our justification and righteousness before God. If we trust in God's work through Christ, we will be set free from the captivity of sin and death, and received as children of God. This is God's great 'gift' to us: the free grace of his own pardon, his own life. While the law and the prophets point to and are fulfilled in Christ, it is a powerful revelation Paul has received in being confronted with this man, Jesus, as 'the way' laid down for us.

The question for us is how open we are to this revelation, to the gift of God that is the grace of Christ, to the fullness and sufficiency and completion of God's work for us. Search your own heart: are there parts of you that still resist the ground God has laid? If so, why? Does some part of you still barter? If so, what are you still needing to hear? As one of my friends puts it, 'when you are being baptized, the last thing you want to do is to keep your head above water...'

O Lord, from whom all good things come:
grant to us your humble servants,
that by your holy inspiration
we may think those things that are good,
and by your merciful guiding may perform the same;
through our Lord Jesus Christ,
who is alive and reigns with you,
in the unity of the Holy Spirit,
one God, now and for ever.

COLLECT

Reflection by **Donna Lazenby** | 165

Monday 31 May

Visit of the Blessed Virgin Mary
to Elizabeth

Psalms 85, 150
1 Samuel 2.1-10
Mark 3.31-end

1 Samuel 2.1-10

'Hannah prayed and said, "My heart exults in the Lord"' (v.1)

Hannah's prayer sounds a triumphant note. 'Exult' is a strong word, and her song is echoed in equal measure centuries later by Mary in her Magnificat. Both begin with an outpouring of exuberant joy that is focused on God and his extravagant grace. Both sing of a reversal of fortunes, whereby God brings down the mighty and raises up the poor and weak, people like themselves, who would never have anticipated such attention from God. It is as if they knew themselves blessed beyond measure and the only possible response is worship and adoration.

Hannah's song proclaims a vision of a new world order. God's concern for Hannah and her heartfelt plea, demonstrated his compassion for all who are poor and needy: the feeble, the hungry, the barren and the dispossessed. Who are the dispossessed in our communities today, and how would they know that God sees and cares for them? Hannah's story calls into question all the prevailing powers of her day – social, institutional and theological – and sets the scene for the towering figure of Samuel, God's prophet and faithful servant.

Much later, Hannah's song took shape in a new way, this time through the unsought pregnancy of another insignificant young woman, whose openness to grace led to an even greater revolution. Pray that the Church will enable the poor and weak of our society to 'exult in the Lord'.

COLLECT

Mighty God,
by whose grace Elizabeth rejoiced with Mary
and greeted her as the mother of the Lord:
look with favour on your lowly servants
that, with Mary, we may magnify your holy name
and rejoice to acclaim her Son our Saviour,
who is alive and reigns with you,
in the unity of the Holy Spirit,
one God, now and for ever.

| *Reflection by* **Liz Hoare**

Psalms **5**, 6 (8)
Job 8
Romans 4.13-end

Tuesday 1 June

Romans 4.13-end

'Hoping against hope, he believed ...' (v.18)

Hoping against hope sounds like a recipe for people who do not have a strong grip on reality. Most of us prefer a few solid facts before we decide to commit ourselves – and preferably some assurance of a good outcome. But faith is not like that; otherwise how could it be faith? How much faith do we need before we dare to hope for what we can't see? And what would that look like as we contemplate the future? It all depends on where we place our hope.

Paul began his letter to the Romans by thanking God for their faith that was being proclaimed throughout the world. They were a beleaguered, insignificant group of people who had dared to put their trust in Jesus and not the Roman Emperor, even though Jesus had died on a cross and the might of the Emperor was evident to all. Paul pointed to another powerless situation where Abraham dared to believe God's promise against all the odds. Faith, then as now, calls forth courage and determination.

Lest we protest that it is just too hard, remember that we are being invited to have faith in the God who raised Jesus from the dead. This shifts the onus from us and our faith, which is often weak and feeble, onto God, who is able to call into existence things that do not exist even today.

COLLECT

Almighty and everlasting God,
you have given us your servants grace,
by the confession of a true faith,
to acknowledge the glory of the eternal Trinity
and in the power of the divine majesty to worship the Unity:
keep us steadfast in this faith,
that we may evermore be defended from all adversities;
through Jesus Christ your Son our Lord,
who is alive and reigns with you,
in the unity of the Holy Spirit,
one God, now and for ever.

Reflection by **Liz Hoare**

Wednesday 2 June

Romans 5.1-11

'... this grace in which we stand' (v.2)

God's gifts abound in Paul's letter to the Romans. He has already referred to justification by grace as a gift (Romans 3.24) and now, as he unpacks the consequences of being justified, he turns to the gift of the Holy Spirit that has been given to us. Paul is beginning to draw out the monumental and life-changing implications of 'this grace in which we stand'.

For a start we have peace with God. There is now nothing to fear from the one who has poured his love into our hearts, since 'perfect love casts out fear' (1 John 4.18). Love changes everything; we know this from a human standpoint. How much more the love of God? The assurance that God's love has indeed been poured into human hearts – an image redolent of extravagant abundance – comes from the guarantee of the Holy Spirit and is sheer gift.

Paul will have much, much more to say about the work of the Spirit, but here he is underlining the extent to which God's love reached down to us in Christ. There is nothing we can do to earn grace; we simply receive it as the gift it is. Whatever kind of suffering and endurance life places on us, it is the boundless generosity of God's action in Christ Jesus that enables us to stand firm, upheld by this amazing grace.

Thank God today for the grace in which you stand.

COLLECT
> Almighty and everlasting God,
> you have given us your servants grace,
> by the confession of a true faith,
> to acknowledge the glory of the eternal Trinity
> and in the power of the divine majesty to worship the Unity:
> keep us steadfast in this faith,
> that we may evermore be defended from all adversities;
> through Jesus Christ your Son our Lord,
> who is alive and reigns with you,
> in the unity of the Holy Spirit,
> one God, now and for ever.

| *Reflection by* **Liz Hoare**

Psalm 147
Deuteronomy 8.2-16
1 Corinthians 10.1-17

Thursday 3 June

Day of Thanksgiving for the
Institution of Holy Communion
(Corpus Christi)

1 Corinthians 10.1-17

'We must not put Christ to the test' (v.9)

Christian freedom is a wonderful gift, but one that is easily abused. Life's experience teaches us that true freedom does not mean doing as we please, because that is a sure way for everyone, ourselves included, to get hurt.

The Corinthians were in danger of hurting themselves by treating their new-found freedom in Christ irresponsibly, so Paul reminds them of their history. The people of Israel abused their newly won freedom, he says, and look what happened to them! It seems the Corinthians thought that baptism and the Eucharist would protect them where idolatry was concerned, but sacraments are not a magic talisman. Sharing bread is a means of sharing in the body of Christ, but just as exodus is a terrible warning not to presume on God's loving-kindness, so partaking of the one bread does not bring automatic protection and blessing.

Coming as it does, in the midst of reading Romans, with its emphasis on the glorious freedom given in Christ, the feast of Corpus Christi reminds us of the cost involved in giving us that freedom; it urges us to practise that freedom in a way that matches our new identity. The Eucharist unites us to Christ in faith and loyalty. Keeping Christ as our vision of life in all its fulness and living out of that vision, means that betrayal becomes unthinkable.

COLLECT

Lord Jesus Christ,
we thank you that in this wonderful sacrament
you have given us the memorial of your passion:
grant us so to reverence the sacred mysteries
of your body and blood
that we may know within ourselves
and show forth in our lives
the fruits of your redemption;
for you are alive and reign with the Father
in the unity of the Holy Spirit,
one God, now and for ever.

Reflection by **Liz Hoare**   169

Friday 4 June

Psalms 17, **19**
Job 11
Romans 6.1-14

Romans 6.1-14

'What then ... Should we continue in sin?' (v.1)

Paul begins this section of Romans with a question that only has one correct answer. To understand how he got here involves unravelling some complicated arguments about the law and its efficacy. Although Paul argued that the law was a bad thing because it serves to show up human sinfulness, he then went on to state that it is in fact a beautiful thing, because it demonstrates how gracious God is to continue in faithfulness towards his sinful people.

So, if the law puts God and his mercy in such a good light, should we not carry on sinning so that God's grace may be even more evident? There is a certain logic to this, but it is not in keeping in any way with God's work of grace in a human life. We have been set free from sin, so now let's leave it well alone! Indeed, we have died to sin, so it makes no sense at all to go on living in it. We have died with Christ in baptism and from now on we are to live his life as free individuals.

Freedom and slavery, life and death; these are pairs of opposites, and we cannot have it both ways. We are destined for life and freedom and today is another opportunity to choose the way of life in our actions and decisions.

COLLECT

Almighty and everlasting God,
you have given us your servants grace,
by the confession of a true faith,
to acknowledge the glory of the eternal Trinity
and in the power of the divine majesty to worship the Unity:
keep us steadfast in this faith,
that we may evermore be defended from all adversities;
through Jesus Christ your Son our Lord,
who is alive and reigns with you,
in the unity of the Holy Spirit,
one God, now and for ever.

| *Reflection by* **Liz Hoare**

Psalms 20, 21, **23**
Job 12
Romans 6.15-end

Saturday 5 June

Romans 6.15-end

'... freed from sin and enslaved to God' (v.22)

Paul's logic once again threatens to tie us in mental knots. Has he not just stated that we have been set free and are not slaves to anyone? Is he now claiming that we have been set free from one master only to be enslaved to another? In one sense, this is exactly what Paul is arguing. Christ has broken sin's hold and set us free. We are never truly free if we choose to please ourselves, for that, as so many of us know to our cost, leads straight back to helpless bondage. Sin has its own wages to give, says Paul, and they lead to death, therefore choose enslavement to Christ which leads to fullness of life.

It is as if we have been transferred to a new kingdom where all the laws are designed to make us more fully the human beings we are meant to be. The character of the king determines the laws of the kingdom, so learning to follow Christ who called us friends and laid down his life out of love shows us how to put this into practice.

Each day, we face the choice either of pleasing ourselves or seeking to live according to the ways that Christ showed us in his own life, death and resurrection. We discover as we choose Christ, that we also choose the life that is true freedom.

Holy God,
faithful and unchanging:
enlarge our minds with the knowledge of your truth,
and draw us more deeply into the mystery of your love,
that we may truly worship you,
Father, Son and Holy Spirit,
one God, now and for ever.

COLLECT

Monday 7 June

Psalms 27, **30**
Job 13
Romans 7.1-6

Romans 7.1-6

'... in order that we may bear fruit for God' (v.4)

Paul has not yet finished with explaining the relationship between law, sin and grace. He was insistent that all believers in Rome, both Jewish Christians and gentile ones, understood that they were to live differently. From now on, for Jew and gentile alike, life is about bearing fruit for God in new ways. Bearing fruit is an image associated with the work of the Holy Spirit that puts flesh on what belonging to Christ means for us. It is about inner growth emerging in a human life to produce a character that is Christlike.

The temptation to resort to keeping the rules is as real for Christians today as it was for Paul's contemporaries. Paul's Jewish readers understood the constraints of the law that had defined God's people for so many centuries; the implications of throwing them off must, to say the least, have felt as threatening as it felt liberating.

The image of fruit is helpful here, for as every gardener knows, there are hidden laws at work that we cannot control, but we still have something to contribute towards its appearance. Fruit needs certain conditions if it is to grow and reach full maturity. Just as it is a beautiful fulfilment of the cycle of life in a tree or plant, so our lives will bear fruit when we allow the life of Christ to permeate our own.

COLLECT

O God,
the strength of all those who put their trust in you,
mercifully accept our prayers
and, because through the weakness of our mortal nature
we can do no good thing without you,
grant us the help of your grace,
that in the keeping of your commandments
we may please you both in will and deed;
through Jesus Christ your Son our Lord,
who is alive and reigns with you,
in the unity of the Holy Spirit,
one God, now and for ever.

| *Reflection by* **Liz Hoare**

Psalms 32, **36**
Job 14
Romans 7.7-end

Tuesday 8 June

Romans 7.7-end
'I do the very thing I hate' (v.15)

How many of us have begun a new day with the best of intentions only to find – yet again – that we snap at strangers in our path, grumble about a colleague, shout at the children or … Those repeating sins and ingrained habits we wish we could kick seem to delight in tripping us up, however hard we pray or try to change.

Chapter 7 of Romans expresses our double-mindedness towards sin and righteousness with startling clarity. On the one hand, we may think, if Paul could not master his passion, what chance have we? On the other, we find a heartfelt reflection on human nature with real hope at the end. We feel Paul's anguished battle, before we discover the outcome of his frustration: 'Wretched man that I am! Who will rescue me from this body of death?' But it is here we also find the grounds of his hope. 'Thanks be to God through Jesus Christ our Lord!'

The difficult reality is that in this life we will always be pulled in two directions, but our ultimate destiny is for the two conflicting natures of flesh and spirit within us to be wholly aligned with our new life in Christ. The ambiguity we experience internally reflects the 'now and not yet' of the present age, which is why the hope referred to in Romans chapter 4 is so crucial for the bigger picture.

God of truth,
help us to keep your law of love
and to walk in ways of wisdom,
that we may find true life
in Jesus Christ your Son.

COLLECT

Reflection by **Liz Hoare** | 173

Wednesday 9 June

Romans 8.1-11

'... walk ... according to the Spirit' (v.4)

I once heard someone say that the kingdom of God is about making earth more like heaven by making people more like Jesus. We cannot make this transformation a reality by ourselves; it is a supernatural change that comes from the same Spirit who raised Jesus from the dead. God's Spirit works from the inside out so that our life in Christ becomes fundamental to who we are, not something superimposed that overrides our humanity. Paul's emphasis is on the Spirit coming to dwell in us, which suggests taking up permanent residence rather than occasionally camping or issuing instructions from afar. The Spirit comes with the aim of aligning our whole being with that of Christ, not with a new set of rules to follow.

We are often urged to 'walk the walk' and not just 'talk the talk'. Freedom means being able to chart a path and walk it without hindrance, and spiritually we have been set free to walk a new path through life. The path that God invites us to tread is one of 'life and peace'. While this will look different according to our circumstances, there will be a family likeness that is recognizable. Choosing which path to take is where we need the guidance and help of the Holy Spirit who lives in us.

Pray for the discerning presence of the Spirit of Christ to lead you in your walk today.

COLLECT

O God,
the strength of all those who put their trust in you,
mercifully accept our prayers
and, because through the weakness of our mortal nature
we can do no good thing without you,
grant us the help of your grace,
that in the keeping of your commandments
we may please you both in will and deed;
through Jesus Christ your Son our Lord,
who is alive and reigns with you,
in the unity of the Holy Spirit,
one God, now and for ever.

Reflection by **Liz Hoare**

Psalm **37***
Job 16.1 – 17.2
Romans 8.12-17

Thursday 10 June

Romans 8.12-17

'... children of God ... and joint heirs with Christ (vv.16,17)

Jesus is heir to all that God has in store for him by the nature of who he is. We are heirs by adoption: we have been adopted into the family and thereby share in the inheritance promised to all believers.

There are two wonders here: first, that we have a new identity. All who are led by the Spirit of God are children of God. This, in a world where identities can be stolen, judged, often confused, made up one day and cast aside another, is profoundly reassuring. What is more, we have done nothing to earn this new identity. It is God's gracious gift.

The second wonder is that because we are now children, we have the same inheritance to look forward to as Christ himself. Just as Jesus now shares in the fullness of life in God, his glory and his perfect love, so we too are destined to share in all of that. While we await our inheritance, we are invited to anticipate it by addressing almighty God as 'Abba! father!'. Intimacy with God in our earthly life provides us with a foretaste of what is to come. Grace sets us free, replacing fear of condemnation with confident hope of glory. Accepting the gift of adoption with thankful hearts is the way to open our hearts to receive it and live in its truth.

God of truth,
help us to keep your law of love
and to walk in ways of wisdom,
that we may find true life
in Jesus Christ your Son.

COLLECT

Friday 11 June

Barnabas the Apostle

Psalms 100, 101, 117
Jeremiah 9.23-24
Acts 4.32-end

Acts 4.32-end

'... great grace was upon them all' (v.33)

It's all very well to describe the early Church as being 'of one heart and soul', but how did that become concrete reality? The early Christians, like the Jewish tradition out of which they came, did not make the same distinction that we do today between heart and mind on the one hand and practical living on the other. Belief and practice were inseparable, but it also needed the power of the Holy Spirit to ignite the whole. The belief in Jesus as Lord led the early Church to be ready to regard each other's needs as their own.

Luke is clear that it was the commitment of the whole group that made this possible, but he also has a personal example to illustrate the general principle. Barnabas, a disciple from Cyprus, sold a field and brought the proceeds to the apostles to use as they saw fit. Barnabas features prominently in Acts as the companion of Paul, preaching the gospel, encouraging the believers and looking out for the needs of others. Here is a disciple modelling integrity in the way his belief in Jesus and his practical discipleship mirrored each other. Did he grow into his name, or was he given it because of the way he demonstrated this grace of encouragement? Either way, he gives us a beautiful example to follow of someone growing into the likeness of his Lord.

C O L L E C T	Bountiful God, giver of all gifts, who poured your Spirit upon your servant Barnabas and gave him grace to encourage others: help us, by his example, to be generous in our judgements and unselfish in our service; through Jesus Christ your Son our Lord, who is alive and reigns with you, in the unity of the Holy Spirit, one God, now and for ever.

Psalms 41, **42**, 43
Job 18
Romans 8.31-end

Saturday 12 June

Romans 8.31-end

'If God is for us, who is against us?' (v.31)

The question here is not whether we are on God's side, but whether he is on ours. If he is, then we may be exposed to danger and great suffering, but nothing can threaten our salvation. That God is indeed for us has been the whole thrust of Paul's letter to the Romans so far. The fact of Jesus, his life, death and resurrection, is our guarantee that we have nothing to fear, not even death. God has shown such depths of love at the cross that we cannot doubt his willingness to give us 'everything else'.

I was given this verse at my baptism when I was fifteen, and it continues to remind me of God's faithfulness, especially when my own faith falters. It is especially encouraging to realize that the list of terrors that might fall on us probably came in part, at least, from Paul's personal experience. The testimony of so many who have proved these words faithful and true is a powerful contemporary witness to the knowledge that we cannot be separated from Christ who is Lord of life and death, things present and things to come. This is our motivation for perseverance and hope.

In whatever we are battling with now, or may face in the future, the love of God in Christ is for us, now and forever. When we falter, God holds us fast.

COLLECT

O God,
the strength of all those who put their trust in you,
mercifully accept our prayers
and, because through the weakness of our mortal nature
we can do no good thing without you,
grant us the help of your grace,
that in the keeping of your commandments
we may please you both in will and deed;
through Jesus Christ your Son our Lord,
who is alive and reigns with you,
in the unity of the Holy Spirit,
one God, now and for ever.

Reflection by **Liz Hoare**

Monday 14 June

Psalm **44**
Job 19
Romans 9.1-18

Romans 9.1-18

'... my kindred according to the flesh' (v.3)

Paul's mood shifts dramatically at this point in the letter. His heart turns to anguish over the unbelief of his own people, his Jewish kindred according to the flesh.

Oh, my people! For centuries, prophetic souls have poured out their lamentations to God. How can it be that God's chosen people should be so blind to his grace? Blessed in so many ways, how could they ignore the great covenant promise that is now being fulfilled in Christ? Glorying in the gospel that is extending to include all people – even the gentiles – it must be agonizing for Paul to think that his own kindred might be left out, through unbelief.

Paul turns instinctively to heartfelt prayer and grappling with the Scriptures. There must be a larger pattern. God will hold out a greater hope. This is the deep, existential struggle of the prayer of lament. In the face of human bewilderment, we pour out our dashed hopes and unanswered questions to an ever-gracious Lord.

Great souls are unashamed to bring their lamentations to the Lord. Not hiding from their grievous disappointments, not grasping for simplistic answers, but wrestling wholeheartedly to embrace the ways of a costlier holiness and truth. When did you last pray like that?

COLLECT

Lord, you have taught us
that all our doings without love are nothing worth:
send your Holy Spirit
and pour into our hearts that most excellent gift of love,
the true bond of peace and of all virtues,
without which whoever lives is counted dead before you.
Grant this for your only Son Jesus Christ's sake,
who is alive and reigns with you,
in the unity of the Holy Spirit,
one God, now and for ever.

| *Reflection by* **Margaret Whipp**

Psalms **48**, 52
Job 21
Romans 9.19-end

Tuesday 15 June

Romans 9.19-end

'Those who were not my people ...' (v.25)

It helps, in the struggles of faith, to keep hold of a long view. Paul feels desperately concerned about the terrible unbelief among his Jewish kinspeople. How tragic that, in contrast to a wonderful response to the good news among the gentiles, it seems that his own people are being shut out from this wider experience of grace.

How do we respond when faced with the severe mercies of God? Paul is one of those people who has to argue it out with God, wrestling to make sense of his disappointment and outrage, digging deep into all that he knows of God's goodness down the ages. He is in good company. Believers as far back as Job have brought all their wits to bear on the intractable challenge of reconciling God's mercy with his sovereign purpose.

Perhaps, like Job, Paul finds fresh hope in a humbler perspective. The pattern of God's election, down long centuries of faith, reveals many startling reversals and breakthroughs. Some of the greatest prophets were those who challenged any sense of cosy entitlement. It is not any racial or religious group that holds a monopoly on God's promises. Only the call and the love of God can preserve the identity of a chosen people.

How is this good news for today?

Faithful Creator,
whose mercy never fails:
deepen our faithfulness to you
and to your living Word,
Jesus Christ our Lord.

COLLECT

Wednesday 16 June

Psalm 119.57-80
Job 22
Romans 10.1-10

Romans 10.1-10

'... a zeal for God, but ... not enlightened' (v.2)

When we are baffled by the behaviour of others, it's surprising how clues can often be traced by looking back on our own personal history. Paul, perhaps more than anyone, knew what it was to have a zeal for God that was not enlightened. He was quite candid about the shadow side of his own youthful enthusiasm that drove him to fierce persecution of Christian believers (Philippians 3.6). Now he testifies to the misdirected zeal that, through ignorance, keeps his fellow-Jews from recognizing the revelation of Jesus as Christ.

Religious zeal brings a double-edged quality in any group or society. The Greek word for zeal in verse 2 conveys something that is overheated and intense, like a blazing hot coal or a boiling liquid. Being so preoccupied with their own agenda, the people of Israel had missed out on what God was doing in their midst. In another metaphor (Romans 9.30-33), Paul pictures athletes who run so fast and furiously in a footrace that they trip and fall over a stumbling-stone.

Paul has learned that salvation comes from embracing what God has done, not from working to establish our own righteousness. It was a hard lesson to learn, and a challenge to recognize what this meant for people whose starting point, in religious terms, seemed very different from his own.

Is this what it means to be enlightened?

COLLECT

Lord, you have taught us
that all our doings without love are nothing worth:
send your Holy Spirit
and pour into our hearts that most excellent gift of love,
the true bond of peace and of all virtues,
without which whoever lives is counted dead before you.
Grant this for your only Son Jesus Christ's sake,
who is alive and reigns with you,
in the unity of the Holy Spirit,
one God, now and for ever.

| *Reflection by* **Margaret Whipp**

Psalms 56, **57** (63*)
Job 23
Romans 10.11-end

Thursday 17 June

Romans 10.11-end
'How beautiful are the feet ...' (v.15)

Great texts from the scriptures create classic resonances down the centuries. We may be familiar with the lovely soprano aria in Handel's *Messiah*, which celebrates the beautiful feet 'of them that preach the gospel of peace, and bring glad tidings of good things'.

Paul knew this text from the book of Isaiah (52.7) with its thrilling vision of a runner dashing over the mountains to bring comfort to God's people in exile. Those 'beautiful feet', we might imagine, would be dusty, hot and sweaty. The image suggests a rather different mood from the consoling melody that carries Handel's 'beautiful feet' tripping along to a lilting eighteenth-century dance tune! Every generation, naturally enough, receives the good news in its own particular register.

The frequent echoes of older scriptures in Paul's letters reflect his search for a larger inspiration for his apostolic vision to preach the gospel across the Roman world. His sense of urgency was well-matched to the earlier prophecy, as was the pain of disappointment when his good news was not universally believed (v.16; cf. Isaiah 53.1). Paul's word for 'beautiful' (*horaios*) is drawn from the Greek Septuagint version of the Scripture. It describes something that is timely or seasonable, more than aesthetically attractive.

God calls messengers in every generation to bring good news in an apt and seasonable manner. These hymn lines by Chris Tomlin can be a prayer: 'Take my feet, and let them be swift and beautiful for thee!'

Faithful Creator,
whose mercy never fails:
deepen our faithfulness to you
and to your living Word,
Jesus Christ our Lord.

COLLECT

Reflection by **Margaret Whipp** | 181

Friday 18 June

Romans 11.1-12

'... has God rejected his people?' (v.1)

Some of the greatest evils of western Christianity have sprung from a theologically warped view of supersessionism – the idea, quite contrary to the scriptures, that God has somehow rejected his covenant people, Israel, and replaced them with a new set of chosen people in the Christian Church.

Paul faces this appalling suggestion head on in his letter to the Romans. For him, there could be no greater slur on the character of God. He is adamant that the God who has so richly blessed Israel is never fickle, but steadfastly and eternally faithful. Has he rejected his people – by no means! The gifts and the calling of God are 'irrevocable' (Romans 11.29).

The problems come – and Paul traces a recurring pattern here – when people reject their God, not the other way round. It is as if a kind of spiritual stupor takes over cultures and nations, blinding them to the most vital truths of their own religious heritage. In verse 8, Paul repeats the same tragic insight that both Jesus and the earlier Jewish prophets recognized.

What are we to make of the heedlessness of our own day, as whole nations and cultures slide inexorably into a 'sluggish spirit'? We must read on, and keep praying – because God's redemptive story is not over yet!

COLLECT

Lord, you have taught us
that all our doings without love are nothing worth:
send your Holy Spirit
and pour into our hearts that most excellent gift of love,
the true bond of peace and of all virtues,
without which whoever lives is counted dead before you.
Grant this for your only Son Jesus Christ's sake,
who is alive and reigns with you,
in the unity of the Holy Spirit,
one God, now and for ever.

| *Reflection by* **Margaret Whipp**

Psalm **68**
Job 25 – 26
Romans 11.13-24

Saturday 19 June

Romans 11.13-24
'Now I am speaking to you Gentiles' (v.13)

Relationships between Jewish and gentile believers in Rome were not straightforward. Following Emperor Claudius' expulsion of the Jews from Rome in AD 49, we might imagine that gentile believers took up a dominant position in the Christian congregations. How easy it would be for gentiles to look down on those Jews who subsequently returned, as a community who were now marginal to God's purposes.

Paul will have none of this smugness. God's kindness and creative purpose to include the gentiles in his grace can never be a licence for triumphalism. It is sobering to realize how often such presumptuous dynamics have been repeated in the history of the Church. When one group of believers receives a new outpouring of grace, they are tempted to dismiss and disparage those who have gone before them.

The parable of the olive tree keeps us earthed in a humbler perspective. Whatever blessings may have been entrusted to us – spiritually, materially, intellectually, theologically – we are all profoundly indebted to those forebears in faith whose deep roots in God have made our understanding possible.

Theological and cultural differences, springing up within the natural distinctives of social life, can put a harmful distance between fellow-Christians. An attitude of humble gratitude, rather than arrogance, is the Christlike way to honour and pray for all God's people to flourish.

COLLECT

Faithful Creator,
whose mercy never fails:
deepen our faithfulness to you
and to your living Word,
Jesus Christ our Lord.

Reflection by **Margaret Whipp** | 183

Monday 21 June

Romans 11.25-end

'O the depth of the riches and wisdom ... of God!' (v.33)

Paul's prolonged existential struggle yields an outpouring of praise to the living God. Like so many saints before him, Paul grapples with the inscrutable patterns of history. Lamenting the lack of faith among his own people, the Jews, the apostle digs deep into the character of the God whose mission he longs to serve.

How will this story end? We need not follow every detail of Paul's complex rabbinical argumentation to sense the deep soul-shift in his understanding. Everything that he knows of God, from the long history of the Jewish people, inspires Paul to trust in the outworking of a rich drama of eschatological fulfilment. Despite blindness and disobedience in both Jews and gentiles, the God of surprises is tirelessly at work, patiently bending the arc of history to a wider redemption.

This is the good news of God's righteousness. It is not, and never has been, dependent on the faithfulness or the cleverness of human beings, whether Jews or gentiles. The endless extravagance of God, which Paul dimly discerns, can weave even our tragic failures into a glorious tapestry of hope. This God is the origin, the sustainer, and the ultimate goal of all creation. Through every twist and turn of the story, his astounding wisdom is at work.

Where might the God of surprises be moving today?

COLLECT

Almighty God,
you have broken the tyranny of sin
and have sent the Spirit of your Son into our hearts
    whereby we call you Father:
give us grace to dedicate our freedom to your service,
that we and all creation may be brought
    to the glorious liberty of the children of God;
through Jesus Christ your Son our Lord,
who is alive and reigns with you,
in the unity of the Holy Spirit,
one God, now and for ever.

| *Reflection by* **Margaret Whipp**

Psalm **73**
Job 28
Romans 12.1-8

Tuesday 22 June

Romans 12.1-8

'I appeal to you ... by the mercies of God' (v.1)

Paul turns towards the practical implications of his message, and his words are marked by tenderness and warmth. He does not command or dictate, but puts himself on a level with his fellow-Christians, appealing to their shared dependence on God's grace. The word in verse 1 for the 'mercies' of God translates a Greek noun for the 'bowels' of God, full of compassion and longing. It is from this heartfelt sense of God's kindness that Paul urges Christians to present their bodies to the Lord.

This rich metaphor of the body plays out on a number of levels, each inviting our wholehearted engagement. In the military context so familiar to the Romans, a soldier who 'presents his body' is yielding his life in service to his commander. Christians redeemed from the old order of sin are called to commit decisively to the new rule of Christ (cf. Romans 6.13). The liturgical context of sacrifice would be familiar to Christians, whether from a Jewish background or from the gentile rituals of temple worship. Paul's appeal to present our bodies 'as a living sacrifice' speaks to the potential consecration of every life, transformed by grace, as a 'holy and acceptable' offering to God. Finally, Paul develops the body metaphor to urge his fellow-Christians to play their part, in all humility, in the upbuilding of their common life.

What radical renewing of our minds is needed for such full-bodied commitment?

COLLECT

God our saviour,
look on this wounded world
in pity and in power;
hold us fast to your promises of peace
won for us by your Son,
our Saviour Jesus Christ.

Reflection by **Margaret Whipp**

185

Wednesday 23 June

Psalm **77**
Job 29
Romans 12.9-end

Romans 12.9-end

'... overcome evil with good' (v.21)

There is a timeless quality to Paul's advice here. We don't need to know the particulars of the strains and conflicts in the Roman house churches to recognize that those early Christians still had a lot to learn – just like us. It is one thing to exhort believers to live harmoniously as one body in Christ, but it takes care and pastoral sensitivity to tease out the attitudinal and behavioural changes that make this possible.

The renewing of our minds evokes a beautiful list of Christlike qualities: sympathy, humility, peacefulness, eagerness, positivity, integrity, hospitality, forgiveness, generosity, resilience. It's not surprising that many readers hear echoes of our Lord's own teaching in this section.

At the top of the list we find sincerity: 'let love be genuine'. It can be all too easy, in the everyday conflicts of living together, to paper over the challenge of genuine concern with pious pretences. Perhaps the socially savvy Romans were good at 'faking it'. We dare not slacken our efforts, wherever fear and conflict lie close beneath the surface, to keep working at genuine unity and love. Dark forces of evil are always corroding the goodness of our life in Christ, but we trust in the grace that overcomes evil with good.

In the particulars of our own strains and conflicts, where might that grace make a genuine difference?

COLLECT

Almighty God,
you have broken the tyranny of sin
and have sent the Spirit of your Son into our hearts
    whereby we call you Father:
give us grace to dedicate our freedom to your service,
that we and all creation may be brought
    to the glorious liberty of the children of God;
through Jesus Christ your Son our Lord,
who is alive and reigns with you,
in the unity of the Holy Spirit,
one God, now and for ever.

| *Reflection by* **Margaret Whipp**

Psalms 50, 149
Ecclesiasticus 48.1-10
or Malachi 3.1-6
Luke 3.1-17

Thursday 24 June
Birth of John the Baptist

Malachi 3.1-6
'See, I am sending my messenger' (v.1)

Behold! Look! Open your eyes to what God is doing in our day! The calling of a prophet is to arouse God's people from the slumber of sin. The book of the prophet Malachi (whose name means 'Messenger') stands at the close of what is for Christians the 'older testament'. It leans forward, almost on tiptoe, towards the good news that will unfold in our 'newer testament' to the grace of God. This is the same, eternal, and unchanging God, who is ever patient with his people, 'not wanting any to perish, but all to come to repentance' (2 Peter 3.9).

Today, we thank God for prophets like Malachi and John the Baptist who keep us from sleepwalking into judgement and disaster. Theirs will never be a comfortable calling: they are sent to smelt and to purge so that God might work a much-needed renewal.

Speaking truth to a privileged, complacent people is never popular. John's preaching took place in the searing desert; his message burned like fire, cleansed like the stinking caustic of fuller's soap. Just like Malachi, John could not remain silent in the face of oppression and social abuse, idolatry and listless worship. Nor should we.

The prophet's usefulness is to turn our hearts from vague discomfort to specific action and repentance. 'Teacher, what should we do?' (Luke 3.12, 14)

Almighty God,
by whose providence your servant John the Baptist
was wonderfully born,
and sent to prepare the way of your Son our Saviour
by the preaching of repentance:
lead us to repent according to his preaching
and, after his example,
constantly to speak the truth, boldly to rebuke vice,
and patiently to suffer for the truth's sake;
through Jesus Christ your Son our Lord,
who is alive and reigns with you,
in the unity of the Holy Spirit,
one God, now and for ever.

COLLECT

Reflection by **Margaret Whipp** | 187

Friday 25 June

Romans 13.8-end

'... put on the Lord Jesus Christ' (v.14)

Questions about civic duty and governmental responsibilities are nothing new. Paul, himself a prisoner of the state, wrote to Christians who worked out their faith within the real world. They wrestled, as we must, to balance conscientious criticism with creative engagement in the public affairs of the day.

Paul, as always, puts these debates on a higher plane. We are not, ultimately, citizens of any human empire or state. A whole new age has dawned in Christ; and we are called to live in the full light of his lordship. This means that questions of moral order are more than a matter of mere duty. We are called to live and to love with transformed minds and sanctified bodies, re-imagining our whole selves within the glorious possibilities of God's reign.

All this is powerfully symbolized in the dynamics of baptism, where a believer throws off the old rags of sin and darkness to 'put on the Lord Jesus Christ'. Outwardly as well as inwardly, through an unforgettable drama, new Christians embrace a radical reorientation of life.

Saint Augustine, famously, was converted through reading this passage. A later saint, John Wesley, was gripped by this profound invitation to put on Christ: 'a strong and beautiful expression for the most intimate union with Him, and being clothed with all the graces which were in Him'. How can we put on or be clothed in Christ today?

COLLECT

Almighty God,
you have broken the tyranny of sin
and have sent the Spirit of your Son into our hearts
    whereby we call you Father:
give us grace to dedicate our freedom to your service,
that we and all creation may be brought
    to the glorious liberty of the children of God;
through Jesus Christ your Son our Lord,
who is alive and reigns with you,
in the unity of the Holy Spirit,
one God, now and for ever.

| *Reflection by* **Margaret Whipp**

Psalms **76**, 79
Job 32
Romans 14.1-12

Saturday 26 June

Romans 14.1-12

'Why do you pass judgement?' (v.10)

Really good questions are those that cut through to the heart of the matter. It is a well-known technique to ask the question 'why?' and to keep on asking until we get right down to the root cause of a problem.

Why do Christians quarrel over different opinions? Why do we weaponize certain ideological positions? Why is it that believers hold such deep scruples about matters of behaviour? Why do we feel the need to judge one another?

Paul treads very carefully through the minefield of Jewish–gentile relationships, deftly exposing the underlying theological causes of their tensions. Beneath the strongly held views are people who are all sincerely seeking God. Their observances and their liberties, however differently understood, are all being practised 'in honour of the Lord'. So, although Paul is happy to question the rationale of Christians who come to different conclusions, he respects them enough not to scorn their underlying integrity.

What matters, and what unifies all believers in Christ, is that we present our bodies – our identities and our practices – as the living sacrifice that is holy and acceptable to God (Romans 12.1). We are not called to set ourselves up in moral judgement over one another, but to live 'before God', attuned to his grace in both our attitudes and our actions.

Instead of contentiously labelling one another, why not focus on welcoming our brothers and sisters in the Lord?

God our saviour,
look on this wounded world
in pity and in power;
hold us fast to your promises of peace
won for us by your Son,
our Saviour Jesus Christ.

COLLECT

Reflection by **Margaret Whipp** | 189

Monday 28 June

Romans 14.13-end

'... the kingdom of God is not food or drink' (v.17)

The steady rise in the number of vegans in many Western countries means there may be more people living with (largely self-imposed) dietary laws than for generations. Some vegans are reluctant to share in a meal where others are eating meat or dairy products. A judge at an employment tribunal in England identified ethical veganism as a protected belief system deserving the same legal protections as established religions.

The circumstances may be different, but the sort of issues Paul is addressing in today's reading are thus not unfamiliar today. There had been a dietary revolution among many Jewish believers in Christ. They no longer regarded certain foods as unclean. Foods once forbidden were allowed. But not all Christians had been able to travel so fast. Paul suggests those liberated from food laws should moderate their practice so that others did not think them careless or disrespectful. Don't provoke. Don't scandalize. That's Paul's message. The kingdom of God is far more important than food or drink, he argues, so do not put secondary things first. Give way to the sensibilities of others.

We live at a time when we know that what we eat and how it is produced has a bearing on the future sustainability of our planet. Those questions are not addressed here. But the call for Christians to be aware of the sensibilities of others in such a contested area remains an imperative in our own age.

COLLECT

O God, the protector of all who trust in you,
without whom nothing is strong, nothing is holy:
increase and multiply upon us your mercy;
that with you as our ruler and guide
we may so pass through things temporal
that we lose not our hold on things eternal;
grant this, heavenly Father,
for our Lord Jesus Christ's sake,
who is alive and reigns with you,
in the unity of the Holy Spirit,
one God, now and for ever.

| *Reflection by* **Graham James**

Psalms 71, 113
Isaiah 49.1-6
Acts 11.1-18

Tuesday 29 June
Peter the Apostle

Acts 11.1-18

'... who was I that I could hinder God?' (v.17)

In a pivotal address in Christian history, Peter justifies his willingness to eat with uncircumcised believers who have not embraced the traditional food laws. His critics in Jerusalem may have had no objection to gentiles finding faith in Christ. Since Jews believed in one God, they could imagine a time when gentiles would also recognize the God of Israel as their own. Even so, many of them believed that the law of Moses and all that flowed from it would still hold. United in faith with gentiles, they could not share the same table.

We may think Peter's critics were slow to catch on that Christ had broken through all these barriers between believers. Peter testifies that 'the Spirit told me ... not to make a distinction between them and us'. If both Jewish and gentile believers in Christ had been equally given 'the repentance that leads to life' how could Peter 'hinder God'? Tables must be shared.

Today, Christians still do not share the same table, especially the holy table, but for different reasons. They may be split about issues such as same-sex marriage (the Methodists in the United States have formally divided on the matter) or in relation to the validity of holy orders or a host of other causes. The Church of God does not seem to have fully taken on the significance of Peter's address. How do we still hinder God?

COLLECT

Almighty God,
who inspired your apostle Saint Peter
to confess Jesus as Christ and Son of the living God:
build up your Church upon this rock,
that in unity and peace it may proclaim one truth
and follow one Lord, your Son our Saviour Christ,
who is alive and reigns with you,
in the unity of the Holy Spirit,
one God, now and for ever.

Wednesday 30 June

Romans 15.14-21

'I have written to you rather boldly' (v.15)

There are times when we are more outspoken than we should have been, and possibly bolder than we intended. At the end of his long letter to the Christians in Rome, Paul seems to think his words may not have gone down too well. He gets personal and a little pensive. After all, he had not founded the Church in Rome or even been there. But there are a lot of gentile believers in Rome, and since Paul is God's apostle to the gentiles, he has written to them 'boldly'.

He glories in the fact that his ministry has not been built 'on someone else's foundation'. Yet in this letter he has been very direct in his instructions to fellow Christians, the vast majority of whom do not owe their faith to his preaching and witness. He is building on the foundations of others, even if he does not fully recognize it.

Two thousand years on, with a long Christian history behind us, the vast majority of those who witness to Christ today are building on substantial foundations laid by many others. Sometimes that's hard. The gospel has been preached nearly everywhere. It's been believed, rejected, half-believed, forgotten. It may be the old, old story, but it's also the newest thing around. When we find the gospel fresh and new, we are more likely to speak it boldly to others.

COLLECT

O God, the protector of all who trust in you,
without whom nothing is strong, nothing is holy:
increase and multiply upon us your mercy;
that with you as our ruler and guide
we may so pass through things temporal
that we lose not our hold on things eternal;
grant this, heavenly Father,
for our Lord Jesus Christ's sake,
who is alive and reigns with you,
in the unity of the Holy Spirit,
one God, now and for ever.

| *Reflection by* **Graham James**

Psalms 90, **92**
Job 40
Romans 15.22-end

Thursday I July

Romans 15.22-end

*'... join me in earnest prayer ... that my ministry ...
may be acceptable' (vv.30-31)*

Paul is not afraid to talk about money. His collection for the Church
in Jerusalem comes mostly from gentile converts and is to be given
to Jewish believers in Christ. He wants to build connections between
the two streams of the early Christian Church. It's a strategy for unity.

You may imagine that when Paul thinks about arriving in Jerusalem
with a bagful of money for the poor, he would anticipate being
welcomed with open arms. Yet he is apprehensive. He asks the
Romans to pray that his ministry may be acceptable and speaks of
needing to be 'rescued from the unbelievers in Judea'. Precisely what
lies behind this we don't know. It may be that sections of the
Jerusalem Church are antagonistic to the gentile mission. Paul may
be conscious that his credentials as an apostle are still not accepted
by everyone. He could be fearing that the money will be regarded as
manipulative, and not the free and unfettered gift it's intended to
be. It's a thank offering from gentile Christians for the gift of the
gospel spreading from Jerusalem. Paul is determined to go to
Jerusalem and make the gift himself. He brings his history with him.
The money may not be that easy for everyone to receive. Are we
sometimes unnecessarily suspicious of the generosity of others? And
what does that say about the spirit in which we give?

Gracious Father,
by the obedience of Jesus
you brought salvation to our wayward world:
draw us into harmony with your will,
that we may find all things restored in him,
our Saviour Jesus Christ.

COLLECT

Reflection by **Graham James** | 193

Friday 2 July

Psalms **88** (95)
Job 41
Romans 16.1-16

Romans 16.1-16

'Greet Asyncritus, Phlegon, Hermes, Patrobas, Hermas ...' (v.14)

Personal greetings were customary at the conclusion of Paul's letters. It's a surprise, though, that he names 27 Christians in these few verses. How did Paul know so many people in Rome, all part of a Church he had never visited? It's been suggested that this list was transferred from another letter, perhaps to Ephesus, where Paul had lived for a long time. There seems little reason to think so. It's more likely that this chapter shows how quickly the Christian Church became international and was also one in which women were given honour.

After commending Phoebe, a deacon on her way to Rome, Paul greets Prisca and Aquila. They were expelled from Rome under an edict of Claudius (Acts 18.2) and made their way to Corinth and Ephesus. They are now in Rome again where they host a congregation in their house. People of means did travel in the Roman Empire. Christians could do so without substantial means since they would find a community to receive and support them in the major centres. Paul greets everyone here as part of the same family, members one of another in the body of Christ. Our allegiance to local church congregations may be narrower than the breadth of belonging demonstrated here. In these greetings we see how quickly the Church of God transcended boundaries of gender, background and location. Would the same be said of the churches to which we belong today?

COLLECT

O God, the protector of all who trust in you,
without whom nothing is strong, nothing is holy:
increase and multiply upon us your mercy;
that with you as our ruler and guide
we may so pass through things temporal
that we lose not our hold on things eternal;
grant this, heavenly Father,
for our Lord Jesus Christ's sake,
who is alive and reigns with you,
in the unity of the Holy Spirit,
one God, now and for ever.

194 | *Reflection by* **Graham James**

Psalms 92, 146
2 Samuel 15.17-21
or Ecclesiasticus 2
John 11.1-16

Saturday 3 July
Thomas the Apostle

John 11.1-16
'Let us also go, that we may die with him'. (v.16)

In her poem *Moveable Feast*, Ann Lewin ponders what Thomas would make of his feast day being moved from December 21st (in the Book of Common Prayer) to July 3rd (in the Common Worship calendar). She thinks Thomas is better represented by a flicker of light on the longest and darkest day (at least in the Northern Hemisphere) rather than the full blaze of midsummer sunshine.

Today's reading suggests Ann Lewin's point is well made. Thomas bleakly proposes to the rest of the disciples that they should all die with Jesus. He says this because Jesus proposes they return to Judea, which they left when some of his enemies wanted to stone Jesus to death. Jesus has been teaching on the other side of the Jordan near where John the Baptist ministered. Thomas can only foresee disaster if they go back. Even so, he believes the disciples should stick with Jesus to the very end. 'Let's all die together' shows Thomas is willing to pay the ultimate price. There are no doubts here.

Thomas' words have been described as 'morose'. They are gloomy, but also an expression of the deepest devotion – a willingness to sacrifice everything, even life itself, for the Lord's sake. That is what happens to Thomas many years later – and a blaze of light still shines from him and all the early martyrs. A flicker of light becomes midsummer glory. Thomas deserves both feasts.

COLLECT

Almighty and eternal God,
who, for the firmer foundation of our faith,
allowed your holy apostle Thomas
to doubt the resurrection of your Son
till word and sight convinced him:
grant to us, who have not seen, that we also may believe
and so confess Christ as our Lord and our God;
who is alive and reigns with you,
in the unity of the Holy Spirit,
one God, now and for ever.

Reflection by **Graham James**

Monday 5 July

Psalms **98**, 99, 101
Ezekiel 1.1-14
2 Corinthians 1.1-14

2 Corinthians 1.1-14
'... we were so ... crushed that we despaired of life' (v.8)

Michael Thompson, a New Testament scholar, once described Corinth in the mid-first century AD as 'something like New York, Los Angeles and Las Vegas all rolled into one'. Re-founded in 44 BC as a Roman colony, Corinth was situated on trade routes from the Western Empire to Asia and between northern and southern Greece. It quickly became prosperous and drew many ambitious people, as well as being a place exceedingly tolerant of uninhibited sexual behaviour. It may be a surprise that Corinth proved fertile ground for the gospel, although its Church was disputatious and divided.

The ancient world liked leaders to have strength and stature. That's not so different from today. Paul does not boast of his strength. He claims that through his sufferings and despair he has received the grace of Christ. He's been crushed, and that's one of his chief qualifications to preach the cross of Christ. The idea that God's power is revealed in human weakness could not have been further from what passed for wisdom in Corinth at the time.

Most churches today still want strong and capable people to join them (and certainly to lead them). But church communities do attract the crushed and despairing, and that's a sign of the gospel at work. Are we any better at seeing God revealed in human weakness today than the people of Corinth all those years ago?

COLLECT

Almighty and everlasting God,
by whose Spirit the whole body of the Church
    is governed and sanctified:
hear our prayer which we offer for all your faithful people,
that in their vocation and ministry
they may serve you in holiness and truth
to the glory of your name;
through our Lord and Saviour Jesus Christ,
who is alive and reigns with you,
in the unity of the Holy Spirit,
one God, now and for ever.

Reflection by **Graham James**

Psalm **106*** (*or* 103)
Ezekiel 1.15 – 2.2
2 Corinthians 1.15 – 2.4

Tuesday 6 July

2 Corinthians 1.15 – 2.4
'...we say the 'Amen', to the glory of God' (v.20)

'Amen' is one of the very few Hebrew words to have leapfrogged untranslated from ancient Israel to the present day. Amen never fell captive to suspicion in periods of division and reformation. When battles raged about the use of the vernacular in worship, no one sought to translate Amen. The word finds its home in all Christian traditions as well as Judaism. Only Hosanna and Alleluia may claim something similar. Like Amen, they are also words of emphatic praise.

It was when David had brought the Ark of the Covenant back to Jerusalem that the choir sang a psalm and we read 'all the people said "Amen!"' (1 Chronicles 16.36). Amen is said at the end of countless prayers. As a child, I was taught it meant 'so be it'. That weak phrase shows why it's best left untranslated. Amen's origin in Hebrew is in a verb meaning 'to support' or 'to make firm'. Amen conveys reliability and truth. In his teaching in the Gospels, Jesus frequently uses Amen at the beginning of his most important sayings. Perhaps it's because we are so used to Amen at the end of prayers that, when Jesus says it, we do translate it as 'truly' or 'verily'. It would be better left untranslated there too.

Paul tells the Corinthians that Jesus is the Amen of God, in whom all the promises of God are fulfilled – firmly, reliably, truly. Amen to that.

Almighty God,
send down upon your Church
the riches of your Spirit,
and kindle in all who minister the gospel
your countless gifts of grace;
through Jesus Christ our Lord.

COLLECT

Wednesday 7 July

Psalms 110, 111, 112
Ezekiel 2.3 – 3.11
2 Corinthians 2.5-end

2 Corinthians 2.5-end

'...we are the aroma of Christ' (v.15)

'Aroma' is an unusual metaphor for Christians, but Paul is prompted to use it since he has spoken of Christ leading his followers in 'triumphal procession'. Such processions were common in the ancient world, and incense was frequently burned at them. Victors in a war would lead their forlorn captives through conquered territory to demonstrate their triumph. The incense was the aroma of victory. For Paul, the victory of Christ on the cross was a very different sort of triumph for those with eyes to see it and noses to smell it. Men and women must determine for themselves whether Christ is a life-giving aroma or a deadly fume. Since the salvation of all is dependent on the preaching of the cross, it's no surprise Paul wonders 'Who is sufficient for these things?'

Despite this talk of aromas there is no mention of the use of incense in early Christian worship. Its use both in the sacrificial worship in the Temple and within pagan rituals, including being offered before the Roman Emperor as a sign of his divinity, would have rendered it problematic in the early Christian decades. The imagery was so powerful, though, that we know Christians began to use incense in worship from the fourth century onwards. Incense remains both a reminder of prayers offered to God and that Christ offers us the fragrance of eternal life.

COLLECT

Almighty and everlasting God,
by whose Spirit the whole body of the Church
    is governed and sanctified:
hear our prayer which we offer for all your faithful people,
that in their vocation and ministry
they may serve you in holiness and truth
to the glory of your name;
through our Lord and Saviour Jesus Christ,
who is alive and reigns with you,
in the unity of the Holy Spirit,
one God, now and for ever.

| *Reflection by* **Graham James**

Psalms 113, **115**
Ezekiel 3.12-end
2 Corinthians 3

Thursday 8 July

2 Corinthians 3

'...with unveiled faces, seeing the glory of the Lord' (v.18)

On a holiday in the Lake District, I visited the Lakeland Motor Museum. I expected to see vintage and classic cars but was surprised to find cars popular in the UK from a few decades ago, such as the Metro. Two million were built, but scarcely any survive. There were also bubble cars, which I recalled from my childhood, and an Austin Allegro, one of the least regarded cars of all time. It was gleaming and in sparkling condition, given a new sheen and dignity.

It's probably an occupational hazard for clergy to have theological experiences in unlikely places. At the motor museum I was reminded that what is commonplace and disregarded, unheralded and even despised, may shine with a lustre that is glorious, especially when cared for and cherished. True for cars. True for human beings too.

We speak of new models of cars being unveiled. Here Paul speaks of the unveiled faces of followers of Christ. The full glory of God has been revealed in Jesus Christ. His glory should be reflected in the faces of those who believe in him. But you do not need to be brand new or unblemished to reveal the glory of the Lord. Some of those whose faces shine brightest are those who have known suffering, been depressed or acknowledged their weaknesses and failures. That's when God gets a chance to restore and remake us. We can then gleam with gospel joy.

Almighty God,
send down upon your Church
the riches of your Spirit,
and kindle in all who minister the gospel
your countless gifts of grace;
through Jesus Christ our Lord.

COLLECT

Reflection by **Graham James** | 199

Friday 9 July

2 Corinthians 4

'... we have this treasure in clay jars' (v.7)

Clay pottery – what we would now call earthenware – was commonplace in the first century. Used for domestic purposes in almost every home, clay jars were cheap but fragile.

Paul compares himself and his companions in ministry to these easily broken vessels. It's evident from this part of his letter to the Corinthians that Paul has had some bad reverses in his ministry. We can only guess what they were, but he says he has been afflicted, perplexed, persecuted and struck down. It does not seem he is exaggerating for effect. Paul was probably in his fifties by the time he wrote this letter so he may well have been conscious of his own body weakening and wearing out too. The Corinthians lived in a culture where leaders were expected to show power and control, working from a position of strength. It seems that some of them are critical of Paul because he has had so many disappointments and problems in his ministry.

When churches search for new clergy and write profiles of the qualities they want in their new ministers or priests, they frequently want 'strong leaders'. I've never seen a congregation ask for a broken vessel or fragile jar to lead them. But that is what churches usually get. Sometimes, as Paul testifies, it is the most cracked pots who know the value of the treasure of the gospel they contain and are keenest to share it.

COLLECT

Almighty and everlasting God,
by whose Spirit the whole body of the Church
   is governed and sanctified:
hear our prayer which we offer for all your faithful people,
that in their vocation and ministry
they may serve you in holiness and truth
to the glory of your name;
through our Lord and Saviour Jesus Christ,
who is alive and reigns with you,
in the unity of the Holy Spirit,
one God, now and for ever.

| *Reflection by* **Graham James**

Saturday 10 July

2 Corinthians 5

'... we are ambassadors for Christ' (v.20)

Since Paul had compared himself and his companions to clay pots of little value, it's a surprise to hear him now claiming the title of 'ambassador'. Then, as now, ambassadors were frequently well-regarded dignitaries who were entrusted with a mission and message on behalf of an even more superior person or state. Ambassadors have no purpose without the person, country or entity they represent and serve. But the assignment they are given has always carried some risk. Paul will have known that envoys from other states could be abused, and occasionally even killed. The Spartans, for example, treated them badly. So, modern concepts of diplomatic immunity do not lie behind the image Paul uses here. Ambassadors of Christ are likely to suffer as Christ did, and even face death because of him.

In our own age, we have 'brand ambassadors' or 'celebrity ambassadors'. It is their personal fame, beauty or glory that is meant to add lustre to the products or causes they support. It's a complete reversal of what Paul speaks about here. He tells the Corinthians that their behaviour and attitudes must be shaped by Jesus Christ who suffered and died for all. They cannot separate themselves from Christ. The responsibility to represent the Lord is one for every minute of every day and may well mean suffering with and for him. How do we manage as ambassadors of Christ?

Almighty God,
send down upon your Church
the riches of your Spirit,
and kindle in all who minister the gospel
your countless gifts of grace;
through Jesus Christ our Lord.

COLLECT

Monday 12 July

2 Corinthians 6.1 – 7.1

'As we work together with him' (6.1)

The idea that we are 'co-workers' with God turns up a number of times in the Letters of Paul: in 1 and 2 Corinthians, and 1 Thessalonians. This has proved to be controversial for some, which surprises me, given that we see God drawing human beings into his work right across the Bible. Commentators have tried to deny that the other passages I mentioned really say this, but with the one before us today, there really is no other way to read it: 'we work together with him', that is with God.

This tells us something about the grace of God. Most of all, it involves God doing for us what we could not do for ourselves. That is the heart of the Christian message of salvation. God does not leave it at that, however. As a second aspect of grace, God chooses to do with us, and through us, what God could have done alone, and without us. God – who needs nothing and no one, and can do all things – makes us 'co-workers'. There is something remarkably dignifying about that.

It all starts with Jesus. In him, we see most perfectly that God chose not to redeem us without us, taking our nature upon him, so as to accomplish the salvation of human beings through a human being, the man who was God: Jesus of Nazareth. Cardinal Newman captured this particularly well:

> *O loving wisdom of our God,*
> *When all was sin and shame,*
> *He, the last Adam, to the fight*
> *And to the rescue came.*

COLLECT

Merciful God,
you have prepared for those who love you
such good things as pass our understanding:
pour into our hearts such love toward you
that we, loving you in all things and above all things,
may obtain your promises,
which exceed all that we can desire;
through Jesus Christ your Son our Lord,
who is alive and reigns with you,
in the unity of the Holy Spirit,
one God, now and for ever.

202 | *Reflection by* **Andrew Davison**

2 Corinthians 7.2-end

'Make room in your hearts for us' (v.2)

'Make room in your hearts for us', Paul writes. The Greek does not have 'in your hearts', but the translators were right to read it that way: Paul wants his readers to make room for him in their thought and affections. That remains no purely inward matter, however. Paul soon shows what this 'having room for' looks like: it means living interconnected lives, and being willing to suffer for one another, even to die.

Paul's word for 'making room' comes from a cluster of words that would later give us some of the most sublime theology ever written about God or about Christ. With it, theologians have written about the Persons of the Trinity giving place to each other, or dwelling in one another, and about the divine and human natures of Christ doing the same.

The technical word, with its origin close to 'making room', is 'perichoresis'. It has come into its own for thinking about the most elevated theological topics we can imagine – about the Trinity and the natures of Christ – but it is good to be reminded that it grows out of earthy, practical, bodily images. That suggests that we can enter into theological understanding through action, as well as through study. We have a sense of what these exalted mysteries mean not only by reading works of scholarship, but also by entering into them actively: by 'making room' for one another, and making space for these truths in our lives. The same word gives us 'room for' or 'holding' in Mark 2.2 and John 2.6.

Creator God,
you made us all in your image:
may we discern you in all that we see,
and serve you in all that we do;
through Jesus Christ our Lord.

COLLECT

Wednesday 14 July

Psalm 119.153-end
Ezekiel 12.1-16
2 Corinthians 8.1-15

2 Corinthians 8.1-15

'... by his poverty you might become rich' (v.9)

There is an exchange at the heart of our reading today: 'though he was rich, yet for your sakes he became poor, so that by his poverty you might become rich.' What hangs on that word 'by'? According to one view, we might think it operates somewhat at arm's length. God would have achieved something for us (becoming rich), and Christ's poverty would have been the means, but no more than that: poverty would be God's instrument, to be taken up, and then laid down.

There is, however, a second way to look at this word 'by', which would not see poverty set aside so easily. Looked at this second way, Christ's poverty would be so much part of how God makes us rich that we are called to share in it. In the first sense, the word 'by' applies only to Christ; in the second sense, 'by' applies also to us.

There can be no doubt that Christianity at its wisest and deepest has taken the second line more than the first. Christ did not simply become poor so that we would not have to; rather, Christ's poverty is part of our riches. Christ's poverty does not affect us at arm's length. It is an invitation for us to learn simplicity, to have our priorities reordered. That too is part of the good news.

COLLECT

Merciful God,
you have prepared for those who love you
such good things as pass our understanding:
pour into our hearts such love toward you
that we, loving you in all things and above all things,
may obtain your promises,
which exceed all that we can desire;
through Jesus Christ your Son our Lord,
who is alive and reigns with you,
in the unity of the Holy Spirit,
one God, now and for ever.

| *Reflection by* **Andrew Davison**

Psalms **143**, 146
Ezekiel 12.17-end
2 Corinthians 8.16 – 9.5

Thursday 15 July

2 Corinthians 8.16 – 9.5

*'God who put in the heart of Titus the same eagerness for you
that I myself have' (8.16)*

As we saw a couple of days ago, the idea of working together with God has sometimes been controversial, although it is clearly scriptural. The section of 2 Corinthians before us today might strike us as rather distant from us, dealing as it does with various particularities of Paul's situation and of early Christian congregations. As an illustration of the dynamic of 'working together', however, which runs through this passage, it ought to hold our attention, reminding us that cooperation is central to the Christian life.

Starting towards the end, we have financial cooperation between churches, which Paul handles with delicacy. He writes that there is no need to mention the matter at all, and then devotes a good many words to it (more than 150 in our translation). In the middle of the passage, we have a closer sharing, in the cooperation of Paul and Titus, as his 'co-worker' in the service of the Corinthians. In the opening sentences, we find a cooperation more intimate still: that cooperation between God and God's servants, here with Titus. That provides an excellent example of how God draws us into his works, such that the work is both all God's, and also fully our own. In the first way, we read that God 'put [it] in the heart of Titus' to work with eagerness. In the second sense, the service Titus renders the Corinthians is offered 'of his own accord'.

Creator God,
you made us all in your image:
may we discern you in all that we see,
and serve you in all that we do;
through Jesus Christ our Lord.

COLLECT

Friday 16 July

Psalms 142, **144**
Ezekiel 13.1-16
2 Corinthians 9.6-end

2 Corinthians 9.6-end

'... the one who sows bountifully will also reap bountifully' (v.6)

Any gardener or farmer could tell us that 'the one who sows sparingly will also reap sparingly, and the one who sows bountifully will also reap bountifully'. As a statement, it is obvious and straightforward. The novelty, however, in Paul's hands, is that he associates all this with giving away.

This giving away is bountiful, and the Greek word for 'bountifully' here is itself rich, or bountiful. It means, among other things, 'for a blessing' or with adulation or praise. We are to give for the sake of blessing, so that we will receive blessedly. Taken that way, however, Paul's theology can begin to look like worldly wisdom, like a rule of investment, a principal of hard-nosed finance.

Turning Christianity into a financial masterplan seems unworthy, out of keeping with the simplicity of Christ (although, on the other hand, neither should we glorify hardship or destitution). The problem is created if we approach all of this as if what we have were our own, something we possess, to be multiplied by clever means, including cooperation in some divine dividend scheme. Better, from a theological perspective, to see that we are always already recipients. We are beneficiaries, before anything that we can do or give. I cannot, therefore, give to God as if to make God my debtor in a shrewd transaction. The generosity of God has always come first.

COLLECT

Merciful God,
you have prepared for those who love you
such good things as pass our understanding:
pour into our hearts such love toward you
that we, loving you in all things and above all things,
may obtain your promises,
which exceed all that we can desire;
through Jesus Christ your Son our Lord,
who is alive and reigns with you,
in the unity of the Holy Spirit,
one God, now and for ever.

| *Reflection by* **Andrew Davison**

Psalm 147
Ezekiel 14.1-11
2 Corinthians 10

Saturday 17 July

2 Corinthians 10

'Let the one who boasts, boast in the Lord' (v.17)

This is not among Paul's clearest passages of writing, but this torrent of prose is witness to the depths of his care for the Corinthian church. Absent from them, Paul is aware of newcomers on the scene of church leadership who are trying to take authority for the congregations he so loves: congregations that these newcomers did not found themselves. What is more, these leaders are boasting about their abilities, and running Paul down, not least with the crushing line: 'His letters are weighty and strong, but his bodily presence is weak, and his speech contemptible.'

There is a good deal of heightened emotion here, and plenty of rhetoric, and we might also think that the situation is rather specific and unlike our own. Paul, however, sets out some maxims that apply far more widely, which we might take to heart: let the overarching principle, in dealing with others, be to build up, not to pull down; beware exalting ourselves, but also do not be ashamed; let your confidence be in God, and let God be the one whose commendation we seek; acknowledge that we have a sphere, or field, and look to do what is praiseworthy within that; don't be jealous of the success of others, elsewhere; sometimes in dealing with arrogant people, a little sarcasm does not go amiss.

Creator God,
you made us all in your image:
may we discern you in all that we see,
and serve you in all that we do;
through Jesus Christ our Lord.

COLLECT

Monday 19 July

2 Corinthians 11.1-15
'I feel a divine jealousy for you' (v.2)

We are not used to seeing jealousy approached in positive terms. It is, after all, one of the seven deadly sins. Paul, however, claims to be jealous unabashedly, and goes further still: he writes about 'divine jealousy', which suggests that there is something like jealousy in God, something that Paul then shares, or demonstrates.

To understand what is going on, it might be useful to look at the word more closely. In English, we can note that 'jealous' and 'zealous' are closely related, and wherever we come across jealous used in a positive way, it is likely to do with zeal. In Greek, the word is *zēlóō*, which at root comes down to something like to boiling, whether boiling love or boiling anger. Scholars who study the origins of words suggest that the root might be a sound that like that of boiling water, although I find that a little far-fetched.

There is nothing wrong with feeling a boiling or flaming love, or even a boiling or flaming anger, if the anger is just, and as long as we do not let the love or zeal master us in ways that lead us to act unwisely or unfairly. There is something in God that is pure: a perfect zeal. Paul shows that we can enter into that well, although we know that we can also follow that path detrimentally. Zeal, or 'jealousy' in this sense, is not wrong in itself, but it can go wrong, so in zeal we need to be wise.

COLLECT

Lord of all power and might,
the author and giver of all good things:
graft in our hearts the love of your name,
increase in us true religion,
nourish us with all goodness,
and of your great mercy keep us in the same;
through Jesus Christ your Son our Lord,
who is alive and reigns with you,
in the unity of the Holy Spirit,
one God, now and for ever.

Reflection by **Andrew Davison**

Psalms **5**, 6 (8)
Ezekiel 18.1-20
2 Corinthians 11.16-end

Tuesday 20 July

2 Corinthians 11.16-end

'... in danger from rivers, danger from bandits, danger from my own people, danger from Gentiles, danger in the city, danger in the wilderness' (v.26)

Not for the first time in reading 2 Corinthians, we can stop simply to admire the quality of Paul's writing. He is a particular master when it comes to lists. First, we have lists of comparisons, contrasting himself with the claims of the teachers or 'apostles' whose work opposes his own. Then, moving seamlessly on, we have a list of Paul's hardships, sometimes counted out, sometimes not, later set out with the repeated, tolling note of 'danger'. He even picks up the pace of the writing as the passage draws on. Not a few of the techniques of ancient rhetoric are on display here, in fine style.

Paul, however, does not go about this out of a spirit of one-upmanship, or out of self-pity, or self-indulgence (or, if perhaps we discern just a little of that, we can let Paul off, given what he has been through). Instead, Paul has a theological point to make, although that will become clearer over the page: that in all of this God is good and sufficient, that God is faithful and in control. Paul crowns the passage by hinting at the idea that will come up more fully in the next chapter: that this is all the more evident when Paul is weak, not when he is strong.

COLLECT

Generous God,
you give us gifts and make them grow:
though our faith is small as mustard seed,
make it grow to your glory
and the flourishing of your kingdom;
through Jesus Christ our Lord.

Reflection by **Andrew Davison** | 209

Wednesday 21 July

Psalm 119.1-32
Ezekiel 18.21-32
2 Corinthians 12

2 Corinthians 12

'I know a person in Christ who fourteen years ago was caught up to the third heaven' (v.2)

2 Corinthians 12 offers a theological commentary on what has just gone before, underlining that Paul has known great hardship and struggle, but that God's strength has sustained him and achieved great things, even in Paul's weakness. This passage is also remarkable on its own terms, with its sudden leap quite out of parochial Corinthian matters into heavenly visions, out of this world altogether, indeed, and into the third heaven.

There is a peculiar ambiguity to this section of the letter, in that Paul does not name the person whose revelations he describes here, who travels into the heavens. He talks about him in the third person: 'I know a person … On behalf of such a one I will boast, but on my own behalf I will not boast, except of my weaknesses.' Few commentators, however, doubt that the person Paul is concerned with here is Paul himself.

Paul speaks elliptically, it would seem, out of humility. 'If I must boast, I will boast of the things that show my weakness', we read yesterday, so not the heavenly visions here, but rather the thorn in the flesh. The overarching theme is the faithfulness and sufficiency of God, expressed in one of the few phrases attributed directly to Jesus outside the Gospels, 'My grace is sufficient for you, for power is made perfect in weakness.'

COLLECT

Lord of all power and might,
the author and giver of all good things:
graft in our hearts the love of your name,
increase in us true religion,
nourish us with all goodness,
and of your great mercy keep us in the same;
through Jesus Christ your Son our Lord,
who is alive and reigns with you,
in the unity of the Holy Spirit,
one God, now and for ever.

| *Reflection by* **Andrew Davison**

Psalms 30, 32, 150
1 Samuel 16.14-end
Luke 8.1-3

Thursday 22 July
Mary Magdalene

Luke 8.1-3

'Mary, called Magdalene, from whom seven demons had gone out'
(v.2)

Mary Magdalene appears in all four Gospels. We have this biographical detail from Luke, and a string of references about her place near the crucifixion, at Christ's burial and as a witness to his resurrection. Historically, she has been associated with the woman – a repentant prostitute – who anointed Jesus before his Passion, wiping his feet with her hair. For some commentators, severing that link is the priority in talking about Mary Magdalene, for others less so. That anointing may not be part of her story, but it is of a piece with a figure who comes to us characterized by reform and liberation (those demons) and great love (her faithfulness at the end of Christ's life, and beyond).

This has made her a popular saint. Perhaps the most arresting passage about Mary comes in John, where she mistakes the risen Christ for a gardener and, when she recognizes him, tries to cling to him. When the National Gallery in London was evacuated during the Second World War, one painting was left behind, for the sake of the morale of the city. There was a risk that it would be destroyed, but the risk was worth it, since it would offer solace and inspiration to a city that had been bombarded. By popular demand, the first painting to be displayed was Titian's depiction of Mary encountering the Risen Christ. It brought hope, that single painting in an enormous gallery, a witness amidst death to the resurrection.

Almighty God,
whose Son restored Mary Magdalene to health of mind
and body
and called her to be a witness to his resurrection:
forgive our sins and heal us by your grace,
that we may serve you in the power of his risen life;
who is alive and reigns with you,
in the unity of the Holy Spirit,
one God, now and for ever.

COLLECT

Reflection by **Andrew Davison** | 211

Friday 23 July

James 1.1-11

'James, a servant of God and of the Lord Jesus Christ' (v.1)

The Book of Esther, in the Old Testament, tells the story of God's deliverance of the Hebrews through the labours of the Jewish Queen of Persia. Famously, though, the book does not mention God at all. There is something a little similar about the Letter of James. It distils much of what lies at the heart of a Christian approach to life, and yet it hardly mentions Christ at all, beyond setting out the credentials of the author at the beginning, and a brief mention in passing in chapter 2.

That need not trouble us. No reader, or writer, of the texts of the Early Church would have expected any particular document to do all the work that could be done, and neither should we. Some texts are biographical, some doctrinal and some about how to live; some do several things, but with an emphasis more on one than another. The Letter of James may not mention Jesus a great deal, or recount his life, but it brings together much that he taught and exemplified, and provides some invaluable commentary upon it. As a Letter, the way it goes about things might remind us of a saying from Matthew's Gospel: 'Not everyone who says to me, "Lord, Lord", will enter the kingdom of heaven, but only one who does the will of my Father in heaven.' (Matthew 7.21)

COLLECT

Lord of all power and might,
the author and giver of all good things:
graft in our hearts the love of your name,
increase in us true religion,
nourish us with all goodness,
and of your great mercy keep us in the same;
through Jesus Christ your Son our Lord,
who is alive and reigns with you,
in the unity of the Holy Spirit,
one God, now and for ever.

| *Reflection by* **Andrew Davison**

Psalms 20, 21, **23**
Ezekiel 24.15-end
James 1.12-end

Saturday 24 July

James 1.12-end

*'Every generous act of giving, with every perfect gift,
is from above' (v.17)*

The writer and lay theologian G. K. Chesterton summed up the basis for his faith in terms of gift. The world, he wrote – and his life, all that he had, everything he encountered – struck him as a wonderful gift. And gifts, he went on to say, seem to imply a giver.

That theme of gift, and of God as the supreme giver, finds unsurpassed expression in the first chapter of the Letter of James: 'Every generous act of giving, with every perfect gift, is from above, coming down from the Father of lights, with whom there is no variation or shadow due to change.' James recognizes God not only as the author of gifts, but also of every act of giving. That is important, since the act of giving and the identity of the giver are usually what make a particular gift so precious to us.

These lines from James offer a magnificent endorsement of all that is good about the world around us: goods both natural and social, human and non-human, familiar and friendly. We need not deny any of that as Christians, or downplay them – either as gifts, or as acts of giving – as if that would 'make room' for God, or give God glory. It is in recognizing all that as good, as real, substantial, excellent – 'perfect' even – that we give place and honour to God, as the giver behind all gifts, and all gift-giving. These are true gifts, truly given, by the truly good God.

Generous God,
you give us gifts and make them grow:
though our faith is small as mustard seed,
make it grow to your glory
and the flourishing of your kingdom;
through Jesus Christ our Lord.

COLLECT

Monday 26 July

Psalms 27, **30**
Ezekiel 28.1-19
James 2.1-13

James 2.1-13

'... you have dishonoured the poor' (v.6)

Three centuries after James wrote his letter, the Roman emperor Julian the Apostate was determined to revive the traditional worship of pagan gods, and suppressed Christianity in order to achieve that. In a reproving letter to his high priest Arsacius, he lamented that although shrine worship was widespread its adherents did not match that devotion with social action. No wonder people were converting to Christianity, he wrote, because, 'those impious Galileans support not only their own poor but ours as well – it is obvious to everyone that we are not helping our own people.'

Why should goodness be indiscriminate? Because favouring one person over another is an 'evil thought' that should have no place whatever in the thinking of a believer in Jesus. Because choosing to put your energy into addressing poverty is an echo of God's 'choice' of the poor as examples of how we should depend on him in faith. Because abusing the power that wealth brings is a 'blasphemy' against Christ, who made himself poor on behalf of humankind.

I have to confess to considering that I have a better-than-average morality. I am, after all, neither a murderer nor an adulterer. It is therefore a severe challenge to realize that something as commonplace as favouritism places me under the judgement of God. My only hope lies in the fact that, because of Jesus, 'mercy triumphs over judgement'.

COLLECT

Almighty Lord and everlasting God,
we beseech you to direct, sanctify and govern
    both our hearts and bodies
in the ways of your laws   ·
    and the works of your commandments;
that through your most mighty protection, both here and ever,
we may be preserved in body and soul;
through our Lord and Saviour Jesus Christ,
who is alive and reigns with you,
in the unity of the Holy Spirit,
one God, now and for ever.

| *Reflection by* **Peter Graystone**

Tuesday 27 July

James 2.14-end

'... faith by itself, if it has no works, is dead' (v.17)

Well, this is a bit rude. It's unusual for one of the writers of the Bible to address you as 'dimwit', so listen up!

What does it mean to have life? A person on a life-support machine is technically alive, but not engaging with the world in any meaningful way. Likewise, a person who believes in God but doesn't allow that to impact on their action on behalf of those who are in need is technically a Christian but isn't fully alive to the richness of faith.

Our worship and our work on behalf of those who are vulnerable or poor are not alternatives. Both are imperative as expressions of our relationship with God. Apathy about suffering in our world or in our nation is incompatible with a Christian faith. It renders all we believe about Jesus meaningless. After all, the devil believes in God, but you could hardly call him a champion of social justice!

As examples of people whose life-changing actions validated their faith James cites Rahab and Abraham. Rahab was neither a worshipper of God nor virtuous, but she protected Jewish spies who were using her brothel when Canaanite soldiers came searching for them. Abraham trusted that God would not take his son from him, and his actions earned him the name 'friend of God'.

Lord God,
your Son left the riches of heaven
and became poor for our sake:
when we prosper save us from pride,
when we are needy save us from despair,
that we may trust in you alone;
through Jesus Christ our Lord.

COLLECT

Wednesday 28 July

James 3

'... no one can tame the tongue' (v.8)

Following the service, the vicar had invited the bishop to Sunday lunch. She asked him to say grace, but the bishop replied, 'Why don't we let your young son Charlie say grace?'

Charles froze: 'I don't know what to say.'

'Don't worry,' said the vicar. 'Just say exactly what Dad said to God at breakfast this morning.'

'Oh that's easy,' said the boy, shutting his eyes. 'O God, is it today that boring old man's coming to lunch?'

There are warnings in this chapter (and in the joke) for three groups: teachers, influential people, and anyone who has a tongue. Don't aspire to teach others about the Christian faith unless your life measures up to what you preach. Be conscious of the impact you make on those who depend on you because even small things, like a bridle or a rudder, can have a big impact. And be careful what you say because unchecked words can burn people.

James offers a contrasting way to teach, to lead and to speak. It is characterized by gentleness, which is the way true wisdom is manifested. Verse 17 lists seven more qualities against which our actions can be measured to test whether they are wise. It is worth identifying the seven and dwelling on each for a while.

COLLECT

Almighty Lord and everlasting God,
we beseech you to direct, sanctify and govern
    both our hearts and bodies
in the ways of your laws
    and the works of your commandments;
that through your most mighty protection, both here and ever,
we may be preserved in body and soul;
through our Lord and Saviour Jesus Christ,
who is alive and reigns with you,
in the unity of the Holy Spirit,
one God, now and for ever.

| *Reflection by* **Peter Graystone**

Psalm **37***
Ezekiel 34.1-16
James 4.1-12

Thursday 29 July

James 4.1-12

'Draw near to God, and he will draw near to you' (v.8)

The words that are spoken during a cigarette break about an office colleague who is safely out of earshot. The comparisons that are made in the playground when technology, brands and bodies are lusted over. The gossip that is spread at the church door disguised as something that needs prayer. We know all about cravings, disputes and judgement of neighbours. They seem trivial, but James uses the language of warfare and terrorism to condemn them. They happen, he writes, because we accept in ourselves in petty ways things that we abhor globally.

The world's standards of self-interest can even permeate our prayers. Our instincts are to pray for what we want God to do for us rather than what we want God to do with us.

There are choices to be made. For humility and against pride. For God and against evil. For repentance and against wrongdoing. For integrity and against judgement. In the extraordinary economy of God, humility is a route to victory. Those who are brought to the verge of tears by awareness of their own shortcomings find God drawing close to them. To 'mourn and weep' is the start of a process in which God gives grace, sins are forgiven, and your spirits can rise as high as heaven.

Lord God,
your Son left the riches of heaven
and became poor for our sake:
when we prosper save us from pride,
when we are needy save us from despair,
that we may trust in you alone;
through Jesus Christ our Lord.

COLLECT

Friday 30 July

Psalm **31**
Ezekiel 34.17-end
James 4.13 – 5.6

James 4.13 – 5.6

'If the Lord wishes, we will live and do this' (4.15)

My smartphone is five years old. In human years that ages it akin to Methuselah. The inbuilt obsolescence of its battery means that it can now only just last through a day without failing. Its life is effectively over. However, it will take 500,000 years to biodegrade. I'm afraid I didn't think about that when I bought it.

Its component parts come from many countries. Some are mined in conflict zones where the use of child or slave labour is reputed to finance civil war. The parts are assembled in regions that are reported to have lamentably poor working standards and in factories where wages keep people barely above poverty. I'm afraid I didn't think of that either.

The world needs a new set of attitudes if trade and industry are to be conducted as 'the Lord wishes'. And frankly, so do I. There was once a time when we did not know what impact our actions were having on the environment, on the world's poorest communities, and on our grandchildren's chance of survival. Now that we know, doing nothing about it is sin.

Across the ages, James calls to us asking how we can possibly claim not to have known these things when he made them so clear at the end of the first century. God is not blind to the world's suffering. Our future is in his hands, and justice will be done.

COLLECT

Almighty Lord and everlasting God,
we beseech you to direct, sanctify and govern
    both our hearts and bodies
in the ways of your laws
    and the works of your commandments;
that through your most mighty protection, both here and ever,
we may be preserved in body and soul;
through our Lord and Saviour Jesus Christ,
who is alive and reigns with you,
in the unity of the Holy Spirit,
one God, now and for ever.

218 | *Reflection by* **Peter Graystone**

James 5.7-end
'Be patient' (v.7)

The readings of the past few days have brought to our attention those who have been oppressed, impoverished or humiliated by the actions of the wealthy. What if they are tempted to take revenge? 'Be patient,' writes James (or in the original, 'Have restraint', v.8). Poverty does not excuse violence. Those who suffer can take strength from knowing that Christ will come as the bringer of ultimate justice. The coming of the Judge will be greeted with exultation by anyone whose child has died from a curable disease, or whose land is flooded because industrialization has changed the climate, or who is hungry because work is underpaid or non-existent.

There is an alternative to taking the law into your own hands. What part does prayer play in the experience of those who are in distress? It is powerful and effective in all circumstances. There is an uncomfortable suggestion here that the illness of a prayerful person will always be healed. Our experience is that the truth is more complex. Through the centuries, the testimony of faithful Christians is that God sometimes responds to prayer by restoring health, sometimes a cure is withheld until the perfect healing of death, and sometimes the knowledge of being in the forgiving care of God brings peace and grace despite continuing illness. This is mighty good news for the poor, the sick, the happy, the fallible ... and me.

Lord God,
your Son left the riches of heaven
and became poor for our sake:
when we prosper save us from pride,
when we are needy save us from despair,
that we may trust in you alone;
through Jesus Christ our Lord.

COLLECT

Monday 2 August

Mark 1.1-13

'Prepare the way of the Lord' (v.3)

In the third decade of the first century, the Jews, made wretched by the Roman occupation of their land, were hungry for hope. There was a growing longing for the ancient tradition of prophecy to be revived. The writer Malachi had anticipated that the prophet Elijah would reappear to herald the emergence of a great leader, the Messiah (Malachi 4.5). Into that setting strode a firebrand. He dressed himself up to look like Elijah. He lived in the same primitive fashion. He roared and cursed like Elijah. His name was John.

Although John was mistaken for the Messiah, he always made it plain that he was merely the herald of his arrival. Immediately after John baptized Jesus, the focus turned to him.

Why did John baptize Jesus, not the other way round? Because in Jesus, God himself was walking among us, human in every way. God was identifying with all the bruises, weaknesses and temptations of human life – including the need to be baptized.

Take a moment to reflect on the marvel of God's incarnation as a human being. In Jesus, God looked up in wonder at the same stars, took the same delight in the smell of food cooking, felt the same splash over his head as he dipped under water. Try to imagine God walking on earth among us in 2021. Where do you picture him? Or her? Among the people of what country? Or religion?

COLLECT

Almighty God,
who sent your Holy Spirit
to be the life and light of your Church:
open our hearts to the riches of your grace,
that we may bring forth the fruit of the Spirit
in love and joy and peace;
through Jesus Christ your Son our Lord,
who is alive and reigns with you,
in the unity of the Holy Spirit,
one God, now and for ever.

| *Reflection by* **Peter Graystone**

Psalms **48**, 52
Ezekiel 37.15-end
Mark 1.14-20

Tuesday 3 August

Mark 1.14-20

'... the kingdom of God has come near' (v.15)

Surely this cannot have been the first occasion on which Jesus met these fishermen. He had proclaimed his message in three sound bites of which any media-savvy leader today would be proud: 'The time has come ... The Kingdom of God has come near. Repent and believe the good news!' (v.15, NIV). Virtually everything Jesus subsequently taught is encapsulated in those three announcements, but he could have fitted them all in a tweet and still had room for an emoji. Now, with what seems like an orderly strategy, the time had indeed come to challenge his chosen group to move from interest to commitment.

What made Jesus so compelling that they took the jeopardous risk of following him? Was it his intense compassion, his visionary mind, his technicolour imagination, his enthralling righteousness, his unrivalled ability to match his words with action?

I find myself wondering how the Jesus who loved and blazed his way into those first followers' lives comes to be described today in a way which is worthy, saintly and slightly bland. To follow him through Galilee and beyond must have involved beauty, thrill and danger. Like fireworks! It's a challenge to those of us who have the opportunity to speak of Jesus, either in private conversation or in public address, to portray him with the energy that once captivated a group of workmen so completely that they staked everything on going with him.

Gracious Father,
revive your Church in our day,
and make her holy, strong and faithful,
for your glory's sake
in Jesus Christ our Lord.

COLLECT

Wednesday 4 August

Psalm **119.57-80**
Ezekiel 39.21-end
Mark 1.21-28

Mark 1.21-28

'... he taught them as one having authority' (v.22)

The people of Capernaum were quick to recognize the compelling teaching of Jesus and his ability to match words with action, which featured in yesterday's reflection. Mark has a word for it – authority. He uses that word repeatedly to describe what distinguished Jesus from other leaders, and the power that his followers were given in order to serve others in God's name (Mark 6.7).

Behind Mark's use of the word authority lies the great Messianic and symbolic figure of the Son of Man who appears in the vision of Daniel (Daniel 7.13,14). In that vision the Son of Man, in the presence of God, is given authority to rule a kingdom that is both eternal and indestructible. Mark decodes the prophecy by showing Jesus in a continuous ascendancy over Satan. It began in the wilderness, where Jesus fought and resisted temptation (Mark 1.13). It was on display in Capernaum in a life-changing healing, a precursor of the healing that will be humankind's universal experience when evil ends, once and for all, in the perfection of heaven. And it gave Jesus the power to forgive sins, releasing into fulfilment people who had been alienated from God (Mark 2.10).

Remarkably, every tiny act of service we do in the name of Jesus asserts that he has authority over evil. It is part of the victory he has already won and which will triumph in the kingdom of eternal goodness.

COLLECT | Almighty God,
who sent your Holy Spirit
to be the life and light of your Church:
open our hearts to the riches of your grace,
that we may bring forth the fruit of the Spirit
in love and joy and peace;
through Jesus Christ your Son our Lord,
who is alive and reigns with you,
in the unity of the Holy Spirit,
one God, now and for ever.

| *Reflection by* **Peter Graystone**

Thursday 5 August

Mark 1.29-end

'Moved with pity, Jesus stretched out his hand' (v.41)

The Talmud (the 5th century compilation of Jewish law and tradition) taught this: 'Four are to be compared with a dead man – the lame, the blind, the leper and the childless.' Shocking as this seems to today's ears, it gives an insight into the worldview of those who met Jesus in Galilee. The situation of many that he healed was no longer worth calling life. What Jesus did was more than healing; it was resurrection.

Jesus' teaching and healing together build his central purpose – 'to destroy the works of the devil' (1 John 3.8). Each transforming action here is at one with the salvation that was brought about through his death and new life. If you raise sickness and possession to their most powerful state, you confront death; if you raise healing and the rout of evil to their height, the result is resurrection.

What happens next is unexpected. While the village sleeps, Jesus slips out of town in the dark. Simon Peter, even at this early stage a leader, fronts the search for him. He finds it incomprehensible that Jesus would not want to capitalize on his success in Capernaum. But Jesus has been guided toward something bigger. How is he so sure what he should do next? Because he is meeting the enormity of the need he sees from the enormity of the power that is available to him in prayer.

Gracious Father,
revive your Church in our day,
and make her holy, strong and faithful,
for your glory's sake
in Jesus Christ our Lord.

COLLECT

Friday 6 August
Transfiguration of our Lord

Psalms 27, 150
Ecclesiasticus 48.1-10
or 1 Kings 19.1-16
1 John 3.1-3

1 Kings 19.1-16
'... a sound of sheer silence' (v.12)

The context of this story is that Elijah had confronted pagan prophets and God had proved himself spectacularly to be one who answers prayer – fire blazed, rain torrented, blood flowed. But Elijah's exhilaration gave way to fear. The incident brought him powerful enemies, and he ran away. God gave him superhuman power to run, so he clearly fled with God's approval (1 Kings 18.46). Christians don't have to face every difficult situation like the X-Men. Sometimes, obedience to God can mean admitting defeat and making an exit.

Equally, Christians don't have to pretend that they never get depressed. Elijah, godly man though he was, showed symptoms that anyone who has lived with depression today will recognize. God supplied three immensely practical gifts, which are also recognizable as helpful responses to those who are living with a depressive illness – sleep, company, and food and drink.

But God's most restorative gift to this spiritually empty man was to take him back to the circumstances in which his faith and trust began. Horeb was probably another name for Sinai, the mountain where God revealed himself to the Hebrew people in law and covenant. There, Elijah rediscovered the presence of God in a way he hadn't expected. It wasn't in spectacle but in tranquillity. This is the kind of touch of God on our lives that we might completely miss. But it brings a transforming assurance: 'You are not alone.'

COLLECT

Father in heaven,
whose Son Jesus Christ was wonderfully transfigured
before chosen witnesses upon the holy mountain,
and spoke of the exodus he would accomplish at Jerusalem:
give us strength so to hear his voice and bear our cross
that in the world to come we may see him as he is;
who is alive and reigns with you,
in the unity of the Holy Spirit,
one God, now and for ever.

| *Reflection by* **Peter Graystone**

Psalm **68**   **Saturday 7 August**
Ezekiel 47.1-12
Mark 2.13-22

Mark 2.13-22

'I have come to call not the righteous, but sinners' (v.17)

Imagine you are a Pharisee in the first century. You are a good and respectable person, deeply religious, and longing to restore the Jews' place in God's affection by reversing lax attitudes to obeying the law.

Next, imagine you are a Jewish tax collector in the same era. Under the Roman occupation of your country, you've seen a business opportunity, taking money from the enemy to do a job for which your countrymen would loathe you.

Finally, imagine that you are a resident of Capernaum intrigued by Jesus. What a shock you must feel when Jesus asked the tax collector to follow him, not the Pharisee. My word, Jesus surrounded himself with some lowlifes!

The next step won't require any imagination. See yourself as a decent, Bible-reading churchgoer. You are deeply loved by God.

However, such is his boundless compassion that people who are completely unlike you are loved by him too. If you are going to be like Jesus, you need to make room in your life and your church to journey alongside some people whom you view more like tax collectors than like Pharisees – people with complicated sexual histories, or whose behaviour is unusual because of mental or physical illness, or who don't share your beliefs and make no secret of it, or whose pasts have taken them through the prison system or drug abuse. Can you imagine yourself making them welcome?

Almighty God,
who sent your Holy Spirit
to be the life and light of your Church:
open our hearts to the riches of your grace,
that we may bring forth the fruit of the Spirit
in love and joy and peace;
through Jesus Christ your Son our Lord,
who is alive and reigns with you,
in the unity of the Holy Spirit,
one God, now and for ever.

COLLECT

Reflection by **Peter Graystone**   225

Monday 9 August

Psalm **71**
Proverbs 1.1-19
Mark 2.23 – 3.6

Proverbs 1.1-19

'Let the wise also hear' (v.5)

The Book of Proverbs opens by setting out its purpose – to convey wisdom – and its intended audience. Three groups are specifically addressed: 'the simple', 'the young' and 'the wise'. The inclusion of the last is surprising. Why should the wise need to acquire wisdom, we might wonder, since they already have it? Wisdom is their intellectual property.

We can only ask that if we see wisdom as an object that we acquire, possess and guard. Such commodified thinking is certainly common today. So, for example, libraries are renamed as 'idea stores', and education is described as 'knowledge transfer'. As long ago as 1934, T. S. Eliot prophetically lamented this trend in his poem 'The Rock', where he observed how wisdom had given way to knowledge, and knowledge to information.

Biblical wisdom is not an asset over which I can claim ownership, or exercise copyright. It is an orientation of my whole being to walk in a particular direction of life, the way that God has set before those who seek his will. That means that gaining wisdom is a continuing and lifelong process.

Proverbs warns about other ways that are also open to me; whatever stage I have reached on my journey, the danger of choosing foolishness is always present. So I can never rest content with whatever measure of wisdom has been given me, but must daily recommit to learning more. Humble fear of the Lord is the beginning of knowledge, but the slippery slope of foolishness starts with the self-satisfied pride of thinking that I know it all.

COLLECT

Let your merciful ears, O Lord,
be open to the prayers of your humble servants;
and that they may obtain their petitions
make them to ask such things as shall please you;
through Jesus Christ your Son our Lord,
who is alive and reigns with you,
in the unity of the Holy Spirit,
one God, now and for ever.

| *Reflection by* **Michael Ipgrave**

Psalm **73**
Proverbs 1.20-end
Mark 3.7-19*a*

Tuesday 10 August

Proverbs 1.20-end

'... in the squares she raises her voice' (v.20)

Proverbs can at times seem like a slightly tedious collection of rather obvious truisms and maxims; but this passage gives a picture of a woman on a mission, reaching out with passion and urgency to shout her message in the squares of the city. Wisdom here has a prophetic edge in its proclamation in the public life of the community.

Surely this speaks into our own confused and anxious times. Verse 22 lists three of the enemies against which public wisdom has to contend: the deliberate choice of simplistic slogans, rather than reasoned argument; the scoffing option of cynicism, instead of engagement with the issues; and the straightforward rejection of knowledge, to deny the claims of truth. All these trends are strong in our national and international life, and they are amplified by social media, where reason and truth are hard to find and questioning voices are shouted down.

The temptation for those of us seized by the wisdom of God is to withdraw into our own space, away from the clamour of conflicting voices. But divine wisdom in this passage not only goes into the city, but also seeks out the busiest corners, as well as the entrances of the gates. These are the places where everybody will pass by. Breaking out from self-referential monologues, wisdom is reaching out in a passionate dialogue with all in the city. It is challenging for the Church in our time to speak with conviction and clarity into the great issues of public life, but we have to trust that the divine wisdom will stand beside us and inform us.

Lord of heaven and earth,
as Jesus taught his disciples to be persistent in prayer,
give us patience and courage never to lose hope,
but always to bring our prayers before you;
through Jesus Christ our Lord.

COLLECT

Reflection by **Michael Ipgrave**   227

Wednesday 11 August

Psalm **77**
Proverbs 2
Mark 3.19*b*-end

Proverbs 2

'... from his mouth come knowledge and understanding' (v.6)

There is a remarkable double reference to the source of wisdom in this passage. At the outset, the speaker, in the role of a parental figure, refers to 'my words', 'my commandments'. Later, though, the text makes clear that wisdom is the gift of God, from whose mouth come knowledge and understanding. So it seems that the parent in some sense speaks the words of God; or, at least, that the parent co-creates and co-delivers wisdom with God.

This may seem odd to a society grown suspicious of the handing on of traditional learning from one generation to another (and where many families are not very good at that task). But if we think not only of parents but also of teachers and others *in loco parentis*, we can see in these verses a foundation for an education that reaches out to help shape for good the lives of many in the community.

A Muslim friend who had gone to a church primary school once said to me: 'I want to thank the Church of England for what it has given me. It has made me the kind of Muslim I am. I want to be part of our society, and I want to help the common good'.

I thank God and pray for all those involved in education who pass on wisdom and good values to young people of all faiths and of none. Some may criticize that as falling short of real 'proclamation', but this passage tells me that it comes from God.

C O L L E C T

Let your merciful ears, O Lord,
be open to the prayers of your humble servants;
and that they may obtain their petitions
make them to ask such things as shall please you;
through Jesus Christ your Son our Lord,
who is alive and reigns with you,
in the unity of the Holy Spirit,
one God, now and for ever.

| *Reflection by* **Michael Ipgrave**

Psalm **78.1-39***
Proverbs 3.1-26
Mark 4.1-20

Thursday 12 August

Proverbs 3.1-26
'... write them on the tablet of your heart' (v.3)

The language used in these verses by the parent to commend wisdom to the child is the same language that the Hebrew Bible uses elsewhere to speak of the law. In verse 1, 'my teaching' is literally 'my *torah*'; 'my commandments' uses the same word as for the 613 commandments that traditionally make up the Jewish Law. The author goes on to urge the binding of loyalty and faithfulness around the neck, in words that echo the instructions in Deuteronomy 11.18 to wear phylacteries containing texts of *Torah*. Writing the words 'on the tablet of your heart' is what God promises Jeremiah he will do for his people with the Law in a new covenant (Jeremiah 31.33).

We often put 'law' and 'wisdom' into different parts of our mind. We think that law comes as command, while wisdom is offered as advice. Almost the only bit of my training as an archdeacon that I can now remember were words of a very senior naval commander: 'You have to be very clear if you are issuing a chap with an order or just giving him some advice; otherwise you will get into an awful mess, Padre'.

There is common sense in what he said about ways of communicating in a hierarchical organization, and as an archdeacon I heeded his words carefully. But with divine wisdom, the distinction is not so clear. Her words are written on our heart, and they become the voice of conscience speaking within us. For Christians, obedience to conscience is not just taking advice; it is obeying the law of God speaking within us.

Lord of heaven and earth,
as Jesus taught his disciples to be persistent in prayer,
give us patience and courage never to lose hope,
but always to bring our prayers before you;
through Jesus Christ our Lord.

COLLECT

Friday 13 August

Proverbs 3.27 – 4.19

'Listen, children, to a father's instruction' (4.1)

Chapter 4 begins with a parental summons to listen that is echoed in the opening words of one of the foundational documents of Western civilization, the *Rule of St Benedict*:

*Listen carefully, my son, to the master's instructions,
and attend to them with the ear of your heart.*

Listening means not mere hearing, but attention, reflection, a readiness to put into practice, so the whole 'ear of the heart' is involved. That is foundational to the reception of wisdom. In a busy and noisy society, we need to find spaces to listen for wisdom with others – in a family, in a religious community, in a group for prayer and Bible study.

Proverbs, and later Benedict, make clear that this listening requires obedience. Aware as we are of the dangers of authority being abused, this may make us feel uneasy. But the father in this chapter reminds his children that he too was once a son, learning wisdom from his own father. As a teacher, he must now remember what it means to be a learner. In the same way, the Benedictine abbot, knowing that he must give account to the Lord for the souls of all his monks, must also submit a reckoning for his own.

Whatever my role in my family, my position in the Church, my place in a community, Lord, remind me that I am a child of God and a disciple of Jesus, and make me ready to listen so I may receive wisdom.

COLLECT

Let your merciful ears, O Lord,
be open to the prayers of your humble servants;
and that they may obtain their petitions
make them to ask such things as shall please you;
through Jesus Christ your Son our Lord,
who is alive and reigns with you,
in the unity of the Holy Spirit,
one God, now and for ever.

| *Reflection by* **Michael Ipgrave**

Psalms **76**, 79
Proverbs 6.1-19
Mark 4.35-end

Saturday 14 August

Proverbs 6.1-19
'Go to the ant, you lazybones' (v.6)

In its older version, 'Go to the ant, thou sluggard', this was one of the earliest Bible verses I remember from my childhood. Its combination of imagery, wisdom and genial abuse appealed to me as a young boy, and I fear I insulted friends and family with it liberally.

However, this verse is not just about taking the random example of a small insect to make a moral point. The use of imagery drawn from nature is an integral part of Solomon's wisdom. According to 1 Kings 4.33, 'He would speak of trees, from the cedar that is in the Lebanon to the hyssop that grows in the wall; he would speak of animals, and birds, and reptiles, and fish'. Out of the natural world created by God, he was able to read guidance and wisdom for daily life.

The idea of 'two books', one of nature and one of the scriptures, is an ancient one in Christianity. It is magnificently expressed by the seventeenth-century physician Sir Thomas Browne in his *Religio Medici*:

> *Thus there are two Books from whence I collect my Divinity; besides that written one of God, another of His servant Nature, that universal and publick Manuscript, that lies expans'd unto the Eyes of all: those that never saw him in the one, have discover'd Him in the other.*

In an age of ecological awareness, many find it more attractive to read the 'book of nature' than the book of the scriptures, and are more deeply and urgently persuaded by its message. How can we rebuild bridges of meaning between these two volumes?

Lord of heaven and earth,
as Jesus taught his disciples to be persistent in prayer,
give us patience and courage never to lose hope,
but always to bring our prayers before you;
through Jesus Christ our Lord.

COLLECT

Reflection by **Michael Ipgrave** | 231

Monday 16 August

Psalms **80**, 82
Proverbs 8.1-21
Mark 5.1-20

Proverbs 8.1-21

'Take my instruction instead of silver' (v.10)

Material wealth is a subject addressed with some subtlety in Proverbs. Later in the book, we read: 'Give me neither poverty nor riches ... or I shall be full, and deny you ... or I shall be poor, and steal' (30.8-9). These balanced phrases express the state of life in which the writer hopes to find himself; they concern what he asks in prayer to receive, rather than what he sets out through action to acquire.

That distinction must be borne in mind. In verse 10, wisdom is prioritized over wealth, but soon after that we read that wisdom brings with her material blessings. This reflects the choice of Solomon when he explicitly rejected riches in favour of wisdom, but then was told by God that he would in any case 'give you also what you have not asked' (1 Kings 3.13). So actively seeking wealth is not acceptable, but being rewarded by it is. The choice in this verse is the same as that starkly posed by Jesus: 'No one can serve two masters ... You cannot serve God and wealth' (Matthew 6.24).

In our contemporary capitalist world, where we are all entangled in financial arrangements immeasurably more complex than those of Solomon's time, it is not so easy to draw a clear line between the financial benefits we receive and those we actively seek. That makes it all the more urgent to ask: Where do we really expend our energy – to get wisdom or wealth?

COLLECT

O God, you declare your almighty power
most chiefly in showing mercy and pity:
mercifully grant to us such a measure of your grace,
that we, running the way of your commandments,
may receive your gracious promises,
and be made partakers of your heavenly treasure;
through Jesus Christ your Son our Lord,
who is alive and reigns with you,
in the unity of the Holy Spirit,
one God, now and for ever.

| *Reflection by* **Michael Ipgrave**

Psalms 87, **89.1-18**
Proverbs 8.22-end
Mark 5.21-34

Tuesday 17 August

Proverbs 8.22-end

'The Lord created me at the beginning of his work' (v.22)

To whom does this passage refer? For much of Christian history, it has been assumed to be about Jesus Christ. Some (such as the fourth-century theologian Arius) argued that these words prove that the Son of God is a created being; others (the orthodox) replied that 'brought me forth' would be a better translation than 'created me', and so in fact the verse shows the pre-existence of Christ.

This may seem a strange argument to us. Surely, we think, the passage obviously refers to some sort of feminine personification of Wisdom. To say that it must really be about Christ is to behave like the (probably apocryphal) boy in Sunday School who was asked the question: 'Who lives in trees, gathers nuts, and has a bushy tail?' Puzzled, he replied: 'Well, it sounds like a squirrel, but this is Sunday School, so I guess it must be Jesus'.

More seriously, we must ask if the assumption that 'it must be Jesus' is an unacceptable Christian appropriation of a Jewish text. That is a question that runs through all Christian reading of the Hebrew scriptures. We certainly need to approach these texts with sensitivity, and with a readiness to learn from the riches of Jewish interpretation. Nevertheless, as Christians, it is in Jesus that we see divine wisdom most fully expressed, so it is natural that when we read this passage we should find ourselves being pointed forward to him, the firstborn of all creation.

God of glory,
the end of our searching,
help us to lay aside
all that prevents us from seeking your kingdom,
and to give all that we have
to gain the pearl beyond all price,
through our Saviour Jesus Christ.

COLLECT

Wednesday 18 August

Psalm 119.105-128
Proverbs 9
Mark 5.35-end

Proverbs 9

'Wisdom has built her house' (v.1)

Behold the great Creator makes
Himself a house of clay
A robe of virgin flesh he takes
Which he may wear for ay.

As a child, I was intrigued by that hymn, which in my village church we sang on the Sundays after Christmas. Its author was Thomas Pestel, a Leicestershire vicar and loyal Royalist during the English Civil War. It was the line about 'a house of clay' that particularly struck me. Drawing on earlier Christian writers, Pestel saw the building of wisdom's house being fulfilled in Christ's taking on of human flesh in the Incarnation. In the Eastern Christian tradition, the 'house of seven pillars' is also seen as the Church, resting on the orthodox faith formulated by the great ecumenical councils.

All that may seem quite fanciful, but the description in this passage of Wisdom preparing a feast and dispatching servants to summon the guests does have echoes in Jesus' parable of the great wedding banquet. Wisdom reaches out in generous invitation to 'the simple'. The word means 'those who are easily led'; it is through the gentle guidance of the Holy Spirit that I can find my way to the table of God's welcome. As a Christian, I have come to know God's supreme communication of truth in the 'body language' of Jesus, the incarnate Son who shares my flesh and blood. I find nourishment and growth in his Church as Wisdom's house.

COLLECT

O God, you declare your almighty power
most chiefly in showing mercy and pity:
mercifully grant to us such a measure of your grace,
that we, running the way of your commandments,
may receive your gracious promises,
and be made partakers of your heavenly treasure;
through Jesus Christ your Son our Lord,
who is alive and reigns with you,
in the unity of the Holy Spirit,
one God, now and for ever.

| *Reflection by* **Michael Ipgrave**

Psalms 90, **92**
Proverbs 10.1-12
Mark 6.1-13

Thursday 19 August

Proverbs 10.1-12

'... love covers all offences' (v.12)

The language of people 'covering' the offences of others is common in the Bible, as is that of God 'covering' sins. The great Jewish observance of the 'Day of Atonement', *Yom Kippur*, means just this: the 'covering' by God of his people's sins. Out of mercy and generosity, the past is blotted out, its damaging guilt no longer taken into account. In the New Testament, there is a close echo in 1 Peter 4.8: 'love covers a multitude of sins'.

In our own times, though, the language of 'covering' what has happened can feel distinctly uncomfortable. It suggests 'covering up', minimizing harm done, even colluding in wrongdoing. Surely, honesty and transparency are what is needed where there has been offence. Is it even possible that there can be reconciliation without truth? However, the biblical meaning of covering is not to deny the reality of the harm that has happened, but to agree on how to deal with it – and to limit its destructive impact on individuals, relationships and communities.

We need to learn to discern here, in the way that a physician will discern how best to treat a wound. Sometimes, the answer will be to probe, clean and expose damaged tissues to fresh air; sometimes, it is stitches and bandages that are needed.

Lord, give me the wisdom to discern aright, and always remind me that my sin is covered by the mercy of your blood.

God of glory,
the end of our searching,
help us to lay aside
all that prevents us from seeking your kingdom,
and to give all that we have
to gain the pearl beyond all price,
through our Saviour Jesus Christ.

COLLECT

Friday 20 August

Psalms **88** (95)
Proverbs 11.1-12
Mark 6.14-29

Proverbs 11.1-12

'By the blessing of the upright a city is exalted' (v.11)

This proverb teaches that the virtue of individuals is not just a private attainment, but something to be shared in society, bringing transformation in the community. Within the theological framework of Proverbs, though, it is unclear how this happens, or what 'the blessing of the upright' means. Is it that God bestows a blessing on them, which then is extended to the whole? Or is their presence itself a direct blessing to the city?

The first interpretation calls to mind the story of Abraham pleading for the preservation from destruction of the city of Sodom on the grounds of fifty, or forty-five, or forty, thirty, twenty, or even just ten righteous people being found in it (Genesis 18.23-32). God is prepared to count such a small number as decisive for the whole. The second interpretation matches Jesus' exhortations to his disciples to be salt and light in the world, and his image of the kingdom of God as yeast leavening a whole mass of flour. There is something contagious about goodness that can change a whole society.

These two ways of reading the verse are not mutually exclusive, and we need to hold them together. Writing to the exiled people of God, Jeremiah urged them to 'seek the welfare' of the city where they live and also to 'pray on its behalf' (Jeremiah 29.7). We are to act in our communities and to pray for them, and by God's grace, both prayer and action will effect transformation.

COLLECT

O God, you declare your almighty power
most chiefly in showing mercy and pity:
mercifully grant to us such a measure of your grace,
that we, running the way of your commandments,
may receive your gracious promises,
and be made partakers of your heavenly treasure;
through Jesus Christ your Son our Lord,
who is alive and reigns with you,
in the unity of the Holy Spirit,
one God, now and for ever.

| *Reflection by* **Michael Ipgrave**

Psalms 96, **97**, 100
Proverbs 12.10-end
Mark 6.30-44

Saturday 21 August

Proverbs 12.10-end
'Truthful lips endure for ever' (v.19)

The author of Proverbs is well aware that there is no situation in which we can simply assume that everybody is telling the truth. Nevertheless, he insists that truthfulness has a durability that will outlive all forms of lying and deceit. He teaches us that this is the only lasting foundation on which we can build our lives – as Jesus promises, 'the truth will make you free' (John 8.32).

As members of all Christian Churches, we have had to learn that lesson painfully in relation to the legacy of cases of abuse of children, young people and vulnerable adults, and those we have excluded or failed to welcome. These have in the past often been dealt with in deeply unsatisfactory ways: victims ignored, abominable behaviour excused, collusion in some cases extended to complicity. To invert the language of Proverbs, for a whole range of reasons 'truthful lips' were silenced.

But truth will have its day. To speak of the durability of truth is to bear witness that, whatever attempts are made to deny or to ignore its claims, it will not go away; truth is always waiting for us to come to its side, and to learn that its embrace can free us. There is still a painful journey to make for us, as Churches and as individuals, in facing the truth. Acknowledging our past failing is a matter of deep shame for us. Yet it is the only way in which we can travel with integrity. The legacy of the past is still with us, but we are given hope for a new way of living. May God give us all courage to embrace that challenge.

God of glory,
the end of our searching,
help us to lay aside
all that prevents us from seeking your kingdom,
and to give all that we have
to gain the pearl beyond all price,
through our Saviour Jesus Christ.

COLLECT

Reflection by **Michael Ipgrave** | 237

Monday 23 August

Psalms **98**, 99, 101
Proverbs 14.31 – 15.17
Mark 6.45-end

Proverbs 14.31 – 15.17

'A soft answer turns away wrath' (15.1)

The best science of the age in which Proverbs was written, and indeed Jesus' time, was that speech was directly related to the heart, the ruling centre of the whole person. Until the second century, when the work of the Greek physician Galen revealed the role of the larynx in speech, it was assumed that words were 'sent forth by the heart'. This makes sense of the fact that the compiler of Proverbs returns again and again to the way we use words as a mark of our godliness. An individual's words reveal what kind of a person he or she is. A fool can be identified by nonsense gushing. But you can recognize wise people because of the well-researched knowledge that comes out of their mouths.

There is practical advice here not just for individual Christians, but for our national life. It is care over the use of our words that will prevent emotions getting out of hand and arguments ensuing. The decisions we make about what we say can heal or crush others.

What if our words disguise what we are really thinking? We may deceive others, but the truth is plain to God. He has a mighty concern to see justice done, particularly when the poor are oppressed. But true fulfilment in life is measured not by being rich or poor, but by being devout, loved and content.

COLLECT

Almighty and everlasting God,
you are always more ready to hear than we to pray
and to give more than either we desire or deserve:
pour down upon us the abundance of your mercy,
forgiving us those things of which our conscience is afraid
and giving us those good things which we are not worthy to ask
but through the merits and mediation
of Jesus Christ your Son our Lord,
who is alive and reigns with you,
in the unity of the Holy Spirit,
one God, now and for ever.

| *Reflection by* **Peter Graystone**

Psalms 86, 117
Genesis 28.10-17
John 1.43-end

Tuesday 24 August
Bartholomew the Apostle

John 1.43-end
'We have found him' (v.45)

This is day five of a remarkable week during which Jesus, many miles from home because he had been drawn to his cousin John's teaching, gathers those who will be his closest companions. They are all seekers, longing for God's Messiah and eager for baptism as a sign of repentance and readiness (John 1.28).

Among them is Nathanael. What was he thinking about under that fig tree? Maybe he was daydreaming about Jacob who, in the middle of a desert (both metaphorical and actual), had a dream in which cascades of angels made him aware of the presence of God (Genesis 28.10-17). Perhaps Nathanael was longing for an encounter with God as profound as Jacob's. He is given the first hint that, in Jesus, that is what has happened.

Philip is a model of how to talk to people about faith. He doesn't get into an argument about Nazareth in spite of Nathanael's initial sarcasm. Instead, he gently invites his friend to investigate Jesus. The result is a revelation.

Nathanael drops out of sight as far as the Gospels are concerned. Philip becomes one of Jesus' inner circle, but Nathanael doesn't (unless, as some have suggested, his alternative name is Bartholomew). But, in the days after the resurrection, he is there on the beach when the fishermen share breakfast with the risen Jesus. On that occasion nobody dared ask, 'Who are you?' (John 21.12). Nathanael already knew.

COLLECT

Almighty and everlasting God,
who gave to your apostle Bartholomew grace
truly to believe and to preach your word:
grant that your Church
may love that word which he believed
and may faithfully preach and receive the same;
through Jesus Christ your Son our Lord,
who is alive and reigns with you,
in the unity of the Holy Spirit,
one God, now and for ever.

Reflection by **Peter Graystone** | 239

Wednesday 25 August

Proverbs 18.10-end

'... a true friend sticks closer than one's nearest kin' (v.24)

Sometimes proverbs state a fact, and it is only by reference to others that their intention is clear. For instance, a gift does indeed improve a relationship with someone who can use their influence on your behalf, but is that a good thing or a bad thing? The condemnation of bribes in 17.23 gives the answer. In fact, there is nothing about wealth that unites us. It isolates people, who believe it makes them invulnerable. It makes them contemptuous of the needs of the poor. That arrogant sense of entitlement cannot last forever.

So, if pursuing money cannot guarantee a fulfilled life, what should we invest our energy in? Our relationships.

Friendship, so undervalued in our sexualized and online generation, is highly prized in Proverbs. The strength and support it brings can be even more valuable than family ties. The key to fostering friendship is taking the time to listen. And a true friend can recognize that someone who has been emotionally wounded (or maybe lives with mental ill-health) needs even more care than someone who is physically unwell. Friendship needs time and effort, because there is nothing more difficult to heal than a friendship that has turned sour. Across the centuries, the proverb-writers challenge the superficiality of Facebook friendship. It is in talking together that friendship of real value is forged.

COLLECT

Almighty and everlasting God,
you are always more ready to hear than we to pray
and to give more than either we desire or deserve:
pour down upon us the abundance of your mercy,
forgiving us those things of which our conscience is afraid
and giving us those good things which we are not worthy to ask
but through the merits and mediation
of Jesus Christ your Son our Lord,
who is alive and reigns with you,
in the unity of the Holy Spirit,
one God, now and for ever.

Reflection by **Peter Graystone**

Psalms 113, **115**
Proverbs 20.1-22
Mark 7.24-30

Thursday 26 August

Proverbs 20.1-22

'Diverse weights and diverse measures are both alike an abomination' (v.10)

Who would the wise men and women who wrote these proverbs have in their sights if they were observing our shops and websites today?

Deceitful sellers have not disappeared over the course of three millennia. The writers would certainly lambast the car salesman who turns back a milometer or the publican whose taps are fixed to provide more froth than drink. I am sure they'd scorn the online retailer who photographs a tiny hotel room to look as though it's worth more than it actually is.

However, they would castigate a dishonest customer just as severely. They would deride the shopper who pretends that a shirt is faulty in order to get the price reduced, then brags, 'Half price, and the shop assistant didn't even notice she was being fooled!' Or the person who keeps quiet about being given too much change.

Who today has the short-term pleasure of 'bread gained by deceit'? Maybe the house purchaser who takes advantage of a seller's difficulty to reduce her offer below the true value. The reference to gravel is about conscience. Real satisfaction comes from belongings that are purchased fairly.

And what about the possessions that are acquired quickly and then don't bring a blessing? I can't help thinking the writers might mutter verse 21 as they walk past the queue for lottery tickets.

These are values that we should not only uphold ourselves, but teach our children.

COLLECT

God of constant mercy,
who sent your Son to save us:
remind us of your goodness,
increase your grace within us,
that our thankfulness may grow,
through Jesus Christ our Lord.

Reflection by **Peter Graystone** | 241

Friday 27 August

Proverbs 22.1-16

'Those who are generous are blessed' (v.9)

God is the maker of all things, and that is a repeated refrain of this book. But the Proverbs are resolutely practical. It's no good having an exemplary spiritual life, but ending up lonely, socially inept, compassionless, in trouble with the law and, worst of all, broke! This chapter, amid the usual scattergun variety of subjects, has a lot to say about money.

To begin with, all we own is put in context. No amount of money is as important as having a good reputation. When people associate your name with love and faithfulness, you have achieved worth both in the eyes of humans and of God (Proverbs 3.3,4).

Subsequently, four facts about money help us develop a balanced view of it. First, it can be one of the signs of a life that God has blessed, although it is not the only one and not the most significant. Second, it is one of the ways in which people exercise power and we need to recognize that fact of life even if we detest it. Third, generosity is a wonderful thing, not just because of its impact on those whose plight it eases, but because those who give find themselves blessed by doing so. And fourth, gaining wealth through any trade or industry that keeps fellow-humans locked in poverty is despicable and will lead to moral (or maybe actual) bankruptcy.

COLLECT

Almighty and everlasting God,
you are always more ready to hear than we to pray
and to give more than either we desire or deserve:
pour down upon us the abundance of your mercy,
forgiving us those things of which our conscience is afraid
and giving us those good things which we are not worthy to ask
but through the merits and mediation
of Jesus Christ your Son our Lord,
who is alive and reigns with you,
in the unity of the Holy Spirit,
one God, now and for ever.

242 | *Reflection by* **Peter Graystone**

Psalms 120, **121**, 122
Proverbs 24.23-end
Mark 8.1-10

Saturday 28 August

Proverbs 24.23-end

'Partiality in judging is not good' (v.23)

We live in an age when it has become possible for courts to be vilified by sections of the media for upholding what's right in a way that does not please some of the population. One tabloid headline described the judges of Britain's highest court as 'Enemies of the People' when they upheld a law in a way which did not fit the worldview that the newspaper espoused. This is dangerous. So it is timely to remind ourselves what standards the Old Testament sets for justice, and to cherish them as God's intentions for a society that operates freely and peacefully.

First, any form of favouritism that allows wrongdoers to escape the consequences of their behaviour is detestable. Oppose corruption in the justice system anywhere that it manifests itself, and pray for any parts of the world in which the judiciary is threatened or curbed by governments.

Second, insist on honesty. That applies to politics, journalism and policing. But if we are looking for it in public life, the place to model it is in our private lies – in conversation with friends, dealings at work, and the way we nurture children. This lip-smacking proverb makes truth really attractive.

And third. resist any temptation to take the law into your own hands. Revenge can only possibly lead to a chaotic breakdown of order. When systems of justice are thriving, we don't need vengeance in order to settle scores.

God of constant mercy,
who sent your Son to save us:
remind us of your goodness,
increase your grace within us,
that our thankfulness may grow,
through Jesus Christ our Lord.

COLLECT

Reflection by **Peter Graystone** | 243

Monday 30 August

Proverbs 25.1-14

'A word fitly spoken is like apples of gold' (v.11)

'Who wants to be the leader?' Me, me me! 'OK, you can be the leader.' Hooray! I'm the leader. What are we going to do now?

Proverbs has plenty of advice for leaders. It is addressed to kings, but its wisdom applies to managers, clergy, teachers, school prefects, parents and anyone who is in a position to influence others.

First, think things through. There are some things about God that no one will ever understand, but your task is to wrestle with them. Don't skimp on the time you spend in prayer and study. Aim high and reflect deeply.

Second, draw around you people who have integrity. That doesn't just apply to work colleagues, but to the friends you keep. They are the ones who will help you keep your moral standards high, won't seek your company solely for what they can get out of it, and won't misrepresent you to others.

Third, if you have to disagree with someone, do it face to face, in a context of mutual listening, and if it gets really serious, find a resolution without having to call in solicitors.

And finally, don't make promises that you can't fulfil. In a dry and dusty land, people need refreshing rain, not pretty clouds that never deliver a drop.

Which of these ancient proverbs leaps over a gulf of thirty centuries to challenge you?

C O L L E C T

Almighty God,
who called your Church to bear witness
that you were in Christ reconciling the world to yourself:
help us to proclaim the good news of your love,
that all who hear it may be drawn to you;
through him who was lifted up on the cross,
and reigns with you in the unity of the Holy Spirit,
one God, now and for ever.

| *Reflection by* **Peter Graystone**

Psalms **132**, 133
Proverbs 25.15-end
Mark 8.22-26

Tuesday 31 August

Proverbs 25.15-end

'If your enemies are hungry, give them bread' (v.21)

Here, assorted in a way that is entirely typical of the book, are proverbs about times when things are going badly and others about times when things are going well.

Here is wisdom that will help you uphold someone who is experiencing hardship. Be aware that a shallow attempt to cheer someone up may be entirely unhelpful, particularly if they are living with a depressive illness. There are many things that can cause distress – being lied about or spoken badly of, which Twitter has magnified in a way that could not be imagined in the days of Solomon; unhappiness in a marriage, which is timeless; or seeing the bad guys win, which sometimes happens even under the shelter of God. Those are the circumstances in which a person needs the sympathetic support of a good friend, because being let down by someone when you are vulnerable is devastating.

And wisdom for good times? Don't overindulge, because it won't bring the pleasure you anticipate. Use the blessings you have received to be generous to those who have stood in your way – teaching that was even more telling when Jesus repeated it in the context of being oppressed under a tyranny (Matthew 5.44). And enjoy the good news – perhaps even more so now that it can reach us from miles away in an instant (a much better use for Twitter).

Almighty God,
you search us and know us:
may we rely on you in strength
and rest on you in weakness,
now and in all our days;
through Jesus Christ our Lord.

COLLECT

Wednesday 1 September

Psalm 119.153-end
Proverbs 26.12-end
Mark 8.27 – 9.1

Proverbs 26.12-end

'Whoever digs a pit will fall into it' (v.27)

Meet the sluggard – rather disappointingly translated by the NRSV as 'the lazy person'. He (although there's no reason why it shouldn't be she) is one of the great fictional characters of the Old Testament. The sluggard is so idle that although he can just about manage to stick his fork in a pile of pasta, he then can't summon the energy to lift it to his mouth. He is certainly not going to work today because there are rumours of wild animals at large and leaving the house would be inviting death. In fact, even leaving bed is a risk not worth taking.

He has already made an appearance in Proverbs where, after plenty of jokes, the laughter freezes when poverty becomes a reality (Proverbs 6.9-11). In contrast to the sluggard, there is an exemplary role model – the ant. Self-motivated and forward-planning, the tiny ant thrives while the lumbering sluggard dozes (Proverbs 6.6-8).

Proverbs is, however, not negative about sleep. A good experience of sleep and 'sound wisdom and prudence' are closely connected (Proverbs 3.21-24). It's typical of the book's practical advice about a balanced life. This also includes taking time to consider when it's right to get personally involved in someone else's difficulty and when to hold back. It means knowing when to stop a joke before it goes too far. And it involves learning what to do in order to take the heat out of a quarrel.

COLLECT

Almighty God,
who called your Church to bear witness
that you were in Christ reconciling the world to yourself:
help us to proclaim the good news of your love,
that all who hear it may be drawn to you;
through him who was lifted up on the cross,
and reigns with you in the unity of the Holy Spirit,
one God, now and for ever.

| *Reflection by* **Peter Graystone**

Psalms **143**, 146
Proverbs 27.1-22
Mark 9.2-13

Thursday 2 September

Proverbs 27.1-22

'Let another praise you, and not your own mouth' (v.2)

The way of Jesus demands integrity in everyday, mundane life. That is where the book of Proverbs leads us, and with a little imagination its message becomes startlingly relevant to the twenty-first century. The proverbs speak of wine (Proverbs 23.31-35), pledges (Proverbs 22.26-27) and dark alleys (Proverbs 7.6-9). But actually they are communicating with us about cannabis, payday loans and hookup apps.

Some proverbs anticipate 2021 in an uncanny way. The advice about relationships in this chapter seems to anticipate our generation in which siblings and children may live a great distance away. We need to take friendship seriously. We learned from the COVID-19 lockdown the relative values of a friend who can be physically present and the image of a relation on Skype. Both are wonderful, but in an emergency, Skype can't leave a bag of groceries on a doorstep.

Other advice about friendship seems timeless. True friends find ways to be open with each other without damaging the relationship, even when they need to be critical. Indeed, constant flattery is not a sign of friendship at all. Honest friendship makes you a better person and brings contentment into your life (v.9, the Hebrew is confusing but suggests the need for comfort in times of distress). The chapter recognizes, however, that a friend who is trying too hard to be upbeat and gregarious can be a pain in the neck. Are you prompted to contact a particular friend for any reason today?

Almighty God,
you search us and know us:
may we rely on you in strength
and rest on you in weakness,
now and in all our days;
through Jesus Christ our Lord.

COLLECT

Friday 3 September

Psalms 142, **144**
Proverbs 30.1-9, 24-31
Mark 9.14-29

Proverbs 30.1-9, 24-31

'... give me neither poverty nor riches' (v.8)

Nobody knows who Agur was, but this chapter has kept his reputation alive for centuries. On the basis of these riddling verses I find him immensely likeable.

I like his humility. He introduces himself as someone who is no great shakes as an academic, but muddles through as best he can because of his awe when he considers God. The answer to his question in verse 4 is, 'Not me; not anybody. God alone!' His sense of the magnitude of what God wants to communicate with us is a caution to all who preach or write. Their role is not to draw attention to themselves but to make sure that people can hear from God directly.

I like his contentment with having just enough. His prayer for neither too little nor too much is a formidable riposte to anyone who teaches that the more faithful you are to God the more prosperous you will become.

I like his witty way with a poem. The repeated pattern of listing three things and adding a fourth draws attention to the importance of the final one (vv.24-31). He encourages those who feel as insignificant as a lizard that they should not underestimate their potential to influence people (v.28). He urges political leaders to prioritize uniting their people (v.31). In verses not included in today's reading Agur reveals himself to be sweetly romantic, and I can't help liking that too (Proverbs 30.18,19).

COLLECT

Almighty God,
who called your Church to bear witness
that you were in Christ reconciling the world to yourself:
help us to proclaim the good news of your love,
that all who hear it may be drawn to you;
through him who was lifted up on the cross,
and reigns with you in the unity of the Holy Spirit,
one God, now and for ever.

| *Reflection by* **Peter Graystone**

Psalm 147
Proverbs 31.10-end
Mark 9.30-37

Saturday 4 September

Proverbs 31.10-end

'... a woman who fears the Lord is to be praised' (v.30)

I fully acknowledge the irony of someone who is both male and single commenting on a Bible passage about a noble wife. I also acknowledge my discomfort that the chapter seems to describe Superwoman. There is something dispiriting about magazines that expect that every woman will have a thriving career while maintaining an immaculate home in which she overturns gender stereotypes by being the one who clears the gutters, meanwhile caring for perfect children, being endlessly creative in bed, and staying up to date with the music that is playing at 3am in the clubs.

Might women find this chapter equally dispiriting? One way to avoid that is by recognizing that it is not a checklist, but a poem. In Hebrew it is an acrostic, each verse beginning with a different letter of the alphabet. In that context it's helpful that it doesn't focus on body image. Instead, it makes virtues of skill, earning, compassion, wisdom and faith. It also insists on the contribution that husbands and children must make. None of these things are to be taken for granted; they are to be honoured.

I prefer to think of the last chapter of Proverbs not as an instruction list, but as a glorious tribute to 22 ways in which women can be magnificent – an A to Z of thank-yous by a man to the wives of the world.

COLLECT

Almighty God,
you search us and know us:
may we rely on you in strength
and rest on you in weakness,
now and in all our days;
through Jesus Christ our Lord.

Monday 6 September

Psalms 1, 2, 3
Wisdom 1 *or*
1 Chronicles. 10.1 – 11.9
Mark 9.38-end

Mark 9.38-end

'Whoever gives you a cup of water ...' (v.41)

The demands of the Christian faith often seem impossibly great. Yet even in this passage, which is a warning, we are not being asked to end world poverty or solve global warming single handed; rather, to give a cup of water to one who bears the name of Christ. I know a priest in the Solomon Islands, where it is always hot, who usually has queues of people waiting outside his house to see him. 'What's your secret?' I asked him. 'Oh, it's not me they come to see,' he replied with humility. 'It's the ministry of cold water. I keep plenty in my fridge.' Kindness is often shown in the very smallest acts. A cup of water seems so insignificant, but as a sign of the way we treat others, it is everything.

Christ cries out from the cross 'I thirst.' I wonder what we are going to do for a thirsting Christ.

We may think Christ is extreme when he talks of losing a hand, leg or eye, but we do not have to look far to see the hell that is created when others are treated with contempt. We will be judged by the way we treat others, and in the smallest of actions the world is transformed: 'When I was thirsty you gave me something to drink... for whatever you did for the least of my brothers and sisters you did it for me.' It's not much to ask. At the same time it's everything. If everyone followed this teaching, there would be no poverty or global warming.

COLLECT

Almighty God,
whose only Son has opened for us
a new and living way into your presence:
give us pure hearts and steadfast wills
to worship you in spirit and in truth;
through Jesus Christ your Son our Lord,
who is alive and reigns with you,
in the unity of the Holy Spirit,
one God, now and for ever.

| *Reflection by* **Richard Carter**

Tuesday 7 September

Mark 10.1-16

'... the two shall become one flesh' (v.8)

Seeing two become one is the most wonderful thing to witness; it is even greater to experience. It involves a love so steadfast that the *me* of the self becomes *us*. It is the realization that we are completed by love. Two becoming one flesh suggests the beauty and tenderness of sexual intimacy, but it also reminds us that love is an eternal thing. When my father was very frail and elderly and needed constant care, I offered to give my mother a day off, intending to give my father the best day ever; however, my father spent the whole day looking out of the window and saying, 'I wonder when your mother is coming home'. The two had become one; their love completed each other.

Yet, as we read this passage, we are aware too of the many times when love that was intended to be steadfast becomes divided and jagged, and all involved live with the pain and consequences of that. Divorce, or the breaking down of a relationship of intimacy and love, can never be taken lightly. It wounds. It is not what God intends for us. But though these words of Christ have often been used to condemn, it is Christ who shows us that the wounds of our past can also become signs of resurrection, and that whatever the failure, we can be set free. Christ will not divorce us; nothing will separate us from his love, for he has become one flesh with us. Through him we will learn the true meaning of a love that never ends and his longing for us to know that at-one-ment.

Merciful God,
your Son came to save us
and bore our sins on the cross:
may we trust in your mercy
and know your love,
rejoicing in the righteousness
that is ours through Jesus Christ our Lord.

COLLECT

Reflection by **Richard Carter** | 251

Wednesday 8 September

Psalm 119.1-32
Wisdom 3.1-9 *or*
1 Chronicles 15.1 – 16.3
Mark 10.17-31

Mark 10.17-31

'... what must I do to inherit eternal life?' (v.17)

I remember many years ago a friend coming to see my father, who was the vicar, to ask him if he thought it would be immoral, when there was so much poverty in the world, if he spent £70,000 on a new car he wanted. My father was not usually one to judge, but he looked at the man with love and said that he did think it was immoral. The man went away with sadness and bought the car nonetheless. I wonder how many people could have been helped out of poverty for the cost of that one car.

Jesus seems to demand a lot of the rich man: go, sell what you own, give your money to the poor, come, follow me. We often struggle with a single demand on us – there are five life-changing ones here. But there is also an incredible offer too: 'you will have treasure in heaven'. I wonder how often we focus on what we think is the depletion of self and miss the generous gift. Perhaps we are not being asked to let go of our worldly wealth but simply open the hands that we clench in fear in order to receive something infinitely more precious. After all, which would you really rather have, an expensive car or the kingdom of heaven? We become what we are by sharing; we follow Christ, and that is the most beautiful gift of all. Try it and see.

COLLECT

Almighty God,
whose only Son has opened for us
a new and living way into your presence:
give us pure hearts and steadfast wills
to worship you in spirit and in truth;
through Jesus Christ your Son our Lord,
who is alive and reigns with you,
in the unity of the Holy Spirit,
one God, now and for ever.

| *Reflection by* **Richard Carter**

Psalms 14, **15**, 16
Wisdom 4.7-end *or*
1 Chronicles 17
Mark 10.32-34

Thursday 9 September

Mark 10.32-34

'... those who followed were afraid' (v.32)

We get the sense in Mark's Gospel that the disciples are really following Jesus into the unknown, amazed and afraid at the same time. However much we may want to plan our future and know our destination, this is not always possible, especially when it is Christ who is leading us. The very meaning of our faith is that we are called to trust him, and trust is not at all easy in our modern culture, which has taught us to distrust. Perhaps when we set out on any adventure, there is always that sense of both amazement and fear, but like those disciples, we may sometimes wish that we had stayed at home.

Jesus predicts his own betrayal, condemnation, death and resurrection, but the disciples certainly don't want to believe that. Suddenly, discipleship has become high risk, costing everything. We too, putting our trust in Christ, may experience doubt ringing in our ears suggesting that this is all folly. So I wonder why we follow. Perhaps once we have met Jesus and tasted what it means to follow, we know our lives will never be the same – that however difficult this path becomes, to abandon it would be to let go of the most precious gift we have ever known. The more we taste God's love, the more we long for the fullness of that love and to return it. As St Augustine wrote: 'Love God and say it with your life.'

Something real is at stake here. What does Christ ask of us? The whole of our lives.

COLLECT

Merciful God,
your Son came to save us
and bore our sins on the cross:
may we trust in your mercy
and know your love,
rejoicing in the righteousness
that is ours through Jesus Christ our Lord.

Reflection by **Richard Carter**   253

Friday 10 September

Mark 10.35-45

'Are you able to drink the cup that I drink?' (v.38)

I have a very powerful memory of my great aunt. She was lying in hospital looking lost, vulnerable and frightened – and so alarmingly thin. I knew she was dying. 'I can't possibly stay here,' she was saying with great authority. 'I want to go home immediately. Tell the doctors to do something.' And I was acutely aware that there was nothing more they could do. My beloved aunt was dying, and I recognized how unprepared for suffering she seemed.

The problem is that we think we have time. We have only *now*. Our modern society often treats suffering as if it's an anomaly for which there is a solution or, if not, someone to be blamed. 'Are you able to drink the cup that I drink, or be baptized with the baptism that I am baptized with?' Jesus asks. 'Bring it on,' the sons of Zebedee respond. And yet they are so obviously not at all ready. They are still looking for their high place with Jesus in glory, one on the right and one on the left. And who can blame them? I wonder if we ourselves are ready to drink the cup of suffering with Christ, or are we not still looking for that same hope of somehow being up there above it all?

Suffering is a great leveller that few of us will escape. Yet Christ's promise is to be there with us. 'For the Son of Man came not to be served but to serve, and to give his life a ransom for many.'

COLLECT

Almighty God,
whose only Son has opened for us
a new and living way into your presence:
give us pure hearts and steadfast wills
to worship you in spirit and in truth;
through Jesus Christ your Son our Lord,
who is alive and reigns with you,
in the unity of the Holy Spirit,
one God, now and for ever.

| *Reflection by* **Richard Carter**

Psalms 20, 21, **23**
Wisdom 5.17 – 6.11 *or*
1 Chronicles 22.2-end
Mark 10.46-end

Saturday 11 September

Mark 10.46-end

'What do you want me to do for you?' (v.51)

Bartimaeus' prayer for mercy is similar to that of the tax collector found in Luke 18.13 and they become the model for one of the oldest prayers in Christendom: 'Lord Jesus Christ, Son of God, have mercy on me'. This is the Jesus Prayer. Pray these words humbly, in the middle of the night when you can't sleep, or as you wake up anxious about the day. Pray them as you walk along the road, or face the problem that has no obvious solution. Pray them for the person you struggle to love or help, or forgive, or be forgiven by: 'Lord Jesus Christ, Son of God, have mercy on me.' Breathe the mercy of God into the deepest part of you.

Now imagine Jesus standing still and attentive, calling you to come to him. He sees all of you, both the seen and the unseen. And now he speaks: 'What do you want me to do for you?' What do you really want, want beyond all else? This is your simple request: 'My teacher, let me see again.' You are standing face to face with Christ. Simply by that standing you are faithful. I wonder what you see. I wonder what this seeing teaches you. I wonder what you want to do next.

Now take this prayer with you and pray it today and each day in every struggle: 'Lord Jesus Christ, Son of God, have mercy on me.' And every time you pray it, see the still face of Jesus and hear his words, 'What do you want me to do for you?' and whisper your response 'My teacher, let me see again'.

Merciful God,
your Son came to save us
and bore our sins on the cross:
may we trust in your mercy
and know your love,
rejoicing in the righteousness
that is ours through Jesus Christ our Lord.

COLLECT

Reflection by **Richard Carter** | 255

Monday 13 September

Mark 11.1-11

'Blessed is the one who comes in the name of the Lord!' (v.9)

'Preach the gospel – use words only if you have to.' St Francis of Assisi is reputed to have said. The last week of Jesus' life begins with an unforgettable dramatic action: Jesus will show us rather than tell us, and Jerusalem will become his stage. Notice the way everything is prepared and ready: the tied colt by the door, the bystanders who ask them what they are doing, and then the ride into Jerusalem. And we too must be ready and prepared to enter this action. You can't describe the humility of God; you can only *be* that humility and that blessing. Jesus rides into the place of conflict, with such generous self-offering and is met with spontaneous celebration and joy. The joy will, of course, not last. His disciples will abandon him, and the crowd of supporters will dissolve into the night as he is arrested and condemned. Yet this action will never be forgotten.

This is the king who comes in complete humility, who comes bringing blessing not curse. Even in the agony of the cross, when the inscription reads in mockery, accusation – or is it recognition: 'The King of the Jews' – hold onto this vision of his kingdom, this donkey, these leafy branches cut from the fields in celebration, these songs of joy – this servant king. And pray this: that like Jesus, we can live that same joy of the Beatitudes, that same song of blessing, without being poisoned by hatred or violence, not only telling but showing what it means to come in the name of the Lord.

COLLECT

God, who in generous mercy sent the Holy Spirit
upon your Church in the burning fire of your love:
grant that your people may be fervent
in the fellowship of the gospel
that, always abiding in you,
they may be found steadfast in faith and active in service;
through Jesus Christ your Son our Lord,
who is alive and reigns with you,
in the unity of the Holy Spirit,
one God, now and for ever.

| *Reflection by* **Richard Carter**

Psalms 2, 8, 146
Genesis 3.1-15
John 12.27-36*a*

Tuesday 14 September
Holy Cross Day

Genesis 3.1-15

'... knowing good and evil' (v.5)

This story of our fall is such a powerful story of disobedience and division, and it's still taking place today. We, who have been called to share in the abundance of God's creation, are tempted to disobey the God of life. Notice the way the very act of disobedience excites: the serpent suggests that it is God who is the deceiver and the life-denier. Yet once we disobey God, we ourselves become the life-deniers – divided from each other, divided from creation, divided from God. Hear all around you, hear within yourself, the voice of the life-denier posing as the life-giver. This voice whispers that it is you alone that matters, that there is no need for compassion, no forgiveness, no redemption, no trust, no truth, no heaven other than what you can possess as your own territory, no need to care for creation just profit, no God greater than self. When we see the divisions and violence of our nation and our world, whole cities riddled with bombs and bullets, millions fleeing violence and poverty, we see how this disobedience and denial of love can lead to the hell of human making.

Who can save us from this death? 'Thanks be to God, through Jesus Christ our Lord' (Romans 7.25). We know this because we see the Son of God's open arms on a cross. And this cross, this sign of death, becomes the sign of forgiveness, hope and resurrection: a cross which through God's love can change God's enemies into God's friends.

We adore you, O Christ, and we bless you, because by your Holy Cross you have redeemed the world.

COLLECT

Almighty God,
who in the passion of your blessed Son
made an instrument of painful death
to be for us the means of life and peace:
grant us so to glory in the cross of Christ
that we may gladly suffer for his sake;
who is alive and reigns with you,
in the unity of the Holy Spirit,
one God, now and for ever.

Reflection by **Richard Carter**

257

Wednesday 15 September

Psalm **34**
Wisdom 7.15 – 8.4 *or*
1 Chronicles 29.1-9
Mark 11.27-end

Mark 11.27-end

'By what authority are you doing these things?' (v.28)

The banks of a canal are created to channel water; if you create high banks, but they channel no water, there is no point to them other than to create an obstacle. Rules can become like that. They are created to protect and enhance life, but if they are used to deny life, then what is their purpose? Authority can become like that too. True authority is the flow of wisdom that guides, protects, empowers, like a wise leader or teacher. True obedience to God is a deeper listening.

Yet often authority becomes about status: 'I am in control. I am following the rules, I don't care if the rule makes no sense whatsoever, obey me.' Again and again, Jesus comes up against this intransigence that poses as religion. It's often based on fear or pride. Fear that one's own certainties and securities are being challenged. Pride that one's power is being ignored or undermined. But actually true authority is life giving. Watch Jesus how he heals on the Sabbath, how he eats or meets with sinners, tax collectors, gentiles – how he even forgives sins. Blasphemy!

By whose authority is Jesus acting? By the authority of the One who called John to prepare the way of the Lord – John, who recognized the beloved, and who realized he was not fit to untie Christ's sandals. Notice the way John realizes his own ministry of baptism is just the beginning, not the final word; the one who comes after him will baptize with the Holy Spirit and fire. Exercising God's authority is revealed in a readiness to step out of the way oneself, to let God be seen beyond our own power or control.

COLLECT

God, who in generous mercy sent the Holy Spirit
   upon your Church in the burning fire of your love:
grant that your people may be fervent
in the fellowship of the gospel
that, always abiding in you,
they may be found steadfast in faith and active in service;
through Jesus Christ your Son our Lord,
who is alive and reigns with you,
in the unity of the Holy Spirit,
one God, now and for ever.

| *Reflection by* **Richard Carter**

Psalm **37***
Wisdom 8.5-18 *or*
1 Chronicles 29.10-20
Mark 12.1-12

Thursday 16 September

Mark 12.1-12

'They will respect my son' (v.6)

How quickly we can become territorial, wanting to possess and to defend what we believe to be ours. You can see this even among holidaymakers or tourists on a beach staking out their areas with wind breaks, towels and deck chairs or loungers as if to say: 'This bit of the beach is mine! Do not intrude.' We defend territory and fear the intruder, whether it be a new boss or colleague at work encroaching on our freedom or responsibility, or a neighbour building an extension, or the contactor who wants to build affordable housing far too near our local school, which should be for our kids not others from outside the area. 'This is mine!' But is it? Is not all we possess the gift of God? 'No,' you may think. 'This is mine! I did the work. It was me who sweated, and built. It was me who earned the profit.'

'Really? Who gave the land? Who gave the land the gift of life? Who gave you the gift of life? I gave it to you in order to steward. But you have changed my giving into taking.' Look around the world and see how many of the conflicts of the world are conflicts of territory. 'This is mine!' See the hatred and the prejudice and the violence when the 'mine' is threatened. And yet Jesus challenges this 'mine', saying 'Let your mine become *ours*. I gave it to you in order to share with others the fruits of creation. You are putting to death the stranger who comes not to rob you but to bless you with the gift of life beyond self.'

In what ways do you receive God's son and allow someone else the space to flourish? How do you let the 'me' become 'us'?

> Lord God,
> defend your Church from all false teaching
> and give to your people knowledge of your truth,
> that we may enjoy eternal life
> in Jesus Christ our Lord.

COLLECT

Friday 17 September

Psalm 31
Wisdom 8.21 – end of 9 *or*
I Chronicles 29.21-end
Mark 12.13-17

Mark 12.13-17

'... the things that are God's' (v.17)

When the Christian Order of Melanesian Brothers came on a mission to the UK, the churches that welcomed them often asked them questions like: 'Which would you like, tea or coffee?' To which the Brothers would respond: 'Both of them.' 'No you have to choose', I tried to explain. 'But I like both of them,' the brother responded. They also treated the vicars they met, the churchwardens and the local mayor with the same respect they treated the homeless man with whom they sat down on the bridge at Charing Cross. It seems we love to create binary alternatives: in or out, rich or poor, friend or unfriend, like or unlike, good or bad, spirit or flesh, righteous or sinner, saved or condemned, spiritual or secular. But I wonder what it means if God includes both of them. They are not in separate silos. God so loved the world. We are not called to make war in the world but live the love of God in the world.

They try to trap Jesus, to prove that he is not in but out, not good but bad, not righteous but a sinner, not saved but condemned. Instead, Christ opens up a wider vision of the kingdom, where God embraces the whole world, and the Word becomes flesh and lives among us, inside and out. How can we take God out of the church and into the street, into the place we are working, or struggling with material needs and allegiances. What does it really mean to show no 'deference' and no 'partiality': to live God's kingdom on earth as it is in heaven?

COLLECT

God, who in generous mercy sent the Holy Spirit
 upon your Church in the burning fire of your love:
grant that your people may be fervent
in the fellowship of the gospel
that, always abiding in you,
they may be found steadfast in faith and active in service;
through Jesus Christ your Son our Lord,
who is alive and reigns with you,
in the unity of the Holy Spirit,
one God, now and for ever.

| *Reflection by* **Richard Carter**

Psalms 41, **42**, 43
Wisdom 10.15 – 11.10 *or*
2 Chronicles 1.1-13
Mark 12.18-27

Saturday 18 September

Mark 12.18-27

'God not of the dead, but of the living' (v.27)

I tried to talk to him, but his reading of the Scriptures tied me up in knots. It seemed so literalistic, so oppressive, like chains rather than good news. Ah, but did I believe this or that? And if I believed that, it must mean I would be separated from the sheep and burn in unquenchable fire. Verse after verse he quoted at me. I'm sure he was trying to save me. Whereas all I longed for was to save him from a reading of the Bible that felt so oppressive. Eventually, I said 'I simply cannot believe in a God who is love who would burn most of those he has created in his image in fire forever'.

Sometimes, you just have to read the Bible with your heart. It's not a theory, it's not an argument, it's not a weapon, it's not words – it's the Word made flesh. It's God's love deeper and wider and more expansive than your dreams. This passage is like a puzzle they set for Jesus to tie him up in knots. Whose wife would the woman be in heaven? Jesus names this kind of moral maze for what it is: nonsense. They have not understood the truth about God and the coming of the kingdom. This is the God of Abraham and Isaac. He is the God of the living not of the dead. He is a God beyond our formulas and mind games, who formed and created all things. It's like being invited to the heavenly banquet and arguing over the seating plan. Surely by then we will have let go of self and be lost and found in wonder, love and praise.

COLLECT

Lord God,
defend your Church from all false teaching
and give to your people knowledge of your truth,
that we may enjoy eternal life
in Jesus Christ our Lord.

Monday 20 September

Mark 12.28-34

'Which commandment is the first of all?' (v.28)

Today's reading reminds us that not all the Pharisees and scribes opposed Jesus. Here is one who openly and respectfully commends Jesus for his answers and whose question to Jesus is not another attempt by an opponent to trip him up on a point of theology. The question reflects a familiar concern in his day. Which laws matter more or less? Once I know, I can be sure I am obedient. This easily results in piety based on measures and achievements. Jesus told stories against those 'confident of their own righteousness' (Luke 18.9, NIV), and it was this kind of box ticking, rule-keeping faith he had in mind.

Rather than picking one commandment, Jesus merges two. There is no love of God that is not a love of neighbour. They are one and the same. The command to 'love your neighbour as yourself ' is directly from the book of Leviticus. There, 'neighbour' is defined as 'any of your people' (Leviticus 19.18). 'Your neighbour' is therefore anyone within the same particular racial, religious, cultural or kinship group as you. The boundaries of love are clearly prescribed and precisely defined.

Throughout his ministry, Jesus actively confronted and demolished such a territorially bounded understanding of love. In this passage, the repeated stress on 'all' has the same effect. To love God with the whole of your being involves loving all and everyone in exactly the same way.

COLLECT

O Lord, we beseech you mercifully to hear the prayers
    of your people who call upon you;
and grant that they may both perceive and know
    what things they ought to do,
and also may have grace and power faithfully to fulfil them;
through Jesus Christ your Son our Lord,
who is alive and reigns with you,
in the unity of the Holy Spirit,
one God, now and for ever.

| *Reflection by* **David Runcorn**

Psalms 49, 117
1 Kings 19.15-end
2 Timothy 3.14-end

Tuesday 21 September
Matthew, Apostle and Evangelist

2 Timothy 3.14-end
'All Scripture is inspired by God' (v.16)

To be inspired is to breathe in and be filled. We use the word to describe the impact of music, literature, art or people that somehow leave us feeling more full of life, creatively energized and motivated. So when this word is used of Scripture, we mean something much more than that it contains the words and instructions of God. We mean Scripture is filled with God's very own life. An alternative translation of this phrase captures this well – 'all Scripture is God-breathed' (NIV).

If you are close to someone's breath, you are close to their very being. They are present in the most intimate and personal way to you. How might that thought change our relationship with the Bible? I always value it when churches keep a quiet pause after the Bible is read in a service. We need a space to breathe it in deeply – to be inspired.

The image of breath connects with another place where life is God-breathed in the Bible. At the beginning of creation, while still lifeless clay, God breathed into Adam's nostrils and he became a living being. God personally in-spires his life in us. Humanity is God-breathed.

Breathing is essential. There is no life without it. We are reminded here of the central habit and discipline of being inspired by the God-breathed Scriptures if we are to be truly alive in his grace and wisdom.

O Almighty God,
whose blessed Son called Matthew the tax collector
to be an apostle and evangelist:
give us grace to forsake the selfish pursuit of gain
and the possessive love of riches
that we may follow in the way of your Son Jesus Christ,
who is alive and reigns with you,
in the unity of the Holy Spirit,
one God, now and for ever.

COLLECT

Reflection by **David Runcorn** | 263

Wednesday 22 September

Psalm **119.57-80**
Wisdom 13.1-9 *or*
2 Chronicles 5
Mark 13.1-13

Mark 13.1-13

'Not one stone will be left here upon another' (v.2)

The temple in Jerusalem was one of the wonders of the ancient world. It was simply enormous. The Jewish historian, Josephus, records that some of its stones were 40 feet long, 12 feet high and 18 feet deep. The impact on pilgrims coming in from the countryside to worship and pray would have been immense. It was vast, solid and surely indestructible – like the holy faith it was built to house.

But when the disciples emerge, gasping and exclaiming with wide-eyed awe, Jesus will have none of it. He bluntly predicts the utter destruction of that colossal building that must have looked indestructible. For his disciples, that outburst must have been like a slap in the face and a total contradiction of what they expected. But Jesus knows that seeking security in things that, despite all outward appearances, will not endure, is the deadliest enemy of gospel faith.

Up to this point, Mark's Gospel has been a record of Jesus' public ministry. But the focus is about to shift to Jerusalem and the condemnation, suffering and death of Jesus. Here, between these two movements of the Gospel, we eavesdrop on Jesus alone with his disciples and the teaching he gives them privately as he prepares them for what is coming and its meaning. It is tough, uncomfortable and uncompromising. But such is the way of salvation in a turbulent world.

COLLECT

O Lord, we beseech you mercifully to hear the prayers
    of your people who call upon you;
and grant that they may both perceive and know
    what things they ought to do,
and also may have grace and power faithfully to fulfil them;
through Jesus Christ your Son our Lord,
who is alive and reigns with you,
in the unity of the Holy Spirit,
one God, now and for ever.

| *Reflection by* **David Runcorn**

Psalms 56, **57** (63*)
Wisdom 16.15 – 17.1 *or*
2 Chronicles 6.1-21
Mark 13.14-23

Thursday 23 September

Mark 13.14-23
'... be alert' (v.23)

These are some of the most disturbing teachings in the Gospels and we hear them from the mouth of Jesus himself. His reference to the 'desolating sacrilege' would have evoked horrific memories for faithful Jews of the time when the Seleucid Emperor Antiochus Epiphanes set up a heathen altar in their holy temple in 168 BC. But here the memory foretells far worse to come. Bible prophecy comes condensed and layered. In the more immediate future it is very likely that Jesus is foretelling the destruction of Jerusalem that happened in AD 70. But his vision also extends to the terror of the end times that he speaks of elsewhere.

There are many places in the world today where all too many know exactly what it is like to have to flee in the face of overwhelming evil with little warning, taking minimal belongings, women pregnant and parents with young children. We are also a world of fake news, falsehood and propaganda in which it is hard to know what and who to trust for our security and wellbeing.

Faith in such a world of terror involves an utter realism about the story we are part of.

We have been warned. We are to pray for protection and deliverance. 'Stay alert', says Jesus. Above all, we must never underestimate the depths from which we need redeeming and from which this world needs saving.

COLLECT

Lord of creation,
whose glory is around and within us:
open our eyes to your wonders,
that we may serve you with reverence
and know your peace at our lives' end,
through Jesus Christ our Lord.

Friday 24 September

Psalms 51, 54
Wisdom 18.6-19 or
2 Chronicles 6.22-end
Mark.13.24-31

Mark.13.24-31

'... from the ends of the earth to the ends of heaven' (v.27)

Jesus continues to teach using highly poetic and apocalyptic language. What he describes is nothing less than the cosmic turbulence and upheavals of a world in final collapse. But those listening to him would have been aware that his words are soaked in the spirit and imagery of the Old Testament prophets. Echoes of Isaiah, Joel, Amos, Daniel, Ezekiel are all found here. This serves to emphasize that, for all their terror, these events are actually signs of something far greater and altogether more wonderful. Something is happening that those ancient prophets longed for and were anticipating from afar off. It is the final consummation of heaven and earth in the coming of Christ and the revelation of the new age of the kingdom.

It takes a certain courage and trust to look terror in the eye and find there signs of hope. But that is what this passage seems to do. Leviathan, the sea monster described in Job, is an untameable and chaotic presence in the world, but God says that 'its eyes are like the eyelids of the dawn' – a new day is hinted at precisely when destruction is the only outcome anticipated (Job 41.18).

As so often, the prophetic vision collapses time. So Jesus promises that those present who will shortly witness his cross, resurrection and ascension and receive the spirit of Pentecost will have truly crossed the threshold of all that his words promise and foretell.

COLLECT

O Lord, we beseech you mercifully to hear the prayers
    of your people who call upon you;
and grant that they may both perceive and know
    what things they ought to do,
and also may have grace and power faithfully to fulfil them;
through Jesus Christ your Son our Lord,
who is alive and reigns with you,
in the unity of the Holy Spirit,
one God, now and for ever.

| *Reflection by* **David Runcorn**

Psalm **68**
Wisdom 19 *or* 2 Chronicles 7
Mark 13.32-end

Saturday 25 September

Mark 13.32-end

'Keep awake' (v.35)

Ancient teachings on spiritual life across all religions characterize our basic human condition as sleeping or sleepwalking. It is a state of unawareness. Christian discipleship is a call to a disciplined alertness and vigilance. 'Wake up!' 'Keep awake', are repeated themes in the New Testament.

What does the call to keep awake demand of us? We tend to speak of tiredness in simple physical terms – 'I just couldn't keep my eyes open'. And sometimes it is sheer exhaustion. But it can also be an emotional or social defence – a way of shutting out and avoiding having to face things we can't cope with. We have a familiar phrase when an unexpected crisis hits a society: we say it is a 'wake-up call'. It often takes the shock of a tragedy to get our attention, and in such moments we become uncomfortably aware of situations that have been neglected or forgotten for too long. At such times 'I did not know' is no more an excuse than pleading 'I overslept'.

The earliest icons of the saints and apostles, with childlike simplicity, picture them all with very large, startled eyes – opened wide by the wonder of the revelation of Christ; and very large ears – for listening for the word of the Lord. As they stand before us in holy attentiveness they witness to the core priority of Christian faith: to 'keep awake'.

Lord of creation,
whose glory is around and within us:
open our eyes to your wonders,
that we may serve you with reverence
and know your peace at our lives' end,
through Jesus Christ our Lord.

COLLECT

Monday 27 September

Psalm **71**
1 Maccabees 1.1-19 *or*
2 Chronicles 9.1-12
Mark 14.1-11

Mark 14.1-11

'Why was the ointment wasted in this way?' (v.4)

'Why this *generosity*?' would have been a more accurate question than 'why this waste?' The story is happening just a few days before Jesus' self-offering on the cross – also a gift poured out beyond any practical measure or costing. But excessive generosity has been a consistent feature of so much of Jesus' ministry and teaching. When he wants to speak of the gift and character of the kingdom, Jesus tells stories of lavish feasts and banquets at which those who have no way of ever earning or deserving an invitation find honoured place.

So why this waste? Because this is how God loves. Divine love has no interest in restricting itself to what is 'necessary'. The cross is not a proportionate, costed response to the needs of the world. Jesus' love is not means tested, or tied to productivity or deserving. His sacrifice cannot be summarized in sober moral equations or legal judgements. God's love is simply not sensible like that. It is beyond measure, poured out in overwhelming excess over an ungrateful, uncomprehending world.

In this story, told in the shadow of the coming cross, is someone who understands all this. An unnamed woman mirrors the wastefulness of God. She is loving as God loves. She is poured out like God and *for* God, beyond thought of cost and beyond any notion of what is 'sensible'.

COLLECT

Almighty God,
you have made us for yourself,
and our hearts are restless till they find their rest in you:
pour your love into our hearts and draw us to yourself,
and so bring us at last to your heavenly city
where we shall see you face to face;
through Jesus Christ your Son our Lord,
who is alive and reigns with you,
in the unity of the Holy Spirit,
one God, now and for ever.

| *Reflection by* **David Runcorn**

Tuesday 28 September

Mark 14.12-25

'... one of you will betray me, one who is eating with me' (v.18)

This account of the preparations for Jesus' last meal with his disciples reveals the degree of danger he was now living under. Two disciples are sent into Jerusalem with very precise instruction to follow and words to say. A rendezvous has been arranged. The owner of the venue remains unidentified. Jesus has been making careful arrangements in secret, not even involving his closest disciples. These are precautions you would expect of people who know they are being watched and who are living under hostile occupation.

Those of us who have never had to live under such threat may at least pray for those who do in today's world. I still recall the shock of discovering that a close friend from a country under a politically repressive regime, had long been taking very practical steps to guard information about his friendships, contacts and personal beliefs.

But the betrayal, when it comes, is from within. There is surely no pain like that. 'It is not enemies ... I could bear that ... But it is you, my equal, my companion, my familiar friend' (Psalm 55.12,13). 'They were our neighbours', cried the bewildered survivor of yet another deadly ethnic conflict.

In some parts of the world today, this meal is still hazardous and risky. Christ offers himself to us through the breaking of bread. This meal is still offered in the midst of conflict, betrayals and deadly divisions in this world. And we are all invited.

Gracious God,
you call us to fullness of life:
deliver us from unbelief
and banish our anxieties
with the liberating love of Jesus Christ our Lord.

COLLECT

Wednesday 29 September
Michael and All Angels

Psalms 34, 150
Tobit 12.6-end *or* Daniel 12.1-4
Acts 12.1-11

Daniel 12.1-4

*'At that time Michael, the great prince, the protector of
your people, shall arise' (v.1)*

Something decisive is being foretold here. But what does it mean?

Some parts of the Bible are best understood by standing well back –
like viewing the main features of a whole landscape. There is a place
for the finer detail, but it is easy to get bogged down and miss the
point. This scene proclaims the defeat of the northern King,
Antiochus, who had sought to destroy and replace the Jewish faith.
But it is told from a heaven-side perspective. It seems that in the
heavenly court each nation had its advocate. Michael, Israel's great
protector, overcomes the protector of the northern king. What is
overcome in heaven is overcome on earth. Deliverance and new life
is declared. The wise guides who were previously despised and
persecuted are now revealed for who they are, shining like stars with
special honour.

One theme here is found elsewhere and is surely one that every age
longs for when chaos or evil threatens to overwhelm. There will be
a time when all things will go to their the proper place – good and
evil, truth and falsehood, faithfulness and apostasy. All will be
revealed for what they truly are. Then a new world becomes possible
in reality and truth.

But here in Daniel, as in our own world, that day is glimpsed but is
yet to be. For the time being, the faithful must live, and endure,
where significant chaos reigns.

COLLECT

Everlasting God,
you have ordained and constituted
   the ministries of angels and mortals in a wonderful order:
grant that as your holy angels always serve you in heaven,
so, at your command,
they may help and defend us on earth;
through Jesus Christ your Son our Lord,
who is alive and reigns with you,
in the unity of the Holy Spirit,
one God, now and for ever.

| *Reflection by* **David Runcorn**

Psalm **78.1-39***
1 Maccabees 2.1-28 *or*
2 Chronicles 13.1 – 14.1
Mark 14.43-52

Thursday 30 September

Mark 14.43-52

'All of them deserted him and fled' (v.50)

The tension has been building and now reaches the moment of decision. A warrant has been issued. Led by Judas, guards arrive to arrest Jesus well out of sight of any excitable crowds. The scene is shadowy and faceless. No one is named except Jesus and Judas. The weapons are absurdly over the top. Jesus feels this keenly and protests at being treated as a common criminal. But he will shortly be crucified alongside two thieves.

The most personal detail in this harrowing account is unique to Mark's Gospel. As all flee, someone makes a grab at a 'certain young man' who was wrapped only in a linen cloth. He slips out of it and runs away naked. There is every indication he had dressed in a hurry to be there. He is named as a follower. Who was he? A linen cloth is a sign of wealth. Had he heard of the plot to arrest Jesus and come to warn him? We know no more. It is possibly Mark's own way of saying 'I was there'.

He flees naked. In fact the whole scene is now stripped bare – bleak and desolate beyond measure. What is left of love, honour, loyalty, courage and faithfulness? Jesus is abandoned and must face his death alone.

We too must face those scenes that expose the worst in us and leave us stripped of our most honourable intentions. We are naked too. We must find our own way of saying, 'I was there'.

Almighty God,
you have made us for yourself,
and our hearts are restless till they find their rest in you:
pour your love into our hearts and draw us to yourself,
and so bring us at last to your heavenly city
where we shall see you face to face;
through Jesus Christ your Son our Lord,
who is alive and reigns with you,
in the unity of the Holy Spirit,
one God, now and for ever.

COLLECT

Reflection by **David Runcorn** | 271

Friday 1 October

Mark 14.53-65

'"Are you the Messiah?" Jesus said, "I am"' (vv.61,62)

The trial was a rushed affair and plainly loaded towards one outcome. The Passover festival was just hours away so time was short. The religious authorities were seeking to use a provision in Jewish law for a capital trial on festival days in the event of serious offence so that 'All the people will hear and be afraid' (Deuteronomy 17.13). But Jewish law also required a trial and condemnation to happen immediately after arrest.

So the trial proceeds through the night at a hurriedly arranged venue. Witnesses have been found but their testimonies were inadmissible as evidence because they contradicted each other. Proceedings were going nowhere until the High Priest personally intervened and questioned Jesus, first on the basis of statements already rejected as flawed. Jesus remains silent until he is asked directly if he is the Messiah. Until this point Jesus has carefully avoided answering this question, most likely because popular political and nationalistic hopes would have hopelessly distorted the meaning of the word. But now he answers directly and unambiguously – 'I am' – and strengthens his answer by quoting prophecy. They have what they need. Their hatred is now unrestrained. The beating and mocking begins.

As events have been unfolding upstairs, another 'trial' has been happening in the courtyard below. Peter has been following Jesus 'at a distance', staying out of sight. That in itself is a contradiction of what discipleship means. But he has been spotted and challenged.

COLLECT

Almighty God,
you have made us for yourself,
and our hearts are restless till they find their rest in you:
pour your love into our hearts and draw us to yourself,
and so bring us at last to your heavenly city
where we shall see you face to face;
through Jesus Christ your Son our Lord,
who is alive and reigns with you,
in the unity of the Holy Spirit,
one God, now and for ever.

| *Reflection by* **David Runcorn**

Psalms **76**, 79
1 Maccabees 2.49-end *or*
2 Chronicles 15.1-15
Mark 14.66-end

Saturday 2 October

Mark 14.66-end

'I do not know this man you are talking about' (v.71)

Mark tells the stories of the trial of Jesus and Peter's denial in parallel and his account alternates between them. As one proceeds in the court upstairs, the other unfolds in the courtyard below. By the fire someone recognizes Peter and is loudly telling everyone around who he is. It is not hard to imagine how frightening that would have been for a known follower of Jesus. The mood was threatening and unpredictable with more than an edge of violence in the air. Peter himself had attacked someone with a sword a few hours earlier. But once he starts denying it, his accent betrays him further.

Peter's denials here function as a dramatic extension of the public abandonment of Jesus that all the disciples were guilty of. *All* fled.

In some parts of the world, Christians have a tradition of being tattooed with the sign of the cross (usually on the wrist). So there is no hiding when the world turns violent. 'You are one of them.' And what of me, I ask myself? How easily would I be recognized – by association or by the way I talk? Do I bear any recognizable marks of believing? And if confronted and challenged, would I stand by the one I too call 'the Christ' and to whom I am pledged, through baptism, to follow with my life?

But if I were to deny and flee, I pray I too may hear a cock crowing and receive the redeeming gift of tears.

Gracious God,
you call us to fullness of life:
deliver us from unbelief
and banish our anxieties
with the liberating love of Jesus Christ our Lord.

COLLECT

Monday 4 October

Psalms **80**, 82
I Maccabees 3.1-26 *or*
2 Chronicles 17.1-12
Mark 15.1-15

Mark 15.1-15

'... he handed him over to be crucified' (v.15)

The Jewish leaders lacked the authority to convict someone of a capital crime. They therefore bring Jesus before Pilate, making the most of the heightened nationalist sentiment that accompanied the celebration of Passover in Jerusalem and accusing him of making treasonous claims to political kingship. The introduction to the narrative of Barabbas, a rebel who had committed murder during the insurrection, confirms why the Roman authorities would be jittery about another claimant to power.

Jesus, however, is silent after his initial reply to Pilate, which indicates that he is a king, but not as Pilate understands it. There are echoes here and throughout the Passion narrative of the Suffering Servant of Isaiah: 'He was oppressed, and he was afflicted, yet he did not open his mouth' (Isaiah 53.7). Jesus is presented as the righteous one of God, handed over in accordance with God's purposes. Those purposes are highlighted by the contrast with Barabbas, which means 'son of the father'. Matthew's Gospel heightens the comparison by telling us Barabbas' first name is Jesus (Matthew 27.16-17). Here the true Son of the Father is condemned to death, in the place of the convicted murderer who goes free. For as the First Letter of Peter puts it, 'Christ also suffered for sins once for all, the righteous for the unrighteous, in order to bring you to God' (1 Peter 3.18).

The innocent one takes the place of the guilty. The story is not just about Barabbas, but about us all: Jesus dies our death, so that we might share his life.

COLLECT

Almighty and everlasting God,
increase in us your gift of faith
that, forsaking what lies behind
and reaching out to that which is before,
we may run the way of your commandments
and win the crown of everlasting joy;
through Jesus Christ your Son our Lord,
who is alive and reigns with you,
in the unity of the Holy Spirit,
one God, now and for ever.

274 | *Reflection by* **Anna Matthews**

Psalms 87, **89.1-18**
1 Maccabees 3.27-41 *or*
2 Chronicles 18.1-27
Mark 15.16-32

Tuesday 5 October

Mark 15.16-32
'Hail, King of the Jews!' (v.18)

Jesus has been condemned as 'the King of the Jews'. Now a travesty of a coronation takes place. Clothed in purple and crowned with thorns, beaten with his royal sceptre (the reed) and offered mocking homage, the soldiers taunt Jesus in his weakness and claims to power. For the early Christians, though, for whom 'God's weakness is stronger than human strength' (1 Corinthians 1.25), Jesus really is a king, and here his throne is the cross.

Jesus' crucifixion tells us of our complicity in the sin of the world. But it also tells another story: of God's love and his unwillingness to leave us in our sin. The 'King of kings and Lord of lords' (Revelation 19.16) who is one with God from all eternity is also the one who in taking on flesh came to be on our side.

This is what true kingship, God's kingship, looks like. The one to whom all glory and dominion belong empties himself of power and takes on the poverty of a servant. The truth incarnate, the Word made flesh, endures contempt and insults. The Judge of all takes the side of the guilty, that we might be forgiven, and the King of kings uses his royal power to stand with and for the suffering, persecuted, lost and forgotten ones – and by our acclamation of him as king asks us to stand with him.

God, our judge and saviour,
teach us to be open to your truth
and to trust in your love,
that we may live each day
with confidence in the salvation which is given
through Jesus Christ our Lord.

COLLECT

Wednesday 6 October

Psalm 119.105-128
I Maccabees 3.42-end *or*
2 Chronicles 18.28 – end of 19
Mark 15.33-41

Mark 15.33-41

'Truly, this man was God's Son' (v.39)

Mark opens his Gospel 'The beginning of the good news of Jesus Christ, the Son of God' and in the first chapter we see the heavens torn apart as God's voice acclaims Jesus as his beloved Son (Mark 1.10-11). Here, in these verses, we see a similar action and acclamation: the veil of the temple is torn in two (Mark uses the same Greek verb as in chapter 1) to show that the way to God stands open through the death of Jesus; and on the lips of a gentile Roman soldier Jesus is confessed as the Son of God.

Jesus dies having cried out in words from Psalm 22.1: 'My God, my God, why have you forsaken me?' There is identification with humanity estranged from God; here also, drawing on the fullness of Psalm 22, an expression of righteous suffering and confidence in God. On the cross, Jesus' ministry looks like it has ended in abject, tortured failure. Yet it is at Jesus' death that Mark gives us the fullest confession of faith in his Gospel: it is not in his works of power but in his suffering and death that Jesus is revealed as God's Son. This was an affront to Jewish and gentile ideas of divinity, and we should not let familiarity with images of the crucifixion lessen its shock. It is God who hangs on the cross – God who loves us so much he goes to the place our sin puts us, who gave 'his life a ransom for many' (Mark 10.45).

COLLECT

Almighty and everlasting God,
increase in us your gift of faith
that, forsaking what lies behind
and reaching out to that which is before,
we may run the way of your commandments
and win the crown of everlasting joy;
through Jesus Christ your Son our Lord,
who is alive and reigns with you,
in the unity of the Holy Spirit,
one God, now and for ever.

| *Reflection by* **Anna Matthews**

Psalms 90, **92**
I Maccabees 4.1–25 *or*
2 Chronicles 20.1-23
Mark 15.42-end

Thursday 7 October

Mark 15.42-end

'... laid it in a tomb' (v.46)

The account of the burial of Jesus deals with early objections that Jesus did not really die – some of which would resurface in a different form in biblical criticism in the 19th and 20th centuries. Mark's narrative anticipates what Christians confess in the Creed: that Jesus 'was crucified, died, and was buried' – and adds the detail that all three events were witnessed by the women, who will be the first to whom the resurrection is revealed.

Jewish Law demanded that a crucified corpse be buried before sunset (Deuteronomy 21.23). Given the timings, the burial rituals would have been rushed, though the intervention of Joseph of Arimathea, a member of the Jewish Sanhedrin (Council) ensured they were observed – Romans preferred to leave decaying bodies on their crosses as deterrents to others.

Why does it matter that Mark insists on Jesus' burial and that the Church makes this fact part of the Creed? It matters because if Jesus did not really die, then neither did he rise from the dead. When Jesus' body is laid in the tomb, death, 'the last enemy' (1 Corinthians 15.26) has claimed him. But death will not hold him. Mark tells of his burial in a borrowed tomb. But as the hymn puts it, 'mine the tomb wherein he lay' (from *My song is love unknown*). And thanks to Jesus' death and resurrection, death is conquered, and we are promised that our tomb, like his, lies empty.

God, our judge and saviour,
teach us to be open to your truth
and to trust in your love,
that we may live each day
with confidence in the salvation which is given
through Jesus Christ our Lord.

COLLECT

Reflection by **Anna Matthews** | 277

Friday 8 October

Mark 16.1-8

'... they were afraid' (v.8)

The first Easter morning brings not joy and the peace of the risen Christ, but bewilderment, fear and flight. It's an odd ending to the Gospel (dissatisfaction with it meant that a shorter and a longer ending were added later), but it says something powerful and true about the resurrection, which is that we sometimes struggle to see it as good news. It doesn't rush us into Easter joy; everything is not instantly resolved. Resurrection doesn't happen tidily. It happens in disarray.

Like the women who flee from the empty tomb, sometimes I flee from resurrection. The new life Jesus promises sometimes feels too unsettling, too unbounded. I find it easier to stay in the tomb of sorrow or fear or unforgiveness, whose contours I at least know, than I do to emerge blinking into the new life Jesus promises, where old certainties are rewritten and my life is made strange and new. If Jesus is risen, then the world is other than I had imagined it to be. The rolled-back stone shows us that tombs do not need to stay sealed. To roll back the stone, to step, tentatively, into the Easter dawn, can be frightening. No wonder the women flee. Because to step out of the tomb, to be resurrected, is to live in a way unbounded by death: to find ourselves not under the dominion of fear or hatred or sin, but under the dominion of love. And that really is good news.

COLLECT

Almighty and everlasting God,
increase in us your gift of faith
that, forsaking what lies behind
and reaching out to that which is before,
we may run the way of your commandments
and win the crown of everlasting joy;
through Jesus Christ your Son our Lord,
who is alive and reigns with you,
in the unity of the Holy Spirit,
one God, now and for ever.

| *Reflection by* **Anna Matthews**

Psalms 96, **97**, 100
1 Maccabees 4.36-end *or*
2 Chronicles 24.1-22
Mark 16.9-end

Saturday 9 October

Mark 16.9-end

'... he appeared first to Mary Magdalene' (v.9)

In most Bibles, the verses after verse 8 of Mark's Gospel are included in brackets. The earliest and best manuscripts do not contain these shorter and longer endings to the Gospel, which use vocabulary not found elsewhere in Mark. Here are added appearances of the risen Jesus, and words of commission and promise. The longer ending is ancient (probably early second century) and clearly draws on the accounts of the other three Gospels.

In all four Gospels, Mary Magdalene is named among the first witnesses of the resurrection. The inclusion here of an encounter between Mary and the risen Christ attests to the consensus in the early Church that she is the first preacher or herald of the resurrection. The subsequent appearance of Jesus to the unbelieving disciples confirms that the Church's testimony is trustworthy – and that the good news has universal significance: it is entrusted to the disciples to be shared with the whole creation.

And the presence of the risen Lord among his disciples is promised, some of the signs mentioned here finding their parallels in the Acts of the Apostles (Acts 2.3-4; 16.18; 28.3-6). Whatever the original ending of Mark, what is clear is that the life of the risen Christ spills out from the pages of the Gospel into the lives of his disciples, in whose witness Christ continues to make himself known in word and deed – and through whom we receive the good news ourselves and are invited to make our response.

God, our judge and saviour,
teach us to be open to your truth
and to trust in your love,
that we may live each day
with confidence in the salvation which is given
through Jesus Christ our Lord.

COLLECT

Monday 11 October

Psalms **98**, 99, 101
1 Maccabees 6.1-17 *or*
2 Chronicles 26.1-21
John 13.1-11

John 13.1-11

'You will never wash my feet' (v.8)

Isaiah describes as 'beautiful' the feet of the messengers of good news (Isaiah 52.7). But these feet are tired and grubby with Jerusalem's dust. Footwashing was a traditional part of hospitality in Jesus' day: when arriving at someone's house, it was expected that the guests' feet would be washed, usually by a servant. Which makes Jesus' action one of both hospitality and humility. He who, right from the start of John's Gospel, has been revealed as the Word made flesh, takes on the role and position of a servant and kneels to wash his disciples' feet.

It's too much for Peter. 'You will never wash my feet' he exclaims. The roles are all wrong: Jesus is his Lord, not his servant. But this humility is the form Jesus' lordship takes. Without imposition, without compulsion, Christ comes to us and asks us to let him serve us.

How tempting it is to echo Peter. Letting Jesus get this close is uncomfortable. Jesus enthroned in heaven is one thing. Even kept safely in the pages of the Bible, Jesus is safe. But kneeling before me? It's the wrong way round. But what Jesus says to Peter he says to us all: 'Unless I wash you, you have no share with me.'

In washing his disciples' feet, Jesus shows that there is no place too lowly, or shameful, or intimate for him to touch, and wash, and love. This is the hospitality of God.

COLLECT

O God, forasmuch as without you
we are not able to please you;
mercifully grant that your Holy Spirit
may in all things direct and rule our hearts;
through Jesus Christ your Son our Lord,
who is alive and reigns with you,
in the unity of the Holy Spirit,
one God, now and for ever.

| *Reflection by* **Anna Matthews**

Psalms **106*** (*or* 103)
1 Maccabees 6.18-47 *or*
2 Chronicles 28
John 13.12-20

Tuesday 12 October

John 13.12-20

'... you are blessed if you do them' (v.17)

Having washed his disciples' feet, Jesus tells them they must wash one another's feet. Their actions and attitudes towards each other are to be a sign of his love. His followers are to be a community shaped by hospitality and humility, where vulnerability is met with tenderness; where the messiness and brokenness of our lives is not hidden, but brought to Christ for healing; where we seek and serve Christ in each other, and in each other let him serve us.

This, says Jesus, is the path of blessing, or beatitude. It's not simply that serving others blesses them: it blesses us, too, by drawing us to him and making us sharers in his divine humility. This is what God's love looks like as it takes on flesh in the lives of Jesus' disciples. It is not in striving for the highest place or honour or achievement or influence that will bring you close to the presence of God, but loving service, through which others will encounter the hospitality of God.

Footwashing is practical and bodily. It's hands-and-knees stuff, lugging bowls and jugs and towels around to touch and wash another, as a sign of God's love. What might this look like in your life? Who can you serve and draw into the hospitality of God's love?

Faithful Lord,
whose steadfast love never ceases
and whose mercies never come to an end:
grant us the grace to trust you
and to receive the gifts of your love,
new every morning,
in Jesus Christ our Lord.

COLLECT

Wednesday 13 October

Psalms 110, **111**, 112
1 Maccabees 7.1-20 *or*
2 Chronicles 29.1-19
John 13.21-30

John 13.21-30

'... reclining next to Jesus' (v.25)

Here we are shown two very different responses to Jesus. He has just washed the feet of the disciples, and broken bread with them. Now Judas goes out into the night, set on the path of betrayal. By contrast 'the one whom Jesus loved' (later identified as the author of John's Gospel) is shown 'reclining next to Jesus' – literally, 'in the bosom of Jesus'.

At the start of the Gospel, Jesus is described as being 'in the bosom of the Father' (John 1.18, KJV – translated by NRSV as 'close to the Father's heart'). The picture of the beloved disciple here shows what Jesus' mission is about: it is to bring us to the place where he is.

From beginning to end, this is the good news that John's Gospel proclaims: Jesus comes to bring us to the place he shares with the Father. As we draw close to Jesus – and it is a picture of great intimacy – so we are drawn close to the Father's heart.

But what of Judas? Jesus knew he would betray him, yet still he loved him; he washed his feet and broke bread with him. Here is a picture of what it means for the Son of God to be handed over: in his love for us, he is vulnerable to betrayal. His love can be accepted in trust, or it can be rejected. Of all of us it demands a choice: to be led like the beloved disciple to the heart of Jesus, or to go our own way into the night.

COLLECT

O God, forasmuch as without you
we are not able to please you;
mercifully grant that your Holy Spirit
may in all things direct and rule our hearts;
through Jesus Christ your Son our Lord,
who is alive and reigns with you,
in the unity of the Holy Spirit,
one God, now and for ever.

| *Reflection by* **Anna Matthews**

Thursday 14 October

John 13.31-end

'... you will follow afterwards' (v.36)

The command to love one another is hardly novel. What makes this a new commandment is what Jesus shows this love to entail: the disciples are told to love one another as Jesus has loved them. He has already shown them what this looks like in the washing of feet and the breaking of bread. With Judas' departure, he now prepares to lay down his life for them. This is the sort of love that is to mark out his disciples.

Peter, impetuous as ever, protests that he is willing to lay down his life for Jesus. But he cannot follow Jesus yet. First will come the fear and the denial, but in Jesus' words there is also the promise of transformation: 'you will follow afterwards'. Here, as the hour of his death arrives, Jesus is still loving his disciples, even in their capacity for making promises they can't keep, in their cowardice and their weakness. And here he holds out hope to us all: that our denials and betrayals and fears will not, finally, have the power to keep us from him; that there is an 'afterwards' for us, too, if we will trust Jesus and the love he offers us – a love that goes to death and hell to bring us to the place where he is.

Faithful Lord,
whose steadfast love never ceases
and whose mercies never come to an end:
grant us the grace to trust you
and to receive the gifts of your love,
new every morning,
in Jesus Christ our Lord.

COLLECT

Reflection by **Anna Matthews** | 283

Friday 15 October

John 14.1-14
'Believe in God' (v.1)

All Jesus' words about his death and departure from them must have alarmed and troubled the disciples. Here he speaks encouragingly to them, assuring them that what to some will look like the failure of his ministry and his abandonment by God is in fact the way to the Father. They are to trust God – and to trust Jesus, who is the revelation of the Father, even as he is arrested, condemned and crucified.

'Show us the Father!' Philip exclaims, missing the revelation of God's truth and life and glory standing right in front of him. It's an easy mistake to make: so often we expect God to reveal himself otherwise than in the person of Jesus Christ. Perhaps we want a God who will spare us from following in the way he goes. But there is unity here: 'Whoever has seen me has seen the Father'. And this is a relationship which Jesus extends to us: 'I go to prepare a place for you', he tells his disciples, promising that through his death they too can enjoy oneness with God.

As you reflect on that, who are those in whose lives you see Jesus' life made visible? How is he visible in yours?

COLLECT

O God, forasmuch as without you
we are not able to please you;
mercifully grant that your Holy Spirit
may in all things direct and rule our hearts;
through Jesus Christ your Son our Lord,
who is alive and reigns with you,
in the unity of the Holy Spirit,
one God, now and for ever.

Psalms 120, **121**, 122
1 Maccabees 13.41-end, 14.4-15 *or*
2 Chronicles 32.1-22
John 14.15-end

Saturday 16 October

John 14.15-end
'I will not leave you orphaned' (v.18)

Contrary to the disciples' fears that they are losing Jesus, he promises an abiding presence with them through the gift of the Holy Spirit. This gift is given to those who love Jesus and keep his commandments, but is not able to be received by 'the world' that rejects Jesus and his revelation of the Father. The disciples, then, are made part of the world of Jesus: they are to live as those who abide in his kingdom, even in the midst of the world that rejects him. And they can do this through the oneness that is the gift of the Spirit. From the start, John's Gospel has made clear the unity between Father and Son. Now the unity between Jesus and his disciples is introduced. The life of Jesus will continue in the lives of believers, just as their lives will continue in him – through love.

It is the gift of the Spirit that will characterize the time after Jesus' death – but in a way that recalls Jesus and makes him present in the lives of his disciples, one of the fruits of which will be the peace which the world cannot give. This promise is given as Jesus' death is imminent, encouraging them to see in his death not the victory of 'the ruler of this world' but the fulfilment of his work of love. This promise sustained the first disciples through all the horror and confusion of the Passion, as it has sustained generations of later disciples through persecution. What might the presence of the Spirit mean for you, and for the way you live as a follower of Jesus in the world today?

Faithful Lord,
whose steadfast love never ceases
and whose mercies never come to an end:
grant us the grace to trust you
and to receive the gifts of your love,
new every morning,
in Jesus Christ our Lord.

COLLECT

Reflection by **Anna Matthews** | 285

Monday 18 October
Luke the Evangelist

Psalms 145, 146
Isaiah 55
Luke 1.1-4

Isaiah 55

'... listen, so that you may live' (v.3)

Who do we listen to when we're faced with any sort of crisis – be it a death in the family, a localized natural disaster or a global threat to health, capable of throwing spanners into the machinations of economic systems, and confronting us with our mortality?

Where will we find wise leadership, truth and selfless compassion?

One word stills our questing mind: listen. Listen carefully. Listen, so you may live. Listen to God who loves us in our vulnerability and gives us strength for the day.

How do we listen? We stop talking. We find solitude. We open our hearts, minds and senses to the whispers of the Spirit always reaching out to us for our good and the world's healing. As we spend time in listening prayer – called contemplative prayer, meditation or the prayer of the heart in the Christian tradition – a clear space within our soul grows stronger, a place where our spirit and the Spirit of Jesus can commune.

Once established, such a listening space allows this sacred communication to continue anywhere: in the midst of trying circumstances, walks in the forest with family, supermarket shopping, even in the valley of the shadow of death.

This spirit-to-Spirit relationship is the food that satisfies, the water that quenches our soul's thirst; not only will *our* comings and goings be full of joy, imbued with peace, but so will the whole of creation.

COLLECT

Almighty God,
you called Luke the physician,
whose praise is in the gospel,
to be an evangelist and physician of the soul:
by the grace of the Spirit
and through the wholesome medicine of the gospel,
give your Church the same love and power to heal;
through Jesus Christ your Son our Lord,
who is alive and reigns with you,
in the unity of the Holy Spirit,
one God, now and for ever.

| *Reflection by* **Sue Pickering**

Psalms **132**, 133
2 Maccabees 6.12-end *or*
2 Chronicles 34.1-18
John 15.12-17

Tuesday 19 October

John 15.12-17

'This is my commandment ...' (v.12)

Jesus has endured the rigours of daily self-emptying and now he leaves his disciples a succinct and stunning commandment.

Instead of the injunction to 'love the Lord your God with all your heart, and with all your soul, and with all your strength, and with all your mind' as recorded in other Gospels (Mark 12.30; Luke 10.27), Jesus offers us a new focus: we are to love each other as he has loved us – personally, persistently, patiently; giving our all, even if it means that we die to everything that we have held dear.

Jesus signals a new way of relating to God by calling his disciples – and us – into an intimate relationship with him, into *friendship*. We are neither slaves, forced by fear or need to do our owner's bidding; nor are we at risk of being 'added' or 'deleted' from a relationship on a whim.

We are offered true friendship as close companions with whom Jesus can share what is closest to his heart. Just as Jesus lived out his humanity in union with God, we are to be united with him, facing trials or rejoicing together, discerning, sustaining and expressing creative ministry wherever we are.

When we live in this way, we know ourselves to be chosen. When we live in this way, we will know how to pray in Jesus' name, for he will be praying with us and in us.

COLLECT

God, the giver of life,
whose Holy Spirit wells up within your Church:
by the Spirit's gifts equip us to live the gospel of Christ
and make us eager to do your will,
that we may share with the whole creation
the joys of eternal life;
through Jesus Christ your Son our Lord,
who is alive and reigns with you,
in the unity of the Holy Spirit,
one God, now and for ever.

Reflection by **Sue Pickering** | 287

Wednesday 20 October

Psalm 119.153-end
2 Maccabees 7.1-19 *or*
2 Chronicles 34.19-end
John 15.18-end

John 15.18-end

'If they persecuted me, they will persecute you' (v.20)

Jesus took the law and the prophets, refining, expanding and living that necessary teaching, until it was distilled as the essence of God: love at its purest, most powerful – and *most vulnerable*.

Jesus risked confronting the religious leaders with their gross failures to be hope-bearers, keepers of the covenant with God. He modelled a life lived according to God's precepts, reaping not only the common people's adulation, but the fury of those who would not face their own shadows, nor change their sinful behaviour.

Now Jesus pulls no punches with his disciples about the consequences of closeness to him. He warns that they too will be targets of persecution – there will be verbal vitriol, rejection, scheming, even death-dealing.

Few of us risk losing our lives physically for professing Christ, yet Jesus' warning still holds true today, when, often in the isolation of a 'post-Christian' context, we try to hold fast to our faith. We may experience subtle but destabilizing emotional persecution; the undermining of our Christian values, beliefs and practices; the exhaustion of being wrongly categorized as being part of extreme expressions of Christianity; being excluded or overlooked – yes, even hated.

It's enough to make any disciple walk away, but, into this talk of hatred and persecution, Jesus introduces the promise of the Advocate, the Spirit of truth, who will be with us to support us. Thanks be to God.

COLLECT

God, the giver of life,
whose Holy Spirit wells up within your Church:
by the Spirit's gifts equip us to live the gospel of Christ
    and make us eager to do your will,
that we may share with the whole creation
    the joys of eternal life;
through Jesus Christ your Son our Lord,
who is alive and reigns with you,
in the unity of the Holy Spirit,
one God, now and for ever.

288 | *Reflection by* **Sue Pickering**

Psalms **143**, 146
2 Maccabees 7.20-41 *or*
2 Chronicles 35.1-19
John 16.1-15

Thursday 21 October

John 16.1-15

'... he will take what is mine and declare it to you' (v.14)

How can Jesus help his friends face what is to come?

He doesn't want them to panic when they find themselves marginalized or threatened by those who have no connection with the truth of the Father's love for all people; nor does he want them to be overwhelmed by losing his physical presence in what he knows will be appalling circumstances.

To calm their sense of growing unease and soothe their sorrow, Jesus assures them that the Advocate will be with them to enable the fullness of Jesus – his glory – to continue to work in the world: convicting people of sin, drawing them closer to the Father, and overcoming forces opposed to the coming of God's kingdom. The Advocate is to keep the connection between Jesus and his disciples alive and purposeful, like an invisible umbilical cord bringing them Jesus' words, inner strength, motivation, courage, inspiration and desire – all they need to grow to their full potential as effective ambassadors of Christ.

They cannot yet know how specific the Spirit's guidance will be for them in the future, nor how the Spirit will become available to every soul who welcomes God's truth. But for now, Jesus is giving them a lifeline – the promise of the Advocate and they must hang on to it to survive.

And so must we.

COLLECT

God, our light and our salvation:
illuminate our lives,
that we may see your goodness in the land of the living,
and looking on your beauty
may be changed into the likeness of Jesus Christ our Lord.

Friday 22 October

Psalms 142, **144**
Tobit 1 *or* 2 Chronicles 35.20 – 36.10
John 16.16-22

John 16.16-22

'A little while ...' (vv.16ff)

Warning of persecutions, promise of the mysterious Advocate, comings and goings of Jesus. What are the disciples to make of all this? The disciples' uncertainty intensifies their anxiety, and they do what many of us do to reduce our fears – they try to get answers by muttering to themselves, talking to each other, seeking some sort of group wisdom, rather than bringing their concerns directly to Jesus. They ponder what Jesus means by 'a little while', forgetting that God's timing is perfect, and missing Jesus' point that change is imminent. They ignore the source of truth standing right in front of them and turn inwards to their own attempts at understanding.

How often do we do the same, taking more than 'a little while' before we recognize our need of God and bring to Jesus our confusion and anxiety?

Jesus knows time is short. He bluntly tells them to expect unimaginable grief but then speaks of natural childbirth in which pain and suffering ultimately lead to joy. They know about this process; they know about the fear and pain of labouring women; they've seen the mix of exhausted, ecstatic joy when new-born and mother are finally, safely, skin to skin.

And so, as happens to this day, an everyday miracle can remind you and me, any wobbly disciple, that no matter our circumstances, Jesus' life in us can transform any hardship and release in us a joy that is indestructible.

COLLECT

God, the giver of life,
whose Holy Spirit wells up within your Church:
by the Spirit's gifts equip us to live the gospel of Christ
    and make us eager to do your will,
that we may share with the whole creation
    the joys of eternal life;
through Jesus Christ your Son our Lord,
who is alive and reigns with you,
in the unity of the Holy Spirit,
one God, now and for ever.

| *Reflection by* **Sue Pickering**

Psalm 147
Tobit 2 *or* 2 Chronicles 36.11-end
John 16.23-end

Saturday 23 October

John 16.23-end

'I have said this to you, so that in me you may have peace' (v.33)

It matters to us when our name is linked with anything reprehensible or we are mispresented. Our name symbolizes our distinctiveness, character and family connections. No wonder we're told to guard against identity theft.

Jesus, however, invites his disciples to *use his name* within the context of the new closeness with the Father through the indwelling Spirit of Jesus. To the extent they follow the Advocate, acting, speaking and thinking with the mind of Christ, his disciples will truly be praying in his name, seeking his will not their own.

When Jesus tells them the Father loves them, the disciples see hints of the perfect joy they will know when they are deeply indwelt by the Spirit. But just as they're beginning to grasp what Jesus has been trying to show them, they are confronted by the cold truth of their impending cowardice, the priority of self-preservation, and, worst of all, the abandonment of their friend.

Jesus hastens to assure his disciples that the Father will be there for him even if they are not. That is what he expects. It's a poignant expectation because we know that, as Jesus absorbs the evil of humankind on the cross, he will also endure a felt sense of separation from his Father.

But for now, Jesus offers them hope and peace in him, rallying them to courage, with his emphatic 'I have conquered the world!'

COLLECT

God, our light and our salvation:
illuminate our lives,
that we may see your goodness in the land of the living,
and looking on your beauty
may be changed into the likeness of Jesus Christ our Lord.

Reflection by **Sue Pickering** | 291

Monday 25 October

John 17.1-5

'... glorify' (vv.1,5)

The burning bush, the Presence in the tent of meeting, and the transfiguration provide visual clues to a creative, intense, relational energy beyond our experience, which we might name as the glory of God.

Like seams of golden light, glory weaves through this passage as Jesus pours out his heart to his Father, asking for an intensifying of the abundance of Being – the eternal 'I AM' – that flows between them through the Spirit.

Though enduring the trials of human frailty and malice, Jesus has still reflected the glory of God by being 'fully alive', as St Augustine expressed it. He has shown us what a human life can look like when indwelt by the Spirit and constantly connected to the Father in filial obedience and joy.

But now, facing the cross, he knows he needs to have available to him that same completeness of divinity that he experienced in union with his Father aeons ago when the earth was still unmade. Only that unimaginably potent and infinite power for creative good, wrapped in the cloak of everlasting compassion, will be sufficient to enable him to absorb the sin of the world, and navigate the untravelled pathway to resurrection.

COLLECT

Blessed Lord,
who caused all holy Scriptures to be written for our learning:
help us so to hear them,
to read, mark, learn and inwardly digest them
that, through patience, and the comfort of your holy word,
we may embrace and for ever hold fast
    the hope of everlasting life,
which you have given us in our Saviour Jesus Christ,
who is alive and reigns with you,
in the unity of the Holy Spirit,
one God, now and for ever.

| *Reflection by* **Sue Pickering**

Tuesday 26 October

John 17.6-19

'Sanctify them in the truth' (v.17)

As he goes on to pray for his disciples, Jesus recounts the story of his developing relationship with the ones whom his Father had given him to be his followers and his friends. God already knows this story, of course, but just as we discover something about ourselves as we tell God our truth in prayer, so, as Jesus recalls the journey they have shared, what they've learned and how they've grown, he is able to gain a richer perspective of the three hectic years of ministry and what they've done together in that time.

What a kindness there is in this – for his disciples and for him.

Jesus longs for them to have his joy, to reach their full potential in the work of the kingdom, to experience the indescribable gladness of being Christ-bearers as they reflect the glory Jesus has given them.

That Jesus loves them deeply is apparent. He wants them to know that, although he is leaving and the Advocate has not yet come, God as Father will be there for them, responsible for their spiritual safety and continuing journey in holiness.

He knows that they will need immense spiritual strength not to succumb to pride at other people's adoration, nor run from the suffering that lies in wait. And so Jesus takes the final, authoritative step: he consecrates himself on their behalf, committing himself to them for eternity.

Merciful God,
teach us to be faithful in change and uncertainty,
that trusting in your word
and obeying your will
we may enter the unfailing joy of Jesus Christ our Lord.

COLLECT

Reflection by **Sue Pickering** | 293

Wednesday 27 October

Psalm 119.1-32
Tobit 5.1 – 6.1*a or* Micah 3
John 17.20-end

John 17.20-end
'... may they also be in us' (v.21)

Jesus wants his disciples – and us – to have no sense of separation from God, to welcome the reality of the indwelling Spirit, breaking open within us the word of God, releasing the power of the risen Christ in our lives.

In a deep, loving relationship, we may become so close to our beloved that we feel as if we are woven together in a way that transcends any differences. It's a glimpse of what is at the heart of the Christian vocation: union with God.

Union with God includes unspoken communication, having one mind with Christ, following the prompts and desires of the Spirit, knowing ourselves to be beloved and letting that love enable us to be Christ's hands, voice and kindness to those we encounter. This is not impenetrable theory; it's been Jesus' lived reality on earth and it can be ours too.

Reclaimed over recent decades, contemplative prayer helps us grow in intimate connection with our personal loving God. In this daily practice, instead of vocal or mental prayer, we sit in silence, and, using a simple word to anchor our wandering mind, we intentionally make ourselves available so God may communicate *directly* with our receptive spirit.

All we have to do is turn up each day and give God space to work within us. It's that simple – and that hard.

COLLECT

Blessed Lord,
who caused all holy Scriptures to be written for our learning:
help us so to hear them,
to read, mark, learn and inwardly digest them
that, through patience, and the comfort of your holy word,
we may embrace and for ever hold fast
the hope of everlasting life,
which you have given us in our Saviour Jesus Christ,
who is alive and reigns with you,
in the unity of the Holy Spirit,
one God, now and for ever.

| *Reflection by* **Sue Pickering**

Psalms 116, 117
Wisdom 5.1-16
or Isaiah 45.18-end
Luke 6.12-16

Thursday 28 October
Simon and Jude, Apostles

Luke 6.12-16
'... and he spent the night in prayer to God' (v.12)

How do you make your choices? Do you gather lots of information, look online, make lists of 'pros and cons', ask others, test things out before you decide? Or do you act on impulse? In this passage we see how Jesus approached his biggest decision: the choice of his closest companions. We're told that he spent the *whole night* in prayer. Most of us struggle to pay attention in prayer for half an hour or an hour at the most, so a whole night might seem impossible.

Maybe Jesus did spend part of this time talking to God aloud about the choices he needed to make, the qualities of the various people who had become his followers and the sort of life he anticipated for them once his ministry began. But, after that thorough unpacking of the issues and possibilities, we can imagine Jesus moving into the deep silence of being as one with his Father, letting all thoughts and feelings and wonderings recede, to be replaced by a stillness of soul that would allow his spirit to focus only on interior communion.

Bound together in the silence of holy union with his Father, Jesus stepped outside familiar, measured time; in the purest practice of contemplation, the hours would pass without exertion or distraction, and Jesus would find refreshment of soul, clarity and a profound peace. From that place of deep knowing, he would name the Twelve, and, in love, care for those not chosen.

COLLECT

Almighty God,
who built your Church upon the foundation
of the apostles and prophets,
with Jesus Christ himself as the chief cornerstone:
so join us together in unity of spirit by their doctrine,
that we may be made a holy temple acceptable to you;
through Jesus Christ your Son our Lord,
who is alive and reigns with you,
in the unity of the Holy Spirit,
one God, now and for ever.

Reflection by **Sue Pickering** | 295

Friday 29 October

Psalms 17, **19**
Tobit 7 *or* Micah 5.2-end
John 18.12-27

John 18.12-27

'... [they] arrested Jesus and bound him' (v.12)

In this passage, Jesus and Peter face the limits of their inner strength. They have choices to make and consequences to face as a result of their decisions. For each of them, the journey through 'the valley of the shadow' awaits.

Harsh hands tie rough rope around Jesus' wrists. He is now, by choice, totally at the mercy of others. From the heights of spiritual communion with his Father and disciples, Jesus is confronted by the physical torment that lies ahead. He who sought others' freedom in radical engagement with those on the margins, now allows himself to be bound, interrogated and struck, each deed intended to undermine his composure. But none of that abuse drives a spear into his soul. The abandonment is yet to come.

Peter lies in order to protect himself, but, in betraying someone he loves, his mask of sturdy competence and his sense of who he is begins to disintegrate. The downward spiral predicted by Jesus has begun. Peter's first denial may have come unconsciously out of self-preservation, but the second and third denials are clearly chosen. Peter's idea of himself as a courageous and determined follower of Jesus splinters into shards of shame, guilt and self-loathing.

The cock's crow announces the beginning, but not just of a new day. Though Peter can't know it in the abysmal darkness of his despair, his journey of transformation towards the light of the risen Jesus has just begun.

COLLECT

Blessed Lord,
who caused all holy Scriptures to be written for our learning:
help us so to hear them,
to read, mark, learn and inwardly digest them
that, through patience, and the comfort of your holy word,
we may embrace and for ever hold fast
    the hope of everlasting life,
which you have given us in our Saviour Jesus Christ,
who is alive and reigns with you,
in the unity of the Holy Spirit,
one God, now and for ever.

| *Reflection by* **Sue Pickering**

Psalms 20, 21, **23**
Tobit 8 *or* Micah 6
John 18.28-end

Saturday 30 October

John 18.28-end

'... for this I came into the world, to testify to the truth' (v.37)

Pilate finds himself alone with Jesus and so begins an interchange that concludes with three words, 'What is truth?'

It's a question that remains particularly relevant today when the postmodern notion that all truth is relative is reinforced by terms like 'alternative facts' and 'fake news'. It is challenging to discern what to believe, whose opinion, version of events or reporting to trust, yet there persists in our shared humanity a compulsion to search for the truth whenever there is confusion or doubt.

Jesus is clear. He dismisses the suggestion that his intention is to establish a conventional kingdom by suppressing enemies and claiming physical territory. His purpose has always been to testify to the truth of God's inclusive mercy and desire to be in loving union with each of us and to point us towards holy living.

Jesus taught, healed, preached, reprimanded and encouraged with an inner consistency based on his relationship with God, and his self-description as 'the way, and the truth and the life' (John 14.6).

He is the yardstick, the 'gold standard' against which our behaviour can be measured. 'What would Jesus do?' may seem a naive question, but if, with a teachable heart, we applied 'WWJD?' to how we vote, spend or share our resources, relate to people, and seek solutions to apparently intractable problems, what a different world it would be.

COLLECT

Merciful God,
teach us to be faithful in change and uncertainty,
that trusting in your word
and obeying your will
we may enter the unfailing joy of Jesus Christ our Lord.

Monday 1 November
All Saints' Day

Isaiah 35.1-9

'... the redeemed shall walk' (v.9)

This passage is full of body parts: hands, knees, heart, eyes, ears and tongue. The prophet promises that each will be made whole by God. Taken together, these different body parts act rather like a 'summary' of the whole human body.

A traditional devotion to Jesus on the Cross called the *membra Jesu nostri* ('the body parts of our Jesus') works in a similar way. It focuses in turn on Jesus' feet, hands, knees, breast and so on, and thus draws the worshipper to sustained contemplation not just of the individual parts of his body but of his bodiliness *as such*.

In Jesus, human flesh is revealed as God's language of preference for telling us about God, and for uniting us with God. And God's taking on of human flesh accomplishes more than the healing of people's individual body parts; it ensures the redemption of our embodied being in all its aspects, making sainthood a real human possibility.

For Isaiah, in this passage, the image of redemption is simple but powerful: walking. Walking is a miracle for those who long to do so and cannot, and in one way or another (mental, social, physical, or - spiritual), that is all of us. Isaiah helps us to realize how all of us can find deliverance in Jesus' words 'Stand up ... and walk!' (John 5.8).

Sanctity is walking on 'God's highway'. No impediment – other than unholiness itself – need bar us from that road.

COLLECT

Almighty God,
you have knit together your elect
in one communion and fellowship
    in the mystical body of your Son Christ our Lord:
grant us grace so to follow your blessed saints
in all virtuous and godly living
that we may come to those inexpressible joys
that you have prepared for those who truly love you;
through Jesus Christ your Son our Lord,
who is alive and reigns with you,
in the unity of the Holy Spirit,
one God, now and for ever.

| *Reflection by* **Ben Quash**

Psalms **5**, 147.1-12 *or* 32, **36**
Isaiah 1.21-end
Matthew 2.1-15

Tuesday 2 November

Isaiah 1.21-end

'... they and their work shall burn together' (v.31)

It is a gift to hymn-writers that 'alloy' rhymes so neatly with 'joy'. The rhyme allows a neat contrast. The righteous know the purity of true joy; the alloyed do not.

Purity is a central concern of the prophet here. Jerusalem and its people are mixed up and need sorting out. The mixed metals of an alloy are just one of several examples of admixture in these verses, which build an accumulated picture of sin. Wine is diluted with water. Silver is corrupted with base matter. Princes consort with thieves. The once faithful city has multiple liaisons, like a prostitute. It is no wonder that the language of judgement is so prominent in this context.

Special condemnation is reserved for 'the strong', whose destruction will be triggered by the work of their own hands. Strength harbours special risks of idolatry – of worshipping one's own achievements. To mix oneself up with God is to create a highly combustible mixture.

When a hymnwriter deploys 'alloy', we suspect that 'joy' is lurking nearby. Similarly, when Isaiah promises judgement on the strong, we can expect a new and better reality to be at hand. It will be God's gift to those who trust in a strength other than their own. For true holiness (and therefore truly holy *joy*) is not the mark of those who mix themselves up with God, but of those who know their need of God's forgiveness.

Almighty and eternal God,
you have kindled the flame of love in the hearts of the saints:
grant to us the same faith and power of love,
that, as we rejoice in their triumphs,
we may be sustained by their example and fellowship;
through Jesus Christ your Son our Lord,
who is alive and reigns with you,
in the unity of the Holy Spirit,
one God, now and for ever.

COLLECT

Reflection by **Ben Quash** | 299

Wednesday 3 November

Psalms **9**, 147.13-end *or* **34**
Isaiah 2.1-11
Matthew 2.16-end

Isaiah 2.1-11

'... out of Zion shall go forth instruction' (v.3)

In Isaiah's picture, all the nations flow to the mountain of Zion and its holy city, and holy instruction goes out from there to enlighten the whole world. Early Church commentators would see a Christian fulfilment of Isaiah's prophecies in Jesus' commission to his disciples after his resurrection. They are instructed to proclaim repentance and forgiveness of sins in Jesus' name to all nations – 'beginning from Jerusalem' (Luke 24.47).

'Anything placed in the centre', wrote St Augustine, 'is common to all.' The celebration of Zion as the centre of the world might sound a little like chauvinism. But that impression is importantly qualified. Jerusalem is more a 'beginning' than an 'end'. 'Common to all', what is initiated there is to be shared everywhere.

So the spirit of this passage is a large and capacious vision of all peoples not as enemies or even just 'others' but as fellow students of God's instruction. The lesson being taught to them is peace.

A sculpture with the title *Let Us Beat our Swords Into Plowshares*, by the Soviet artist Evgeny Vuchetich, was given to the United Nations by the USSR in 1959 and stands outside the UN building in New York City. Long before the end of the Cold War was imaginable, an atheist regime's gift came to adorn its Western enemy's principal city. In the words of its title, Isaiah's hope, which 'began at Jerusalem', continued to be broadcast down the centuries.

COLLECT

Almighty and eternal God,
you have kindled the flame of love in the hearts of the saints:
grant to us the same faith and power of love,
that, as we rejoice in their triumphs,
we may be sustained by their example and fellowship;
through Jesus Christ your Son our Lord,
who is alive and reigns with you,
in the unity of the Holy Spirit,
one God, now and for ever.

| *Reflection by* **Ben Quash**

Thursday 4 November

Isaiah 2.12-end
'Enter the caves of the rocks' (v.19)

This passage opens with a decalogue of denunciations. On the day of the Lord, it will be made plain what displeases him. Above all (and seeking to be 'above all' is exactly the issue!) it is pride. Lofty trees and hills and towers and walls are the outward and visible expression of inward and spiritual arrogance. All of these things will be 'brought low'. Conjuring for us how God's rising up in judgement will terrify the earth, the prophet fires off no fewer than ten 'againsts' in half as many verses.

The only apparent beneficiaries of this great reckoning are the moles and the bats. They know how to take cover. In clefts in the rock and holes in the ground, they provide a lesson for those who are tempted to vaunt themselves and their achievements.

Perhaps these creatures put us in mind of one of Isaiah's great predecessors in the service of God: Moses. He too understood that there was 'terror' to be anticipated in 'the glory of [God's] majesty', and he let God guide him to a cleft in the rock so as to be protected from God's face, looking instead on God from behind (Exodus 33.22–23). To be at God's back is to position yourself as a follower, as a disciple. It is to exchange pride for humility. In Moses' case, this humility was rewarded with a different decalogue: the ten commandments, which invite us beyond terror and into loving relationship with God.

God of glory,
touch our lips with the fire of your Spirit,
that we with all creation
may rejoice to sing your praise;
through Jesus Christ our Lord.

COLLECT

Friday 5 November

Psalms **16**, 149 *or* **31**
Isaiah 3.1-15
Matthew 4.1-11

Isaiah 3.1-15

'... oppressed, everyone by another' (v.5)

Plato knew that political societies are a delicate system of mutual dependence. In his *Republic*, he outlined three classes of citizens: makers and producers, defenders and enforcers, and governors. Each corresponds also to an aspect of the human being. The ordinary civilians who supply the material needs of the whole social body represent appetite. The soldiers and law enforcers represent spirit. The rulers who direct the other two classes represent reason (which is why Plato's ideal ruler is a philosopher).

Isaiah also knows how human flourishing requires complex networks of interdependence – and how easily these networks can go wrong. Among the many types and conditions of people who are referred to in this passage, we recognize some that Plato also identified: warriors and soldiers, judges and elders. But there is something rotten in this state, because the bonds of reciprocity have been forgotten. Ordinary civilians (the producers of things) are victims of their leaders. The 'elders and princes' despoil the poor and devour their vineyards. And when this happens, everyone suffers. All are 'oppressed, everyone by another and everyone by a neighbour'.

Violent and unjust, Jerusalem has become like Sodom, for which there was no remedy but destruction. In this drastic situation, the city needs more than a philosopher king. It needs the wisdom that can only come from fear of the Lord of hosts – just as each of us does if our appetite, spirit and reason are to serve our (and others') flourishing.

COLLECT

Almighty and eternal God,
you have kindled the flame of love in the hearts of the saints:
grant to us the same faith and power of love,
that, as we rejoice in their triumphs,
we may be sustained by their example and fellowship;
through Jesus Christ your Son our Lord,
who is alive and reigns with you,
in the unity of the Holy Spirit,
one God, now and for ever.

| *Reflection by* **Ben Quash**

Psalms **18.31-end**, 150 *or* 41, **42**, 43
Isaiah 4.2 – 5.7
Matthew 4.12-22

Saturday 6 November

Isaiah 4.2 – 5.7

'Let me sing for my beloved my love-song' (5.1)

Instinctively, we would probably put prophets in a very different category from the singers of love-songs. The latter are more likely to conjure up pictures of Romeo beneath Juliet's balcony. Yet this prophetic passage explicitly announces itself as a lover's song.

Once the song is underway, our expectations are further confounded. First, the beloved for whom the song is being sung (the planter of the vineyard) suddenly becomes the singer. And secondly, the sad tale of a vineyard neglected and run wild becomes a fierce pronouncement of judgement upon it: it will be trampled down and made a waste. The song ends desolately with the sound of 'a cry!'

What sort of a love-song is this?

Prophets can often seem like outsiders, speaking from the margins. They look into a situation and see difficult truths that those who are more directly involved with it cannot see. They can seem like people who don't fully belong. But actually, you might say that they suffer from an *excess* of belonging – this is what gives them both their insight into what their audience needs to hear and their costly commitment to trying to get them to hear it. It is precisely because they care so much that they speak with such uncomfortable passion. They act from love, even when their message is judgement. And the source of their fierce passion is God, for whose love-song they are mouthpieces.

God of glory,
touch our lips with the fire of your Spirit,
that we with all creation
may rejoice to sing your praise;
through Jesus Christ our Lord.

COLLECT

Reflection by **Ben Quash** | 303

Monday 8 November

Psalms 19, **20** *or* **44**
Isaiah 5.8-24
Matthew 4.23 – 5.12

Isaiah 5.8-24

'Sheol has enlarged its appetite' (v.14)

The Bible teaches that the justice people embody or disregard in their dealings with one another – and thus the health or ill-health of the human community – is deeply connected to the health or ill-health of the whole creation. When people treat each other badly, the land suffers. When people treat the land badly, people suffer.

The joining of house to house and field to field is a form of excessive consumption by a greedy few, mirrored in the excesses of their pursuit of strong drink. The casualties are the poor (who are 'parched with thirst') and the land (whose yield plummets).

In 1930s America, photographers were commissioned by the Farm Security Organization (FSA) to highlight the extreme poverty of farmers, with the aim of building support for a rural resettlement scheme. Images like Dorothea Lange's *Migrant Mother* (1936) – showing a woman described as having 'all the suffering of mankind in her' – seared themselves on the public imagination. Like such documentary photojournalists, Isaiah faces us with what we prefer to avoid, with the aim of changing our behaviour.

Isaiah is also like the creators of medieval 'Doom Paintings' (or Last Judgement scenes) – not so much there to scare the wits out of all who looked at them as to assure those deprived of justice that it would, one day, be meted out. The guzzling, glugging mouths of the wicked will meet their match in Sheol's measureless maw.

COLLECT

Almighty Father,
whose will is to restore all things
in your beloved Son, the King of all:
govern the hearts and minds of those in authority,
and bring the families of the nations,
divided and torn apart by the ravages of sin,
to be subject to his just and gentle rule;
who is alive and reigns with you,
in the unity of the Holy Spirit,
one God, now and for ever.

304 | *Reflection by* **Ben Quash**

Psalms **21**, 24 *or* **48**, 52
Isaiah 5.25-end
Matthew 5.13-20

Tuesday 9 November

Isaiah 5.25-end

'He will ... whistle for a people' (v.26)

Isaiah's faith is in a God who can create something where formerly there was nothing, a God who can bring into being things which were not.

This is the God who breathed into the mouth of Adam and made of him a living soul, a 'breathing being' in his own right (the Hebrew word translated 'soul' – *nefesh* – is connected with the idea of breath).

This is the God whose Spirit breathed on the waters at the very dawn of creation, when the world was summoned into being from nothing.

For Christians, this is the God who, in Jesus, breathed on his disciples on the day of his resurrection, giving them the Holy Spirit and creating them afresh; equipping them for their tasks in a world made new.

This passage shows that the divine power to create with something as simple as an exhalation is to be feared as well as rejoiced in. In what seems almost like a parody of the act of giving life to Adam, the Lord God blows out breath and summons death. The breath of God issues in a whistle, and a new threat springs into being: 'a people at the ends of the earth', swift and terrifying, appears on the horizon.

What scant comfort there is here must lie in the hope that a God this powerful is, finally, a creator not a destroyer.

God, our refuge and strength,
bring near the day when wars shall cease
and poverty and pain shall end,
that earth may know the peace of heaven
through Jesus Christ our Lord.

COLLECT

Reflection by **Ben Quash**   305

Wednesday 10 November

Psalms **23**, 25 *or* **119.57-80**
Isaiah 6
Matthew 5.21-37

Isaiah 6

'... vast is the emptiness in the midst of the land' (v.12)

Isaiah's overwhelming vision of the Lord in his temple gives us three pictures of fullness: the hem of God's robe fills the temple; the whole earth is described as full of his glory; and the house of worship fills with smoke. Then come three pictures of emptiness: cities lie waste without inhabitants; houses are without people; and 'vast is the emptiness in the midst of the land'. And then there are the three holies, which might be a key to understanding the mysterious relationship of filling to emptying in this passage.

God's is a burning holiness. The smoke filling the temple is more than the incense of worship; it is the cloud of God's glory. Meanwhile, the already empty land is told that it will 'be burned again' – made yet emptier. Perhaps, darkly, we are being asked to suppose that this is a form that holiness must sometimes take. It would explain how the empty land is also 'full' of God's glory.

Alongside the promised destruction, a seed is being planted for new growth – a seed planted in the soil of the prophet by one of the seraphim (etymologically, 'burning ones'). One minute he is a man of unclean lips; the next he is someone whose guilt is taken away and whose sin is forgiven, and who presses to offer himself for the Lord's purposes. Faced with God's glory, he *should* have died, but instead he finds himself newly raised up.

In time, the thrice-holy will become the hymn of Jews and Christians in all corners of the earth, filling it with the praise of sanctified lips.

COLLECT

Almighty Father,
whose will is to restore all things
in your beloved Son, the King of all:
govern the hearts and minds of those in authority,
and bring the families of the nations,
divided and torn apart by the ravages of sin,
to be subject to his just and gentle rule;
who is alive and reigns with you,
in the unity of the Holy Spirit,
one God, now and for ever.

| *Reflection by* **Ben Quash**

Psalms **26**, 27 *or* 56, **57** (63*)
Isaiah 7.1-17
Matthew 5.38-end

Thursday 11 November

Isaiah 7.1-17

'If you do not stand firm in faith, you shall not stand at all' (v.9)

The 'sign' of the young woman who would give birth to a son has, for understandable reasons, been leapt upon by Christian interpreters as a prophecy of Jesus' birth to Mary despite the awkward fact that the word is not best translated as 'virgin'. But signs can mean more than one thing; they are always affected by a context. Tracey Emin's neon message 'I want my time with You', displayed high up in London's St Pancras station, will be received in countless ways by countless travellers with their own particular associations and experiences. Just so, 'Emmanuel' – 'God with us' – can also mean more than one thing to more than one set of ears. The promise of Emmanuel was a message to Ahaz in his time and place. But it could be reiterated anew in an angel's message to a sleeping Joseph hundreds of years later (Matthew 1.23).

Emmanuel takes an activity of God and uses it as a proper name. And because God is the same yesterday, today and forever, it should be no surprise that this name connects the young woman of Isaiah 7 with the young woman betrothed to Joseph in the Gospels. The name is a promise that God will keep company with us in every generation. Whatever armies gather at our gates, we may take heart with confidence, trusting in the power of this name. It may always be true in new ways, but it will never stop being true.

God, our refuge and strength,
bring near the day when wars shall cease
and poverty and pain shall end,
that earth may know the peace of heaven
through Jesus Christ our Lord.

COLLECT

Friday 12 November

Psalms 28, **32** *or* 5 I, 54
Isaiah 8.1-15
Matthew 6.1-18

Isaiah 8.1-15

'... it will rise above all its channels and overflow all its banks' (v.7)

In the Greek geographer Strabo's description of the rebuilt city of Smyrna, written around the time of Christ, he lauds the plans and efforts of its designers and its citizens, noting however one glaring flaw in the work of the engineers (Strabo, *Geography* 14.1.37):

> *'... when they paved the streets they did not give them underground drainage; instead, excrement covers the surface, and particularly during rains, when the cast-off filth is discharged upon the streets.'*

This will be a painful memory for the growing number of people experiencing floods in our own day. Floods, and the detritus and filth they leave strewn everywhere, are a vivid sign of judgement. In Smyrna, it was judgement on the engineers who forgot to make proper sewers. In the twenty-first century, it is judgement on our overheating of the planet, and on the failure of politicians and planners to provide adequate protection for their citizens (and especially for the poorest of them) against changing patterns of weather. In Isaiah's Jerusalem, the 'flood' of a looming foreign invasion is a judgement on the long complacency of the people and on their rulers' failure to fear the right things – above all, God.

As St Paul knew when describing his public ministry as that of an 'offscouring' (1 Corinthians 4.13, KJV) – another waste product – the unwelcome eruption into full visibility of something offensive and invasive is a sign that there is an old order that needs to pass away, and that a new world needs building.

COLLECT

Almighty Father,
whose will is to restore all things
in your beloved Son, the King of all:
govern the hearts and minds of those in authority,
and bring the families of the nations,
divided and torn apart by the ravages of sin,
to be subject to his just and gentle rule;
who is alive and reigns with you,
in the unity of the Holy Spirit,
one God, now and for ever.

| *Reflection by* **Ben Quash**

Psalms **33** *or* **68**
Isaiah 8.16 – 9.7
Matthew 6.19-end

Saturday 13 November

Isaiah 8.16 – 9.7

'... authority rests upon his shoulders' (9.6)

The difference between necromancy and worship is the difference between darkness and light, between muttering in shadowy corners and full-throated rejoicing in harvest sunshine. Why 'consult with ghosts' when the 'Prince of Peace' offers his 'wonderful counsel'?

The exultation in this passage is intoxicating, and for Christians is jubilantly inflected through Christianity's messianic association of this child with Jesus. His gifts will be justice, righteousness and endless peace. Rather than skulking in the 'gloom of anguish', an oppressed world can now reach for the light – as the souls in the underworld reach for the hand of their liberator in so many traditional depictions of the Harrowing of Hell.

This child comes to break the yoke of those who are heavy-burdened. They have a 'bar' across their shoulders. The Prince of Peace has something else across his – 'authority' – which is why the oppressed have such cause to hope in him.

But, as Tertullian pointed out, wouldn't you normally expect to find the signs of authority on rulers' heads (in the form of crowns) and in their hands (in the form of sceptres)? 'What king is there', he writes, 'who bears the ensign of his dominion upon his shoulder?' (*Against Marcion* 3:19).

His answer follows swiftly: 'the one new King of the new ages, Jesus Christ, carried on his shoulder both the power and the excellence of his new glory, even his cross'. By his yoke we are unyoked, and by his burden we are unburdened. The doors of darkness are thrown open.

God, our refuge and strength,
bring near the day when wars shall cease
and poverty and pain shall end,
that earth may know the peace of heaven
through Jesus Christ our Lord.

COLLECT

Reflection by **Ben Quash**   309

Monday 15 November

Psalms 46, **47** *or* **71**
Isaiah 9.8 – 10.4
Matthew 7.1-12

Isaiah 9.8 – 10.4

'The bricks have fallen, but we will build with dressed stones' (9.10)

Accurate dating for the book of Isaiah has proved to be a historical and critical minefield, something we will not engage with here. But the opening theme of today's passage, continued in tomorrow's reading, is depressingly familiar, and could find a place at many points in Israel's history. God's people have – yet again – fallen away from the way of life and standards of behaviour God set for them at the time of their calling as God's people. Their response to God's rebuke is not one of repentance but of pride and arrogance: 'The bricks have fallen, but we will build with dressed stones; the sycomores have been cut down, but we will put cedars in their place'.

There is a recurring phrase in this passage: 'For all this, his anger has not turned away; and his hand is stretched out still.' This would seem to suggest a viewpoint that sees God's anger as a direct response to human misbehaviour; other interpretations see the need to make sense of disaster within a framework that seeks understanding of God *and* history. Either interpretation poses us with the same hard question: in our walk with God, as individuals and as churches, is our first reliance on God, or do we look first to our own innate abilities? To what extent have we replaced God's original 'bricks' in our lives with new (and supposedly superior) 'dressed stones' of our own making?

COLLECT

Heavenly Father,
whose blessed Son was revealed
    to destroy the works of the devil
and to make us the children of God and heirs of eternal life:
grant that we, having this hope,
may purify ourselves even as he is pure;
that when he shall appear in power and great glory
we may be made like him in his eternal and glorious kingdom;
where he is alive and reigns with you,
in the unity of the Holy Spirit,
one God, now and for ever.

| *Reflection by* **Barbara Mosse**

Psalms 48, **52** *or* **73**
Isaiah 10.5-19
Matthew 7.13-end

Tuesday 16 November

Isaiah 10.5-19

'... shall I not do to Jerusalem and her idols what I have done to Samaria and her images?' (v.11)

The tirade against Israel continues, and Assyria is to be the instrument of God's wrath, 'to take spoil and seize plunder, and to tread them down like the mire of the streets'. But Assyria has no reason to be complacent, as God will 'punish the arrogant boasting of the king of Assyria and his haughty pride'. Reading these stern words, whether addressed to the Israelites or concerning the fate of the King of Assyria, we could be tempted to distance ourselves from the issues raised here. We might reflect on the tendency of all world powers, in any age, eventually to overreach themselves, calling to mind that well-known saying of historian Lord Acton: 'Power tends to corrupt, and absolute power corrupts absolutely.'

But the reference to 'Jerusalem and her idols' brings the matter much closer to home, because the root of the problems of both nations lies in idolatry: the tendency to put other things before God. Our general human weakness in this respect is made clear right at the beginning with the stories of the garden of Eden. Those 'things' we idolize can be anything – possessions, talents, money, ideas – and may well be different for each person.

I may not see myself as any kind of leader, but I must still fight daily with the temptation to present my own ideas and plans to God for God's approval, rather than seeking God's will in the first place.

Heavenly Lord,
you long for the world's salvation:
stir us from apathy,
restrain us from excess
and revive in us new hope
that all creation will one day be healed
in Jesus Christ our Lord.

COLLECT

Wednesday 17 November

Psalms **56**, 57 *or* **77**
Isaiah 10.20-32
Matthew 8.1-13

Isaiah 10.20-32

'A remnant will return ... to the mighty God' (v. 21)

The Israelites' suffering under the Assyrians will be severe, but there is a glimmer of light. Not all will be lost; a 'remnant' will return to the Lord. We may feel that this idea of a remnant is not one we can readily identify with today. Sadly though, it is the present reality for all too many people. There is the worsening refugee crisis, with migrants drowning making hazardous sea crossings or dying in refrigerated lorries, and around the world people are displaced as a result of war and the whims of their political leaders. We may never suffer these particular tragedies, but all of us will have felt the effects of the pandemic that swept across the world. Even in normal circumstances, most of us will experience bereavement or illness at some time in our lives, and all too many will know the pain of divorce or redundancy.

We need to be careful here that we don't assume that our misfortunes are somehow 'sent' by God to test us, as if there was some sort of divine assault course we must complete successfully. True, some people do emerge from their trials stronger and firmer in faith than before (the 'remnant') – but not all. The ancient world struggled with the relationship between suffering and a loving God – and so does ours. The potential for the emergence of light in and through the darkness we experience remains a paradox and a mystery.

COLLECT

Heavenly Father,
whose blessed Son was revealed
    to destroy the works of the devil
and to make us the children of God and heirs of eternal life:
grant that we, having this hope,
may purify ourselves even as he is pure;
that when he shall appear in power and great glory
we may be made like him in his eternal and glorious kingdom;
where he is alive and reigns with you,
in the unity of the Holy Spirit,
one God, now and for ever.

| *Reflection by* **Barbara Mosse**

Psalms 61, **62** *or* **78.1-39***
Isaiah 10.33 – 11.9
Matthew 8.14-22

Thursday 18 November

Isaiah 10.33 – 11.9

'He shall not judge by what his eyes see,
or decide by what his ears hear' (11.3)

Today's reading points beyond the time of the faithful remnant, to the difficult-to-imagine future when true peace and justice will prevail. The prophet pictures this in a familiar passage of great beauty and paradox, showing nature's most destructive instincts brought into peaceful harmony. This transformation will be enabled by the ideal ruler, a direct descendent of Jesse the father of King David, who will function with true insight, wisdom and compassion. In the collective memory of Israel, David embodied the ideal of earthly kingship.

The verse quoted above indicates one of the qualities that this ideal king-to-be will possess, which is of relevance to the way we live our lives today. People's attention spans nowadays, we are told, are tiny; so we are fed with easy-to-digest soundbites rather than a rounded picture. Information of every kind must be delivered briefly and in short segments. The breathtakingly rapid rise of social media and the spread of the internet generally have brought many benefits, but the shadow side of this rapid development is seen in the fact that many people do judge by what their eyes see and their ears hear; depth of reflection and a painstaking growth of wisdom are not encouraged.

To what extent has my own life been affected by today's negative tendencies? Do I think before I speak, or am I too quick to leap to superficial judgements?

Heavenly Lord,
you long for the world's salvation:
stir us from apathy,
restrain us from excess
and revive in us new hope
that all creation will one day be healed
in Jesus Christ our Lord.

COLLECT

Reflection by **Barbara Mosse**   313

Friday 19 November

Psalms **63**, 65 *or* **55**
Isaiah 11.10 – end of 12
Matthew 8.23-end

Isaiah 11.10 – end of 12

'You will say on that day: I will give thanks to you, O Lord...' (12.1)

> *'When Adam's flesh and Adam's bone*
> *sits at Cair Paravel in throne*
> *the evil time will be over and done.'*

Anyone who has read C. S. Lewis' *The Lion, the Witch and the Wardrobe* may remember these words of Narnian prophecy. Narnia has been held in thrall by the evil White Witch, and the prophecy looks ahead to the time when the four Pevensie children (who found their way into Narnia through a wardrobe) will occupy the four thrones at Cair Paravel, breaking the evil spell of the witch and ushering in a time of peace and security. Isaiah here continues to point to a similar time in the future when evil will be destroyed and God's reign of peace prevail. Such prophecy is introduced by the repeated phrase, 'On that day ...'.

These promises continue the theme of the returning exiles; the petty jealousies and rivalries that have set tribe against tribe will be healed, and they will unite to vanquish their enemies.

Yet this good news for Israel raises a note of caution we may recognize. The theologian Gene M. Tucker asks, 'Is it necessary to believe that good news for some entails bad news for others?' In our warped world, success for one so often happens at the expense of the health and wellbeing of others, but these prophecies point us to a time when our rivalries will cease, and God will be all in all.

COLLECT

Heavenly Father,
whose blessed Son was revealed
    to destroy the works of the devil
and to make us the children of God and heirs of eternal life:
grant that we, having this hope,
may purify ourselves even as he is pure;
that when he shall appear in power and great glory
we may be made like him in his eternal and glorious kingdom;
where he is alive and reigns with you,
in the unity of the Holy Spirit,
one God, now and for ever.

| *Reflection by* **Barbara Mosse**

Psalm **78.1-39** *or* **76**, 79
Isaiah 13.1-13
Matthew 9.1-17

Saturday 20 November

Isaiah 13.1-13

'Wail, for the day of the Lord is near' (v. 6)

But the day of the Lord will not be dawning with light and peace for
everyone. The words above come from an oracle of Isaiah addressed
to Babylon, whose inhabitants are to be held to account for the
wrongs they have committed against God's people. The language is
fierce, harsh, uncompromising. 'The Lord of hosts is mustering an
army for battle.' Terms like 'cruel', 'wrath' and 'fierce anger' abound;
and 'every human heart will fail ... Pangs and agony will seize them'.

This makes very uncomfortable reading as we seek to share the love
of God with others. Neither can we comfort ourselves by assuming
we aren't like Babylon – such condemnation can't possibly apply to
us! But whatever our nationality, the challenge that this passage
offers all of us comes very much closer to home.

When my husband and I got married, the preacher said something I
have never forgotten. He told the congregation that he believed that
when our earthly lives ended and we stood before the throne of
God, the Lord's question to us would be very simple: 'Did you love?'
and, 'How *much* did you love?' In New Testament times, Jesus taught
this principle on many occasions. When dealing with others, 'the
measure you give will be the measure you get' (Matthew 7.2). We
cannot expect to bask complacently in the sunshine of God's love if
our attitudes towards and treatment of others don't bear scrutiny.

Heavenly Lord,
you long for the world's salvation:
stir us from apathy,
restrain us from excess
and revive in us new hope
that all creation will one day be healed
in Jesus Christ our Lord.

COLLECT

Reflection by **Barbara Mosse**　315

Monday 22 November

Psalms 92, **96** or **80**, 82
Isaiah 14.3-20
Matthew 9.18-34

Isaiah 14.3-20

Your pomp is brought down to Sheol (v. 11)

The prophet's words here look confidently forward to the time when the Lord will give the Israelites rest and relief from all their suffering at the hands of the Babylonians. What follows is slightly unusual, in that what we might expect to hear is God's continuing condemnation of Babylon, the oppressing power. What is given, though, is not so direct. Instead, it reads as if the prophet himself provides the words with which Israel may 'taunt' the defeated Babylon, and these words do not spare their erstwhile enemy. Babylon, which vaunted itself above all the other nations, will be ridiculed by the shades of 'all who were kings of the nations', saying 'You too have become as weak as we are! ... maggots are the bed beneath you, and worms are your covering.'

There is a mood here of glorying in the downfall of the enemy, and a relishing of subsequent feelings of vengeance. Our natural reaction may be to recoil from such feelings as 'unholy'; but unattractive as these feelings may be, they are an entrenched part of the universal human condition. At their best, they may be prompted by a genuine desire for justice, but we have to admit that we are not always that right-minded. Such passages may help us to identify within ourselves the darkness that lurks there alongside the light: the times and situations that spark such feelings and emotion within our own hearts.

COLLECT

Eternal Father,
whose Son Jesus Christ ascended to the throne of heaven
that he might rule over all things as Lord and King:
keep the Church in the unity of the Spirit
and in the bond of peace,
and bring the whole created order to worship at his feet;
who is alive and reigns with you,
in the unity of the Holy Spirit,
one God, now and for ever.

| *Reflection by* **Barbara Mosse**

Psalms **97**, 98, 100 *or* 87, **89.1-18**
Isaiah 17
Matthew 9.35 – 10.15

Tuesday 23 November

Isaiah 17

For you have forgotten the God of your salvation (v. 10)

Today's reading forms part of a patchwork of oracles addressed to various places, among them Damascus, the capital of Syria. Whatever the individual dates of these oracles, commentators tend to see them all as coming from a time of war in the late 8th century BC. Whoever is being addressed, the overall theme is a familiar one: the condemnation of idolatry in one form or another, and the change God will bring about when the day of the Lord comes ('On that day', vv. 4, 7).

And the root cause of idolatry? 'For you have forgotten the God of your salvation, and have not remembered the Rock of your refuge.' It always seems to come down to a misplaced sense of priorities, and the people here are being warned that all that they seek to plant and nurture through their own skill and initiative will fail. This motif runs throughout Scripture, using a variety of imagery: 'Unless the Lord builds the house, those who build it labour in vain' (Psalm 127.1); Jesus' parable of the wise and foolish builders in Matthew 7. In John 15, Jesus uses the imagery of himself as a vine and the disciples as its branches for illustration, while reminding them that 'apart from me you can do nothing'. And all can be summed up in the injunction to 'strive first for the kingdom of God' (Matthew 6.33).

How deep are the foundations on which our own 'houses' are built?

God the Father,
help us to hear the call of Christ the King
and to follow in his service,
whose kingdom has no end;
for he reigns with you and the Holy Spirit,
one God, one glory.

COLLECT

Reflection by **Barbara Mosse** | 317

Wednesday 24 November

Psalms 110, 111, **112**
or **119.105-128**
Isaiah 19
Matthew 10.16-33

Isaiah 19

*'Blessed be Egypt my people, and Assyria the work of my hands,
and Israel my heritage' (v. 25)*

When I was a very new Christian, one of the things that disturbed me when I read the Old Testament was the impression it often gave me that God's choosing of Israel as his people implied a lack of love or concern for anyone else. So imagine my excitement when I came across the following passage in Joshua 5. On the eve of battle, Joshua sees an unknown man (angel?) with a drawn sword standing before him. He asks this man: 'Are you one of us, or one of our adversaries?' And this mysterious man answers: 'Neither; but as commander of the army of the Lord I have now come.' This opened up a whole new perspective to me: the suggestion that other nations as well as Israel had their own relationships with God.

The same perspective can be seen in verse 25 of Isaiah 19, which comes as something of a surprise as it emerges from the preceding oracles and prophecies of doom against various nations (including Israel!). The emerging idea was that of Israel being chosen by God not just for themselves, but so that they could become 'a light to the nations' (Isaiah 42.6). This idea didn't come easily, as witnessed by the New Testament struggles between Jews and gentiles which continued beyond Jesus' lifetime.

How do we cope with this widening of the landscape? How is it possible that God, who calls me and loves me deeply, also loves equally everybody else across the universe and throughout time?

COLLECT

Eternal Father,
whose Son Jesus Christ ascended to the throne of heaven
    that he might rule over all things as Lord and King:
keep the Church in the unity of the Spirit
and in the bond of peace,
and bring the whole created order to worship at his feet;
who is alive and reigns with you,
in the unity of the Holy Spirit,
one God, now and for ever.

318 | *Reflection by* **Barbara Mosse**

Psalms **125**, 126, 127, 128 *or* 90, **92**   **Thursday 25 November**
Isaiah 21.1-12
Matthew 10.34 – 11.1

Isaiah 21.1-12

*'As whirlwinds in the Negeb sweep on, it comes from the desert,
from a terrible land' (v. 1)*

The Negeb, a large desert region in southern Israel, is a familiar theme recurring throughout Scripture, but the feelings it stimulates are ambivalent. Referred to as a 'terrible land', it was nevertheless God's chosen place of safety for the Israelites after their Egyptian captivity and during their 40-year journey to the Promised Land. There are references to the desert as a place of rebellion (Numbers 11.1-6), but also a place of transformation and healing (Isaiah 35.1; 51.3). In the Gospels, the desert also becomes the site of Jesus' most severe, 40-day temptation by the devil.

The events of any human life provide many 'desert' experiences: critical times of trauma, such as bereavement, redundancy or serious illness; or even times of simple boredom when nothing much seems to be happening. The sight of our streets devoid of people and traffic during periods of 'lockdown' have offered a visible and very real desert experience for us all.

The desert has also suggested itself as a powerful symbol for those drawn into a deeper life of prayer. The anonymous fourteenth-century author of *The Cloud of Unknowing* and the sixteenth-century Spanish mystic St John of the Cross exemplify this pathway. Those called to this way of prayer can find it a disorientating experience, leading them out of familiar ways of being and praying, into unknown territory. Prayer here tends to use fewer words, and to take on more of an attitude of silent waiting on God. And from the silent waiting, our action, guided by God, slowly emerges.

God the Father,
help us to hear the call of Christ the King
and to follow in his service,
whose kingdom has no end;
for he reigns with you and the Holy Spirit,
one God, one glory.

COLLECT

Reflection by **Barbara Mosse**   319

Friday 26 November

Isaiah 22.1-14

'Let us eat and drink, for tomorrow we die' (v.13)

Of all the sayings that have come down to us from Scripture, the one above must be among the most famous. But how do we view it, and what do we understand by it? As with so many things, it all depends on the context in which the saying is used.

In today's passage, the saying is found near the end of another of Isaiah's oracles, this one 'concerning the valley of the vision'. What this means precisely is not made clear, but as with the other oracles that look towards the coming day of the Lord ('On that day...' vv. 8, 12), the oracle itemizes some of the many ways the people conduct themselves without seeking the way of the Lord. So there is joy and festivity when the Lord is calling the people to weeping and mourning, and the general tendency to 'eat and drink' forms a major part of this inappropriate behaviour.

Some may protest that Scripture is not consistent here, arguing that Jesus himself saw no problem with celebratory eating and drinking (John 2.1-11). The religious authorities disapproved, criticizing him for being 'a glutton and a drunkard', and a friend of tax collectors and sinners (Matthew 11.19). But Jesus' behaviour was always governed by his closeness to his Father, and his attitude consistently reflected his Father's will rather than his own. When we examine our own attitudes and behaviour, can we say the same?

COLLECT

Eternal Father,
whose Son Jesus Christ ascended to the throne of heaven
    that he might rule over all things as Lord and King:
keep the Church in the unity of the Spirit
and in the bond of peace,
and bring the whole created order to worship at his feet;
who is alive and reigns with you,
in the unity of the Holy Spirit,
one God, now and for ever.

| *Reflection by* **Barbara Mosse**

Psalm **145** *or* 96, **97**, 100
Isaiah 24
Matthew 11.20-end

Saturday 27 November

Isaiah 24
'The earth lies polluted under its inhabitants' (v. 5)

This is a bleak chapter, with very little light to counter the general feeling of darkness and condemnation. As a result of humanity's misuse of creation, the Lord vows to 'waste the earth and make it desolate … twist its surface and scatter its inhabitants'. The punishment is to be universal and carries resonances of the Noah story in Genesis, where God vowed to do away with corrupt humanity and make a fresh start.

But the means this time are different. In Noah's time, a flood was the chosen instrument of punishment and cleansing. Here there is no flood, but its opposite: the earth is drying up and, again, it is the people who are the problem. The prophet sees the reason clearly, and it is a depressingly familiar one: the earth's inhabitants have forgotten their God, and broken the covenant he made with them. There is a surprising interjection of light in verses 14 to 16, but the prophet feels that even this is misplaced, urging the people not to be misled by a false dawn: 'But I say, I pine away … Woe is me! For the treacherous … deal very treacherously'.

With today's ever-present warnings about climate change and plastics clogging our oceans, the pollution of the earth through the actions of humanity has a disturbingly contemporary ring.

Our actions have consequences, and the prophet reminds us disconcertingly of that fact. Do we accept our share of responsibility for the way things are in our world today?

God the Father,
help us to hear the call of Christ the King
and to follow in his service,
whose kingdom has no end;
for he reigns with you and the Holy Spirit,
one God, one glory.

COLLECT

Reflection by **Barbara Mosse** | 321

Seasonal Prayers of Thanksgiving

Advent

Blessed are you, Sovereign God of all,
to you be praise and glory for ever.
In your tender compassion
the dawn from on high is breaking upon us
to dispel the lingering shadows of night.
As we look for your coming among us this day,
open our eyes to behold your presence
and strengthen our hands to do your will,
that the world may rejoice and give you praise.
Blessed be God, Father, Son and Holy Spirit.
Blessed be God for ever.

Christmas Season

Blessed are you, Sovereign God,
creator of heaven and earth,
to you be praise and glory for ever.
As your living Word, eternal in heaven,
assumed the frailty of our mortal flesh,
may the light of your love be born in us
to fill our hearts with joy as we sing:
Blessed be God, Father, Son and Holy Spirit.
Blessed be God for ever.

Epiphany

Blessed are you, Sovereign God,
king of the nations,
to you be praise and glory for ever.
From the rising of the sun to its setting
your name is proclaimed in all the world.
As the Sun of Righteousness dawns in our hearts
anoint our lips with the seal of your Spirit
that we may witness to your gospel
and sing your praise in all the earth.
Blessed be God, Father, Son and Holy Spirit.
Blessed be God for ever.

Blessed are you, Lord God of our salvation,
to you be glory and praise for ever.
In the darkness of our sin you have shone in our hearts
to give the light of the knowledge of the glory of God
in the face of Jesus Christ.
Open our eyes to acknowledge your presence,
that freed from the misery of sin and shame
we may grow into your likeness from glory to glory.
Blessed be God, Father, Son and Holy Spirit.
Blessed be God for ever.

Blessed are you, Lord God of our salvation,
to you be praise and glory for ever.
As a man of sorrows and acquainted with grief
your only Son was lifted up
that he might draw the whole world to himself.
May we walk this day in the way of the cross
and always be ready to share its weight,
declaring your love for all the world.
Blessed be God, Father, Son and Holy Spirit.
Blessed be God for ever.

Blessed are you, Sovereign Lord,
the God and Father of our Lord Jesus Christ,
to you be glory and praise for ever.
From the deep waters of death
you brought your people to new birth
by raising your Son to life in triumph.
Through him dark death has been destroyed
and radiant life is everywhere restored.
As you call us out of darkness into his marvellous light
may our lives reflect his glory
and our lips repeat the endless song.
Blessed be God, Father, Son and Holy Spirit.
Blessed be God for ever.

Blessed are you, Lord of heaven and earth,
to you be glory and praise for ever.
From the darkness of death you have raised your Christ
to the right hand of your majesty on high.
The pioneer of our faith, his passion accomplished,
has opened for us the way to heaven
and sends on us the promised Spirit.
May we be ready to follow the Way
and so be brought to the glory of his presence
where songs of triumph for ever sound:
Blessed be God, Father, Son and Holy Spirit.
Blessed be God for ever.

From the day after Ascension Day
until the Day of Pentecost

Blessed are you, creator God,
to you be praise and glory for ever.
As your Spirit moved over the face of the waters
bringing light and life to your creation,
pour out your Spirit on us today
that we may walk as children of light
and by your grace reveal your presence.
Blessed be God, Father, Son and Holy Spirit.
Blessed be God for ever.

From All Saints until the day before
the First Sunday of Advent

Blessed are you, Sovereign God,
ruler and judge of all,
to you be praise and glory for ever.
In the darkness of this age that is passing away
may the light of your presence which the saints enjoy
surround our steps as we journey on.
May we reflect your glory this day
and so be made ready to see your face
in the heavenly city where night shall be no more.
Blessed be God, Father, Son and Holy Spirit.
Blessed be God for ever.

The Lord's Prayer and The Grace

Our Father in heaven,
hallowed be your name,
your kingdom come,
your will be done,
on earth as in heaven.
Give us today our daily bread.
Forgive us our sins
as we forgive those who sin against us.
Lead us not into temptation
but deliver us from evil.
For the kingdom, the power,
and the glory are yours
now and for ever.
Amen.

(or)

Our Father, who art in heaven,
hallowed be thy name;
thy kingdom come;
thy will be done;
on earth as it is in heaven.
Give us this day our daily bread.
And forgive us our trespasses,
as we forgive those who trespass against us.
And lead us not into temptation;
but deliver us from evil.
For thine is the kingdom,
the power and the glory,
for ever and ever.
Amen.

The grace of our Lord Jesus Christ,
and the love of God,
and the fellowship of the Holy Spirit,
be with us all evermore.
Amen.

An Order for Night Prayer (Compline)

Preparation

The Lord almighty grant us a quiet night and a perfect end.
Amen.

Our help is in the name of the Lord
who made heaven and earth.

A period of silence for reflection on the past day may follow.

The following or other suitable words of penitence may be used

**Most merciful God,
we confess to you,
before the whole company of heaven and one another,
that we have sinned in thought, word and deed
and in what we have failed to do.
Forgive us our sins,
heal us by your Spirit
and raise us to new life in Christ. Amen.**

O God, make speed to save us.
O Lord, make haste to help us.

**Glory to the Father and to the Son
and to the Holy Spirit;
as it was in the beginning is now
and shall be for ever. Amen.
Alleluia.**

The following or another suitable hymn may be sung

Before the ending of the day,
Creator of the world, we pray
That you, with steadfast love, would keep
Your watch around us while we sleep.

From evil dreams defend our sight,
From fears and terrors of the night;
Tread underfoot our deadly foe
That we no sinful thought may know.

O Father, that we ask be done
Through Jesus Christ, your only Son;
And Holy Spirit, by whose breath
Our souls are raised to life from death.

The Word of God

Psalmody

One or more of Psalms 4, 91 or 134 may be used.

Psalm 134

1   Come, bless the Lord, all you servants of the Lord, ◆
    you that by night stand in the house of the Lord.

2   Lift up your hands towards the sanctuary ◆
    and bless the Lord.

3   The Lord who made heaven and earth ◆
    give you blessing out of Zion.

**Glory to the Father and to the Son
and to the Holy Spirit;
as it was in the beginning is now
and shall be for ever. Amen.**

Scripture Reading

*One of the following short lessons or another suitable
passage is read*

You, O Lord, are in the midst of us and we are called by
your name; leave us not, O Lord our God.

Jeremiah 14.9

(or)

Be sober, be vigilant, because your adversary the devil is
prowling round like a roaring lion, seeking for someone
to devour. Resist him, strong in the faith.

1 Peter 5.8,9

(or)

The servants of the Lamb shall see the face of God, whose
name will be on their foreheads. There will be no more night:
they will not need the light of a lamp or the light of the sun,
for God will be their light, and they will reign for ever and
ever.

Revelation 22.4,5

327

Into your hands, O Lord, I commend my spirit.
Into your hands, O Lord, I commend my spirit.
For you have redeemed me, Lord God of truth.
I commend my spirit.
Glory to the Father and to the Son
and to the Holy Spirit.
Into your hands, O Lord, I commend my spirit.

Or, in Easter

Into your hands, O Lord, I commend my spirit.
    Alleluia, alleluia.
Into your hands, O Lord, I commend my spirit.
    Alleluia, alleluia.
For you have redeemed me, Lord God of truth.
Alleluia, alleluia.
Glory to the Father and to the Son
and to the Holy Spirit.
Into your hands, O Lord, I commend my spirit.
    Alleluia, alleluia.

Keep me as the apple of your eye.
Hide me under the shadow of your wings.

Gospel Canticle

Nunc Dimittis (The Song of Simeon)

Save us, O Lord, while waking,
and guard us while sleeping,
that awake we may watch with Christ
and asleep may rest in peace.

1   Now, Lord, you let your servant go in peace:
     your word has been fulfilled.

2   My own eyes have seen the salvation
     which you have prepared in the sight of every people;

3   A light to reveal you to the nations
     and the glory of your people Israel.

Luke 2.29-32

**Glory to the Father and to the Son
and to the Holy Spirit;
as it was in the beginning is now
and shall be for ever. Amen.**

**Save us, O Lord, while waking,
and guard us while sleeping,
that awake we may watch with Christ
and asleep may rest in peace.**

Prayers

Intercessions and thanksgivings may be offered here.

The Collect

Visit this place, O Lord, we pray,
and drive far from it the snares of the enemy;
may your holy angels dwell with us and guard us in peace,
and may your blessing be always upon us;
through Jesus Christ our Lord.
Amen.

The Lord's Prayer (see p. 325) may be said.

The Conclusion

In peace we will lie down and sleep;
for you alone, Lord, make us dwell in safety.

Abide with us, Lord Jesus,
for the night is at hand and the day is now past.

As the night watch looks for the morning,
so do we look for you, O Christ.

[Come with the dawning of the day
and make yourself known in the breaking of the bread.]

The Lord bless us and watch over us;
the Lord make his face shine upon us and be gracious to us;
the Lord look kindly on us and give us peace.
Amen.

REFLECTIONS FOR LENT 2021

**Wednesday 17 February –
Saturday 3 April 2021**

This shortened edition of *Reflections* is
ideal for group or church use during
Lent, or for anyone seeking a daily
devotional guide to this most holy
season of the Christian year.

It is also an ideal taster for those
wanting to begin a regular pattern of
prayer and reading.

£4.99 • 64 pages
ISBN 987 1 78140 182 8
Available November 2020

Authors:
Guli Francis-Dehqani,
David Hoyle, Graham James,
Mark Oakley, Margaret Whipp

**Please note this book reproduces the material for Lent and
Holy Week found in the volume you are now holding.**

RESOURCES FOR DAILY PRAYER

Common Worship: Daily Prayer

The official daily office of the Church of England,
Common Worship: Daily Prayer is a rich collection of
devotional material that will enable those
wanting to enrich their quiet times to develop
a regular pattern of prayer. It includes:

- Prayer During the Day
- Forms of Penitence
- Morning and Evening Prayer
- Night Prayer (Compline)
- Collects and Refrains
- Canticles
- Complete Psalter

896 pages • with 6 ribbons • 202 x 125mm

Hardback	978 0 7151 2199 3	**£22.50**
Soft cased	978 0 7151 2178 8	**£27.50**
Bonded leather	978 0 7151 2277 8	**£50.00**

REFLECTIONS FOR DAILY PRAYER
App

Make Bible study and reflection a part of your routine wherever you go with the Reflections for Daily Prayer App for Apple and Android devices.

Download the app for free from the App Store (Apple devices) or Google Play (Android devices) and receive a week's worth of reflections free. Then purchase a monthly, three-monthly or annual subscription to receive up-to-date content.